THE FORMATION OF THE ENGLISH COMMON LAW

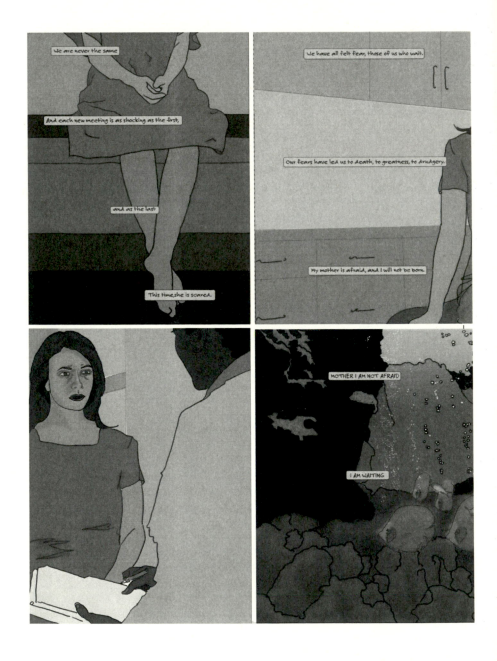

THE MEDIEVAL WORLD
Editor: David Bates

Already published

. . . .

THE FORMATION OF THE ENGLISH COMMON LAW

Law and Society in England from the Norman Conquest to Magna Carta

John Hudson

LONGMAN
London and New York

Addison Wesley Longman Limited,
Edinburgh Gate, Harlow,
Essex CM20 2JE, United Kingdom
and Associated Companies throughout the world.

*Published in the United States of America
by Addison Wesley Longman, New York.*

© Addison Wesley Longman Limited 1996

First published 1996

ISBN 0 582 07027 9 CSD
ISBN 0 582 07026 0 PPR

British Library Cataloguing-in-Publication Data

A catalogue record for this book is
available from the British Library

Library of Congress Cataloging-in-Publication Data

Hudson, John.
The formation of the English common law : law and society in England from the
Norman Conquest to Magna Carta / John Hudson.
p. cm. – (Medieval world)
Includes bibliographical references and index.
ISBN 0-582-07027-9. – ISBN 0-582-07026-0 (pbk.)
1. Common law–England–History. 2. Common law–England–Sources.
3. Justice, Administration of–England–History. 4. England–Social
conditions–1066-1485. I. Title. II. Series.
KD671.H83 1996
340.5′7′0942–dc20   95-49759
                                           CIP

Set by 7p in 11/12pt Baskerville
Produced by Longman Singapore Publishers (Pte) Ltd.
Printed in Singapore

CONTENTS

v

CONTENTS

EDITOR'S PREFACE

England's history is unique for the development at a very early date of a unified system of law, which is normally described as the English Common Law. This Common Law was duly exported to many parts of the globe in the baggage train of the British Empire, and remains highly significant, for example, in North America. In a broad context, the historical foundations of the Common Law have also remained utterly central to all discussion of the distinctive historical identity of a major European nation and to our understanding of the early phases of English and European state-building. Anyone who seeks to understand English identity must very rapidly focus their attention on the formation of the Common Law. Likewise, anyone who seeks to understand the development of the medieval English monarchy and its relations with the kingdom's localities must also focus their attention on the development of the Common Law.

John Hudson's book therefore inevitably takes its place in an important historical tradition. The influence of F. W. Maitland (1850–1906), the intellectual giant, not just of early English legal history, but of social history as well, set an agenda which has exercised a profound influence over all who have followed. Maitland's central thesis was that the reforms of Henry II's reign, set out for all to see in the law book known as *Glanvill*, marked a decisive phase of legal creativity and organizational centralization. The period between 1154 and 1189 to all intents and purposes saw the creation of the Common Law. Many distinguished scholars have followed Maitland and, while there has been a tendency, developed in the works of the likes of R. C. van

Caenegem and Lady Stenton, to trace origins back into the Norman period, the basic lines of Maitland's arguments held until the 1970s. Then, a difficult, but very important, book, S. F. C. Milsom's *Legal Framework of English Feudalism* broke sharply from Maitland's approach by questioning the whole sociological and jurisprudential framework on which Maitland had constructed his ideas. It also doubted the innovatory character of Henry II's reforms, which became no more than devices to facilitate the legal workings of a feudal society already well established. Their results, almost accidentally, were the processes which brought a Common Law into existence in the thirteenth century; the formation of the Common Law owed as much to pressure from suitors and the devices of lawyers as to the centralizing efforts of government.

John Hudson steps with assurance into this complex historiographical discussion. The author of a distinguished book entitled *Land, Law, and Lordship in Anglo-Norman England,* he brings to the subject a much deeper knowledge of the early charter evidence than any of his predecessors. His framework, like Maitland's and Milsom's, sets legal development within the context of social structures and social change, but his view of Anglo-Norman society is very different from either Maitland's or Milsom's. Anglo-Norman society possessed much of the conceptual, social and institutional framework which made possible the formation of the Common Law. The importance of Henry II's régime is greater than Milsom allowed, but it should be seen as a crucial period in an evolving process. John Hudson focuses on all the essential themes of royal power, the central and local courts, crime, dispute-settlement and customary law. His book is a very welcome and necessary contribution to a subject which has become exceptionally technical over recent decades. His analysis, which is both clear and original, is an excellent addition to the Medieval World series.

David Bates

AUTHOR'S PREFACE

This book is an introductory essay. As an essay, it has an argument: that the common law was formed from a variety of elements during the period 1066–1215. I am not searching for the 'origins' of every element of that law, but rather examining the process whereby they cohered. It is introductory in that it attempts to explain what is assumed in many other works on the subject. My reliance on secondary literature is clear at many points. Except briefly in chapter 1, I have deliberately eschewed extensive discussion of historiography, but hope that this book will encourage readers to move on to the classics of the subject, most notably Maitland's *History of English Law*. Equally clear will be the omission of many important subjects, for example law relating to status, the forest, urban and ecclesiastical law, legal learning. I seek to present not a text-book account of the law of the period, but a stimulus to thinking about the workings of law within society. Rather than aim for completeness, I have provided more extended analyses most notably of disputes. I shall often examine law from the perspective not of a legislator or judge but of a party in a transaction or dispute. Through such contextualization I hope to overcome the sense of unreality which often arises in students of the subject when approaching 'legal history'. Instead, law is taken as a way of entering into the history of power and every-day thought.

Those who, like me, attended Paul Hyams' Oxford lecture courses on medieval law will know how much this book owes to him; on occasion I have felt as if I were merely his amanuensis. Three select groups of St Andrews students opted to take my Special Subject on 'Law and

COLOPHON

PRODUCTION

The text on the interior of this book was offset printed in dense black ink on an Itek 3985 sheetfed offset printing press. The color images were printed on a Xerox C75 digital production press. The paper is Mohawk Via Vellum 70# Warm White uncoated text weight stock, selected for its subtle color and texture.

The cover is Classic Crest Eggshell Antique Gray 100# cover stock, and was printed in three colors, using a combination of traditional letterpress printing and foil stamping on a beautiful antique Heidelberg Windmill letterpress.

The endpapers are French Kraft-Tone 70# uncoated text weight stock.

AFTERMATH was edited, designed, printed, cut, and collated in our Brooklyn print shop. Book binding was done across The Hudson River in New Jersey by Bassil Bookbinding.

TEXT

The body typeface is Adobe Garamond Pro, a classic serif font that continues to make us happy every day. The headlines are Expo Sans Bold Condensed. The sub-head on the cover is Prenton RP Condensed Medium.

LABOR

Radix Media is unionized with the Graphic Communications Conference/International Brotherhood of Teamsters. The small insignia on the copyright page (also known as a "union bug") notes that this work was produced by union labor. The union bug has a long, rich history and is inseparable from the labor movement to which we owe so much. We encourage you to read more at: alliedlabel.org.

Society' rather than more immediately appealing options: they contributed greatly to what follows. The coincident presence of Rob Bartlett, Lorna Walker, and Steve White in 1993–94 made St Andrews the ideal place to be working on this book. Thanks are also due to various people for allowing me access to their unpublished work: Joseph Biancalana, Robin Fleming – who thereby helped greatly in remedying my ignorance of Domesday Book – and in particular Patrick Wormald. David Bates first suggested that I write the book, and he, Rob Bartlett, and Lise Hudson have read and commented upon the entire typescript. Help has also been gratefully received from Bruce O'Brien, Dan Klerman, Ros Faith, Hector MacQueen, George Garnett, Paul Brand, and Patrick Wormald. I hope that students will learn from this book, and I hope that I learnt some of the skills of communication so admirably displayed by my own tutors, James Campbell and Harry Pitt: to them I dedicate whatever is of value in this study.

We are grateful to Oxford University Press for permission to reproduce extracts from *The Ecclesiastical History of Orderic Vitalis* edited and translated by Marjorie Chibnall, vol. 3 (1972) and vol. 4 (1973) © Oxford University Press 1972, 1973.

ABBREVIATIONS

ANS	*Anglo-Norman Studies.*
ASC	*Anglo-Saxon Chronicle.*
Bartlett, *Trial*	R. J. Bartlett, *Trial by Fire and Water: the Medieval Judicial Ordeal* (Oxford, 1986).
Borough Customs	M. Bateson, ed., *Borough Customs* (2 vols, Selden Soc., 18, 21, 1904, 1906).
Bracton, Thorne	*Bracton De Legibus et Consuetudinibus Anglie,* ed. and trans S. E. Thorne (4 vols, Cambridge, MA., 1968–77).
Brand, *Legal Profession*	P. A. Brand, *The Origins of the English Legal Profession* (Oxford, 1992).
Brand, *Making*	P. A. Brand, *The Making of the Common Law* (London, 1992).
CMA	J. Stevenson, ed., *Chronicon Monasterii de Abingdon* (2 vols, London, 1858).
CRR	*Curia Regis Rolls* (in progress, 1922–present).
Dialogus	Richard Fitz Nigel, *Dialogus de Scaccario,* ed. and trans C. Johnson, rev. F. E. L. Carter and D. E. Greenway (Oxford, 1983).
EHD	*English Historical Documents,* i, *c.* 500–1042, ed. D. Whitelock (2nd edn, London, 1979); ii, 1042–1189, ed. D. C. Douglas and G. W. Greenaway (2nd edn, London, 1981).
EHR	*English Historical Review.*

Garnett and Hudson, *Law and Government*	G. S. Garnett and J. G. H. Hudson, eds, *Law and Government in Medieval England and Normandy: Essays in Honour of Sir James Holt* (Cambridge, 1994).
Glanvill, Hall	'Glanvill', *Tractatus de Legibus et Consuetudinibus Regni Anglie,* ed. and trans G. D. G. Hall (Edinburgh, 1965).
Holt, *Magna Carta*	J. C. Holt, *Magna Carta* (2nd edn, Cambridge, 1992).
Hudson, *Centenary Essays*	J. G. H. Hudson, ed., *The History of English Law: Centenary Essays on 'Pollock and Maitland'* (*Proceedings of the British Academy,* 89, 1996).
Hudson, *Land, Law, and Lordship*	J. G. H. Hudson, *Land, Law, and Lordship in Anglo-Norman England* (Oxford, 1994).
Hurnard, *Pardon*	N. D. Hurnard, *The King's Pardon for Homicide* (Oxford, 1969).
Hyams, 'Ordeal'	P. R. Hyams, 'Trial by ordeal: the key to proof in the early Common Law', in M. S. Arnold, T. A. Green, S. A. Scully and S. D. White, eds, *On the Laws and Customs of England: Essays in Honor of S. E. Thorne* (Chapel Hill, NC, 1981), pp. 90–126.
Hyams, 'Warranty'	P. R. Hyams, 'Warranty and good lordship in twelfth century England', *Law and History Review* 5 (1987), 437–503.
Lawsuits	R. C. van Caenegem, ed., *English Lawsuits from William I to Richard I* (2 vols, Selden Soc., 106, 107, 1990–91).
LHP, Downer	L. J. Downer, ed. and trans, *Leges Henrici Primi* (Oxford, 1972).
Liebermann	F. Liebermann, ed., *Die Gesetze der Angelsachsen* (3 vols, Halle, 1903–16).
Lincs.	D. M. Stenton, ed., *The Earliest Lincolnshire Assize Rolls, A.D. 1202–1209* (Lincoln Record Soc., 22, 1926).

Milsom, *Legal Framework*	S. F. C. Milsom, *The Legal Framework of English Feudalism* (Cambridge, 1976).
ns	new series.
Orderic	Ordericus Vitalis, *The Ecclesiastical History*, ed. and trans M. Chibnall (6 vols, Oxford, 1969–80).
PKJ	D. M. Stenton, ed., *Pleas before the King or his Justices, 1198–1202* (4 vols, Selden Soc., 67, 68, 83, 84, 1952–67).
Pollock and Maitland	Sir Frederick Pollock and F. W. Maitland, *The History of English Law before the Time of Edward I* (2 vols, 2nd edn, reissued with new introduction by S. F. C. Milsom, Cambridge, 1968).
PR	*Pipe Roll.*
PRS	Pipe Roll Society.
Royal Writs	R. C. van Caenegem, ed., *Royal Writs in England from the Conquest to Glanvill* (Selden Soc., 77, 1959).
RRAN	H. W. C. Davis, C. J. Johnson, H. A. Cronne and R. H. C. Davis, eds, *Regesta Regum Anglo-Normannorum, 1066–1154* (4 vols, Oxford, 1913–69).
SSC	W. Stubbs, ed., *Select Charters and other illustrations of English Constitutional History* (9th edn, Oxford, 1913).
Stenton, *English Justice*	D. M. Stenton, *English Justice between the Norman Conquest and the Great Charter* (Philadelphia, PA, 1964).
Stenton, *First Century*	F. M. Stenton, *The First Century of English Feudalism, 1066–1166* (2nd edn, Oxford, 1961).
Surrey	C. A. F. Meekings, ed., *The 1235 Surrey Eyre, vol. 1* (Surrey Record Soc., 31, 1979).

TAC, Tardif	E.-J. Tardif, ed., *Le Très Ancien Coutumier de Normandie* (Société de l'Histoire de Normandie, Rouen and Paris, 1881).
TRHS	*Transactions of the Royal Historical Society.*

Chapter 1

INTRODUCTION

Like modern film audiences, those listening to literature in the twelfth century enjoyed nothing better than a good court-room drama, preferably spiced by some sex or violence:

> Perrot, who devoted his cunning art to putting into verse the deeds of Reynard and his dear crony Isengrin, left out the best part of his matter when he forgot about the lawsuit brought for judgement in the court of Noble the lion concerning the gross fornication perpetrated by Reynard, that master of iniquity, against Lady Hersent the she-wolf.[1]

In the same period, legal metaphors structured or were incorporated within writings on many subjects, human and divine.[2] Participation in legal matters was widespread. A significant proportion of the male population participated in court decisions, a much larger proportion was involved in the maintenance of law and order.

Law operated in a society which combined various communities with strong hierarchic forces. Communities included the hamlet or village, the family, the hundred and shire, the lordship. Within the smaller of these, all members knew one another, and much of each other's affairs; within the larger, this was true of the more important members of the community. Disputants, members of courts, participants in transactions, were

1. *The Romance of Reynard the Fox*, trans D. D. R. Owen (Oxford, 1994), p. 5.
2. See e.g. below, pp. 86, 109.

unlikely all to be strangers. In such circumstances, one's status, honour, and capacity for forceful action, mattered greatly. The potentially dangerous had to be restrained, deference maintained, support for retribution on occasion mobilized. Any idyll of the small community as always one of peaceful, egalitarian self-regulation should be rejected. It could be rumour ridden or dominated by a few individuals.

Moreover, lordship and kingship were as much part of the setting for law as were local communities. And it was often through local communities that royal and seignorial authority was exercised. Kings, particularly before *c.* 1166, commonly dealt with areas through resident local officials, rather than with a multiplicity of individuals through officers temporarily dispatched from central government. Compared with today or the nineteenth century, eleventh-, twelfth-, and even thirteenth-century England was a country very little governed from the centre. Compared with much of contemporary Europe, however, it was heavily governed, by a combination of lordship, increasingly bureaucratized royal administration, and the exercise of local self-government. Such a combination of the local and the royal was to be essential to the emergence and form of the English common law.

. . .

THE CONCEPT OF LAW

Medieval historians have been usefully influenced by the writings of anthropologists who deny the applicability of the concept of law to the societies they study. However, there can be no doubt that people in Anglo-Norman England wrote, spoke, and thought in terms of law and laws.[3] It

---

3. Note the stimulating discussions in W. I. Miller, *Bloodtaking and Peacemaking: Feud, Law, and Society in Saga Iceland* (Chicago, IL, 1990), ch. 7 and Brand, *Legal Profession*, ch. 1. My concern in this section is with the attitudes of the bulk of those involved with law, not with notions based on book-learning (for the latter, see e.g. R. Sharpe, 'The prefaces of "Quadripartitus"', in Garnett and Hudson, *Law and Government*, pp. 148–72). The primary concern of chapters 2–8 is with activities and ideas contained within this not very tightly defined concept of law; extra-legal activities, such as the cultivation of favour, do not get such extensive treatment for their own sake.

would be hard for any Christian people whose learned members placed great emphasis upon the Bible to do otherwise, and both English and Normans were also aware of the legacy of laws from their own pasts.

Unlike English, many languages distinguish between written laws (*lois* in modern French) and law generally (*droit*). Our late eleventh- and twelfth-century texts reveal a division similar in vocabulary but not in sense. Most of our sources are in Latin, and the first word of obvious interest here is *lex*, in the English or French of the time generally *laga* or *lei*.[4] This can mean written laws, as in the key law for Christians, the Bible and especially sections of the Old Testament.[5] It can also mean learned law, canon and Roman, or twelfth-century texts such as the *Leges Edwardi Confessoris*.[6] It is sometimes used of a specific law, sometimes a new law, as when a chronicler wrote that Henry I made a law that anyone caught in theft be hanged.[7] But *lex* can also mean all Law or laws, written or unwritten. It may refer to the laws of England or the good old law of Edward the Confessor. It is thus not clearly differentiated from custom.[8] A closely related use comes in phrases such as 'according to law', 'against law', or 'compelled by law', employing 'law' to indicate in a general sense what is lawful or what is considered correct procedure.[9] 'Law' is also

4. See e.g. *ASC*, s.a. 1087, 1093, 1100; *Song of Roland*, l. 611; *Leis Willelmes*, Prol., 42, Liebermann, i 492–3, 516. See also A. Kiralfy, 'Law and right in English legal history', *Journal of Legal History* 6 (1985), 49–61.

5. See e.g. *LHP*, 72.1e, 75.4a, Downer, pp. 228, 234; Orderic, i 135, ii 250. *Lex* is also used to describe the basis of good living according to God's instruction, e.g. in the Psalms in the Vulgate. Orderic, ii 46 uses *lex* for the Rule of St Benedict.

6. See e.g. *Lawsuits*, no. 327; on the *Leges*, see below, pp. 249–50.

7. *SSC*, p. 113; see also Orderic, iii 26 on decrees of council of Lillebonne; Domesday lists of customs referred to as *leges*, e.g. Chester, *Domesday Book*, i 262v.

8. See e.g. *Lawsuits*, nos 5, 7; 'Ten Articles of William I', c. 7, Henry I Coronation Charter, c. 13, *EHD*, ii nos 18–19. Canonical collections, of course, made clearer distinctions.

9. See e.g. *Domesday Book*, i 298v; *LHP*, 7.7, 43.1, Downer, pp. 100, 150; *Royal Writs*, no. 72 on a man leaving 'sine judicio . . . et sine laga'; also Holt, *Magna Carta*, pp. 111–12. See also more specific usages such as the right of pillage 'hostili lege', Henry of Huntingdon, *Historia Anglorum*, ed. T. Arnold (London, 1879), p. 275. Note other terms for customary behaviour, such as *mos*; e.g. *Lawsuits*, no. 204.

contrasted with 'agreement', thus giving legal activity confrontational connotations.[10] Sometimes, though, it seems to mean the terms of an agreement.[11] Lastly, 'law' is used in a more technical sense to mean proof, as when a man has to 'make his law', thereby showing that he is a lawful man.[12]

Other relevant words are *ius* and *rectum*, both of which are the equivalent of the Old French *dreit* or of words based on the Old English *riht*.[13] *Ius* is best translated as 'right', as in phrases such as 'the land belonged to him by right'; 'by hereditary right'; 'rights of the church'.[14] Very occasionally in the Anglo-Norman period *ius* is best translated as 'law', and such usage later became more common, probably under the influence of Roman and canon law.[15] *Rectum*, on the other hand, is usually best translated as 'justice' as in phrases such as 'do him justice' or 'for lack of justice'.[16] On occasion, we do see *ius* being used where one might expect *rectum*, and vice versa.[17] In general, however, usage suggests that when people spoke of *dreit* or *riht*, they were capable of employing them not in a vague and general fashion, but specifically and in more than one way.

People in Norman and Angevin England thus were sensitive to the vocabulary of 'law', and they were also well aware of a category of affairs which we can best term legal. Men might be categorized as peculiarly expert or learned in law, as 'lawful' or 'law-worthy',[18] or as 'outlaws'. Certain

10. E.g. *LHP*, 49.5a, Downer, p. 164.
11. See e.g. *RRAN*, iii no. 272; E. Searle, ed. and trans, *The Chronicle of Battle Abbey* (Oxford, 1980), p. 80.
12. Note e.g. *Lawsuits*, nos 123–5; *LHP*, e.g. 9.6, Downer, p. 106.
13. See e.g. *Song of Roland*, ll. 2747, 3891; *Leis Willelmes*, 47, 52, Liebermann, i 518–19; *ASC*, s.a. 1087, 1093, 1100; F. E. Harmer, *Anglo-Saxon Writs* (Manchester, 1952), no. 61. See also *Song of Roland*, l. 1015 for 'dreit' in the sense of right as opposed to wrong.
14. Note also *Lawsuits*, no. 226 using 'in jus militare' to describe landholding by military service.
15. For possible Anglo-Norman instances, see e.g. *Lawsuits*, no. 226, 'iuris peritiores'; this is an ecclesiastical text, perhaps canonically influenced. For the later period, see J. C. Holt, 'Rights and liberties in Magna Carta', in his *Magna Carta and Medieval Government* (London, 1985), pp. 203–15.
16. *Royal Writs*, nos 3, 4, etc.
17. E.g. *Lawsuits*, no. 326; cf. e.g. *Royal Writs*, no. 196, for a clear distinction between the terms.
18. See below, p. 11; e.g. *RRAN*, ii no. 1516.

bodies had a legal function, and were created for that special purpose.[19] Some men were criticized as excessively active in lawsuits, particularly litigious:[20] such people made common what should have been unusual, for legal matters differed from the day to day. Legal customs were different from mere habits: the legal obligation to provide one's lord with a hawk every year was qualitatively different from the habit of going hawking. Also, whilst clearly we are dealing with a society permeated by the Church and religion, some distinction could be drawn between legal and religious matters: there were law books and there were penitentials; there were punishments and there were penances. Law was also differentiated from various forms of self-help and violence, although parties in a dispute might differ as to which forms of the latter were lawful.[21] The violence of disputing outside court is clearly distinguishable from the formalized fighting of the trial by battle, or even the rough and ready treatment meted out in an *ad hoc* court to the wrongdoer caught red-handed.[22]

In part, what made law special was its relationship to some authority, especially an external authority. We can sometimes see medieval men and women 'going to law' rather like characters in a nineteenth-century novel. For several years in the mid-twelfth century Richard of Anstey had to spend heavily and travel as far as southern France in pursuit of his inheritance case.[23] Travel to various authorities and appearance in various courts took litigants and their business outside the usual course of social life. In these settings, some activities could be distinguished as 'legal', and contemporaries reflected this in the categorization of certain court activities as *placita*, 'pleas'. Moreover, whilst court proceedings might involve much exercise of influence and presentation of a wide variety of

19. See below, pp. 63–6, on frankpledge.
20. See e.g. K. R. Potter, ed. and trans, *Gesta Stephani* (Oxford, 1976), p. 24.
21. See e.g. the case of William of St Calais, *Lawsuits*, no. 134; also Hudson, *Land, Law, and Lordship*, p. 2, citing, *inter alia*, Geoffrey of Monmouth distinguishing between violent and just acquisition of property. For permissible self-help, see also below, pp. 211–12.
22. See below, pp. 69–70, 76.
23. *Lawsuits*, no. 408.

ABOUT RADIX MEDIA

Radix Media is a worker-owned printer and publisher based in Brooklyn, New York. Our name comes from the Latin root of the word *radical*, which means *to get to the root*. We strive to stay true to this concept by publishing stories that get to the root of the human experience. We publish work that explores the nuances of life, and asks the reader to step outside of their own experience. Radix Media is committed to sharing stories that reflect these experiences, and to building a platform for the voices that often go unheard.

All of our work is lovingly designed and printed in-house in our commercial print shop. This gives us total control over how our books look and feel and hearkens back to the nineteenth century, when printers and publishers were the same people. We are a union shop and support those who struggle to create a more fair and just world.

Want to see more? Visit us online and let's build together.

On the web: radixmedia.org
Twitter, Instagram: RadixMedia

argument, they also usually included some distinctive and formulaic elements, indicating the existence of a register of language which could signify legal affairs.[24] This is true also of legal activity other than court-room disputes: for example, the drawing up of a charter in Latin had its own special phraseology.

Setting and language can thus distinguish the 'legal', and so too can appeal to norms, or what are usually referred to as customs. Customs are not simply neutral statements of what usually happens; rather they are prescriptions of established and proper action, prescriptions which carry authority.[25] Records of cases occasionally make explicit reference to the custom of the locality or the realm.[26] People at the time allowed a place within law for some exercise of discretion, particularly by one with power. However, they also regarded law as involving the tempering of will by custom, notions of reasonableness, advice, or court judgment.[27]

The categorization of certain affairs as legal does not make law at this time completely distinct from the rest of social life, nor give it as much autonomy as exists for modern or even later medieval law. Clearly the legal business of courts might have been hard to distinguish from their other activities, and not all arguments put forward in law cases were distinctively 'legal' in nature.[28] However, we shall discover that the category was becoming more discrete. Royal administrators, for example, came to specialize in either law or finance. Law came to have some systematic existence of its own, and experts were increasingly capable of manipulating it in order to obtain results distant from the social norms of the day.[29]

---

24. See below, p. 71; out-of-court activity could also, of course, involve formulaic oaths.
25. Had I included an entry for custom in the glossary it might have read 'Custom: (i) a norm, questioning of which might draw the answer "well, that's how we do things here" '.
26. See e.g. below, p. 54.
27. See also below, ch. 8.
28. See also e.g. below, p. 56; also p. 102 on gifts to the Church. Of course, not all arguments put forward in modern law courts are distinctively 'legal'.
29. See below, pp. 227–30.

. . .

THE FUNCTIONS OF LAW

Law is one means whereby societies are regulated and whereby members of those societies achieve their ends. Law includes substantive elements, determining rights, claims, obligations; one example would be a custom that if an eldest son survives a tenant, he will succeed to the whole of the inheritance. It also includes more managerial matters, how the process of succession is to take place, how a charter should be drafted. And it includes the administration of justice, for example the sending of writs, the holding of courts, the giving of judgments.

A first function of law, and the one that medieval, like modern, people might have identified most readily, was to keep the peace and restrain wickedness. In particular, in a society where violence was frequent, law should protect the weak, especially those lacking any more immediate protector. In such circumstances it was often necessary for law to be backed by its own violence, notably to punish offenders, both because it was felt that they deserved the penalty and also to deter others.[30]

Punishment is one way in which a case can end, and the settlement of disputes is another of the functions of law. The settlement may be achieved in or out of court but in either case law provides certain guidance and constraints which may aid the process, removing or channelling emotions which might perpetuate the dispute. Law should also help to ensure that the settlement sticks, for example through publicity or through coercive force. However, its success is far from guaranteed, for parties in disputes can employ law for their own ends. In the medieval period a particular problem was accusation through hatred. Unless the wrongful motive were identified, this might allow the accuser an official setting in which to fight his enemy and, if victorious, an authorized opportunity to inflict terrible punitive violence upon him.[31]

However, to concentrate upon courts, or even upon disputing more generally, is too narrow a focus. Law

30. See e.g. below, p. 139.
31. See below, p. 160.

provides guidance for avoiding trouble or punishment, thereby assuring a more peaceful life and preventing disputes. Law also enables certain actions to be carried out, or reinforces those actions. A man may wish to make a gift to a church which will last beyond his death. His capacity to do so is determined by a variety of factors, but it is greatly strengthened if such a grant is protected by law. Legal practice may also help by indicating the form to be taken by a document recording and hence protecting the gift. Law thus provides authority and protection for a party acting according to its norms, making his action a legal act.

Different ideological slants can be put on law, in part according to the position of the observer. It can be taken as a coherent system or as an incomprehensible intrusion into one's life, and can be regarded as a sign of the proper functioning of government, as a method of control, or of oppression. All such views were taken of the Anglo-Norman and Angevin kings and their use of law.[32] In these various ways, settling disputes, keeping the peace, punishing offenders, controlling or oppressing the people, restraining or restricting the ruler, guiding, enabling or reinforcing actions, law helped to make social life more predictable. Law and custom were intimately related; they were in part determined by common practice, but themselves, in turn, determined such practice.

. . .

DISPUTING AND NEGOTIATING

The functions of law, the existence of a category of the 'legal', and their close integration with other social practices, will become apparent in many ways, but here I concentrate upon the processes of disputing and negotiating. A dispute has arisen: how are you to achieve your ends, or at least obtain the best possible settlement? The available means are diverse. Courts are only one option, and other methods may be pursued instead or in parallel. Even if you have a good case, you may face many problems. Problems of communication may render potential sources of justice, such as the king, very distant. Or the lands which your opponent is claiming to hold from you may be far from the

32. See Holt, *Magna Carta*, p. 88; also e.g. *CMA*, ii 298.

centre of your power. Or he may be able to draw upon various sources of strength unavailable to you. He may be able to withdraw favour from you or your supporters. You may even have to decide that you cannot pursue your case, as the risks are too great or your chances of success negligible.[33] Moreover, you and your opponent are not the only people affected by and therefore involved in the dispute, and others may have different aims. The king or another lord may be most intent on maintaining the peace, asserting his own power, or gaining financially. The various communities of which you are a member have interests of their own, desiring perhaps to restore their peaceful functioning, perhaps to re-adjust the balance of power. All of these different interests may demand difficult decisions as to how to pursue your case.

Disputing within and outside court displayed many similarities. Disputes outside court obviously involved confrontation between the parties, and throughout our period the emphasis in court, too, was upon individuals starting cases conducted in an adversarial fashion: one party brought a complaint or accusation against the other.[34] Certainly, judicial proceedings in court could be distinguished by particular formality at various stages. The party who had brought the case made his formal accusation, his opponent his formal denial. At least part of their statements might be highly formulaic and accompanied by oaths.[35] There were also formal judgments, first as to which party should produce proof of their claim, secondly as to the outcome of that proof. Proof could take many forms, for example, the testimony of witnesses or documents,[36] ordeal by hot iron or cold water, or trial by

33. Some anthropologists and anthropologically influenced legal historians with a liking for technical terms categorize such decisions as 'lumping it'.
34. See below, chs 3 and 4 for greater detail, and discussion of communal accusations; here and later I rely primarily on case reports rather than the *Leges*.
35. See e.g. *LHP*, 64, Downer, pp. 202–6; on the limits of the need to be word perfect in such statements, Brand, *Legal Profession*, pp. 3–4. For arguments concerning the limits of legal representation in court in the Anglo-Norman period, see ibid., pp. 10–13.
36. See e.g. *Lawsuits*, nos 3, 189 (Domesday Book), 226, 243, 257 (false charter).

battle. Alternatively, a variety of forms of oath could be assigned to the party himself, to a representative, to the supporters of one or both parties, or to a body of important people, sometimes but not always the suitors of the court.[37] On occasion a group of local people, often but not always twelve in number, might be delegated to decide the case on oath; such was a decision by jury or inquest.[38]

However, other court proceedings might resemble non-judicial negotiation, for example with lengthy and less formal pleading and discussion. Depending on the origins and status of the parties, and perhaps the type of court, the language of business in the Anglo-Norman period would be French or English. Pleas between great men in the royal court would almost certainly be in French, those between minor men in the hundred in English; intermediate situations are less certain. Use of French in influential contexts, continuing even when English may have been the first tongue great men acquired, helps to explain the importance of French-derived vocabulary in our legal language.[39]

Although parties sometimes produced documents to back their claims, on occasion decisively, and writing was important for other legal purposes, this was a largely oral culture. Each party might tell their story, their *talu* (Old English) or *conte* (Old French). Common knowledge of the parties' affairs limited the scope for invention, and demanded plausibility. Some arguments might be piled up

37. See e.g. *Lawsuits*, nos 166, 193, 215, 280.
38. See e.g. *Lawsuits*, no. 298. I do not discuss questions concerning the Anglo-Saxon or Frankish 'origin of the jury' as I am convinced by Susan Reynolds' argument in *Kingdoms and Communities in Western Europe, 900–1300* (Oxford, 1984), esp. pp. 33–4, that decisions by sworn bodies of neighbours were common to early medieval law in many regions, and that the peculiarity of England comes from royal formalization of jury procedure, especially in the Angevin period; see below, ch. 5. Juries in the Anglo-Norman period were often used for disputes concerning a variety of rights, rather than in land-holding cases, e.g. *Lawsuits*, no. 254B.
39. P. R. Hyams, 'The common law and the French connection', *ANS* 4 (1982), 91–2 is the best discussion of pleading language. On legal language, see Pollock and Maitland, i 80–7; J. P. Collas, ed., *Year Book 12 Edward II* (Selden Soc., 81, 1964). For use of English, see e.g. *Lawsuits*, no. 204.

to influence the audience, others on their own might suffice to win the case.

Views of what was lawful provided guidance. There were no full-time professional lawyers, but a disputant might draw upon the wisdom of a man expert in laws and other relevant matters.[40] Alternatively, an expert might be called in by the president of the court or his superior, as at the great trial at Penenden Heath in 1072 when 'Aethelric bishop of Chichester, a very old man, very learned in the laws of the land, . . . had been brought in a cart at the king's command in order to discuss and expound those old customs of the laws'.[41] More generally, parties took counsel from their friends and peers, although in court this might only be allowed in some circumstances and with the permission of the court-holder.[42]

Implicit or explicit appeal might be made to norms, and discussion turn on the relationship of these to the particular facts of the case. Thus each side might accept the implications of certain forms of land-holding, but argue as to which form was at issue.[43] However, the number of cases decided by a knock-down legal argument was smaller than in modern law, and hard cases could arise for a wider variety of reasons. Some would stem from the lack of obvious right and wrong according to law, but others from differing perceptions of reasonable action, from the irreconcilability of the parties, or from disparity in their power. In such circumstances argument was likely to be less structured, wider ranging. Eloquence, astuteness, and reputation, as well as the bringing of evidence, were of great importance.

40. See e.g. *Lawsuits*, nos 10, 206, *CMA*, ii 2 for *causidici*. On the importance of advisers or suitors with good memories, see e.g. *Lawsuits*, no. 4. For more specialized advice in a case involving canon law, see the Anstey dispute, *Lawsuits*, no. 408.
41. *Lawsuits*, no. 5B.
42. E.g. Orderic, vi 20; *Lawsuits*, no. 321 (p. 274); *LHP*, 47.1, 48.1, Downer, pp. 156–8.
43. See below, pp. 105–8; for still more explicit appeal to norms, and argument over fact, see the Anstey case, *Lawsuits*, no. 408; for argument based on procedural precedent, *Lawsuits*, no. 134; for argument on motive, below, p. 61. The lack of recorded explicit citations of norms reflects not just the tendency to implicit appeal to norms but also the nature of the records.

The opinion of one's 'peers' was therefore highly influential. One's reputation, one's honour counted for much, as did one's word.[44] If not respected, one might at least be feared. We know of lords such as the Clares against whom men reputedly dared not pursue lawsuits. Tenants, too, might seek to deter lordly control by 'promises, threats, and terrorisation'.[45] Particularly less powerful disputants would need backers. Past favours might be recalled, any possible relationships drawn upon. According to the abbey's chronicler, Abbot Vincent of Abingdon preserved his right to the hundred of Hormer and a market at Abingdon not merely because he gave 300 marks to Henry I, but also because he was 'supported by the favour of the barons, as he was loved by everyone since he was munificent and generous'.[46] Money and wealth were always useful in obtaining support, and the difference between an acceptable grant and a bribe might be in part a matter of timing but also one of view-point. Grants were made to officials or others in return for future support, or to a man acting as the 'protector and friend' of a church.[47] An interesting settlement between the abbot of Abingdon and Nigel d'Oilly also reveals the logistical problems of disputing: whenever the abbot had a plea in the king's court, Nigel was to be present on the abbot's side, unless the plea was against the king, and whenever the abbot went to the king's court, Nigel was to provide lodgings for him. If Nigel could find nothing appropriate, he was to give up his own lodgings to the abbot.[48]

44. See below, p. 77. For suggestion that status should affect procedure, see *LHP*, 9.6a, Downer, p. 106.
45. E. O. Blake, ed., *Liber Eliensis* (Camden Soc., 3rd Ser. 92, 1962), pp. 226–7, *Lawsuits*, no. 258. Note also curses, e.g. *Lawsuits*, no. 271; the presence of large groups of men to coerce opponents in court, e.g. *Lawsuits*, no. 174; and warranty, see below, p. 110.
46. *Lawsuits*, no. 246. Note also *LHP*, 57.8, Downer, p. 178 on lords maintaining their men in disputes, as opposed to incurring shame by abandoning them.
47. *CMA*, ii 230, *Lawsuits*, no. 252; note also J. A. Green, *The Government of England under Henry I* (Cambridge, 1986), p. 182, Brand, *Legal Profession*, pp. 9–10; *Lawsuits*, no. 317. For the use of money in compromise settlements, see e.g. *Lawsuits*, no. 238.
48. *Lawsuits*, no. 206. See also J. H. Round, 'The Burton Abbey surveys', *EHR* 20 (1905), 282.

Requests for aid or judgment might also be made to still higher authorities. The king could intervene in person or by writ, by ordering that something be done or by setting a hearing in motion. Such need not be impersonal bureaucratic acts but loans of royal power, applications of the royal will. Sometimes they led to unjust or overly hasty action, and the king had to issue another writ to reverse the effect of the first.[49] Parties might have to bid for royal support, and even then the king's intervention might not be effective.[50]

Lastly, help might come from above, from God or a saint. Such aid could be requested, by reciting a charm for the return of stolen goods or a prayer for the defeat of one's enemies:

> O Lord, master of all, we beseech you who love all justice, avenge the wrong done to your servants and be with us in our present tribulation. ... Thou also holy Mary, perpetual virgin, be with us in our need and tear from our enemy's hand the possession offered to this your holy church. ... See to it, Lady, that the enemy who did not fear to invade your possession does not enjoy it.[51]

God or his saints might respond in various ways. St Dunstan reputedly gave Lanfranc encouragement at Penenden Heath, whilst in a lengthy dispute between Bury and the bishop of Thetford, the king refused to act decisively, but St Edmund

> who had been patient for a long time, at last took revenge for his people. As the bishop was riding through a wood and talking wrongfully with his following [about the dispute], a

49. E.g. *Lawsuits*, no. 218; note also no. 246. For the personal tone of royal orders, see e.g. *CMA*, ii 90. Support, including royal support, might also be presented through a confirmation charter: note e.g. *Lawsuits*, no. 220.
50. See e.g. *Lawsuits*, no. 146; for problems arising from a royal order, see also no. 173.
51. P. R. Hyams, 'Feud in medieval England', *Haskins Society Journal* 3 (1992), 4; see also 17–20 on ecclesiastical involvement. For charms, see e.g. G. Storms, *Anglo-Saxon Magic* (The Hague, 1948), pp. 202–5, 302; the magical as well as the Christian elements of such charms are clear.

branch hit his eye – clearly the effect of the saint's revenge – causing that man, whose eyes were both bleeding copiously, sudden and awful pain. The inside of his eyes was seen to be full of putrid flesh . . . .[52]

As is clear also from the practice of trial by ordeal, this was a society in which the supernatural could determine worldly affairs, especially when ordinary means were proving insufficient.

We are here also moving from peaceful if sometimes threatening acts, which might occur in as well as outside court, into the realm of forceful and violent deeds. Forceful methods ranged from pressure to outright violence. In some instances, for example the temporary taking of cattle which had strayed on to one's land, self-help was generally acceptable. In others, it might raise the temperature of a dispute. There are some notable signs that Anglo-Norman society was relatively peaceful, at least compared to contemporary Continental realms. Most famously, Orderic Vitalis wrote that Henry I accused Ivo of Grandmesnil 'of waging war in England and burning the crops of his neighbours, which is an unheard of crime in that country and can only be atoned by a very heavy penalty'.[53] However, the use of low level violence, particularly against property rather than persons, was not entirely excluded from disputes in post-Conquest England, even under Henry I.[54] Two periods may have seen more serious and frequent violence. We shall turn to Stephen's reign in chapter 5, and here touch upon the decade or two immediately after the Conquest. The *Life of St Modwenna*, written between 1118 and 1150, recalls the following incident from *c.* 1090. Two men living under the authority (*sub iure*) of the abbot of Burton ran away to a neighbouring village, and wished to live under the power (*sub potestate*) of Count Roger the

---

52. *Lawsuits*, nos 5, 9; see also nos 10, 16, 146, and below, p. 76. The proportion of recorded cases involving divine or saintly intervention seems to have been high in William I's reign relative to those of his sons.
53. *Lawsuits*, no. 190.
54. See *Lawsuits*, no. 173 for a riot; no. 272 for violence against property. See below, p. 109, for possible problems with the evidence; p. 96 on distraint.

Poitevin. The abbot therefore ordered that the crops, still in the men's barns, be seized, 'hoping in this way to induce them to return to their dwellings'. The men looked to the count for protection, and in his anger he threatened to kill the abbot wherever he was found.

> Violently angry, the count gathered a great troop of peasants and knights with carts and weapons and sent them to the monks' barns at Stapenhill and had them seize by force all the crops stored there. . . . Not content with this, Count Roger sent his men and knights to lay waste the abbey's fields at Blackpool, encouraging them especially to lure into battle the ten knights whom the abbot had recruited as a retinue from among his relatives.

The abbot sought to restrain his knights, and looked to God instead. His knightly relatives, meanwhile, ignored his prohibition, and set out to do battle, 'few against many'. Despite their numerical superiority, the count's knights were scared off once one of them had his leg broken and another was hurled into a nearby muddy stream.[55]

Here then we have outright inter-personal violence. However, it must be remembered that forceful action could be pursued in conjunction with other deeds in or out of court. Action in a dispute might begin out of court, then involve a court hearing, only to be settled out of court. Or the approaches might be adopted simultaneously. A land claim might be pursued in court. At the same time, or when the court was not actually sitting, negotiation might be conducted in the same place, during feasting or drinking. Meanwhile, in the region of the land itself, the parties might bring all sorts of pressures to bear upon each other.

Pressure in or out of court could compel one party to admit that he was in the wrong.[56] Alternatively, in judicial

---

55. Reference and translation courtesy of Professor Bartlett, whose edition and translation of the *Life* will appear in *Oxford Medieval Texts*. The peasants who were the cause of the trouble died suddenly. On the day when they were buried, they appeared carrying their wooden coffins on shoulders. Not surprisingly, this led the count to repent, and submit.
56. See e.g. *Lawsuits*, no. 164.

proceedings, once proof had been made, the judgment of the court was announced, probably by the person presiding over it. However, throughout the court process there remained the possibility of a compromise settlement. Such compromises, which were very common, might be encouraged by the divided loyalties of those interested in the case; by the self-interest of the parties, perhaps seeking compensation rather than punishment, perhaps unwilling to risk a court decision; and by a general preference for 'love' overcoming 'judgment'.[57] The end result of judicial proceedings therefore might well resemble that of negotiation out of court.

Any settlement or decision – for example, punishment, compensation, or restoration of land – had then to be put into effect and measures taken to ensure that it lasted. Publicity and stability could be obtained through witnessing and through the use of writing. Rhetoric, ceremony, and spectacle might not only strengthen the present decision but also deter other potential offenders or claimants.[58] Like the other elements of disputing, these too can be fitted into a wider and longer process. Even an apparently decisive court judgment need not mark the real end of a dispute. Rather, the parties would be finally reconciled by a marriage, or a dispute over a piece of land ended by its grant to a church.

·   ·   ·

ENGLISH COMMON LAW

To return to our categorizations of law. Clearly, a common law should be one which applies throughout the realm, except perhaps in a limited number of obviously privileged areas. Outside these areas, other jurisdictions should be subordinate to that administering the common law. This law should be generally available, at least to a significant portion of the population. Its operations should show

---

57. See e.g. *LHP*, 6.6, 49.5a, Downer, pp. 98, 164; also S. D. White. ' "*Pactum . . . legem vincit et amor iudicium*": the settlement of disputes by compromise in eleventh-century western France', *American Journal of Legal History* 22 (1978), 281–308, and comments in Hudson, *Land, Law, and Lordship*, pp. 146–8.
58. See e.g. *CMA*, ii 203, *Lawsuits*, no. 254B.

considerable regularity, both in substantive rules and procedure.

Common law must contrast with a regionally based law. The reign of Ethelred the Unready (978–1016) had seen law-codes which applied solely to those who lived in the Danish areas of the realm. Such divisions are recalled in archaicizing twelfth-century texts such as the *Leges Henrici* of 1114–18, with their distinction between the laws of Wessex, the laws of Mercia, and the Danelaw.[59] Yet Anglo-Norman records and legislation do not support such a tripartite division. Customs were either more local or notably unvaried. Perhaps the tripartite division had never been as clear as these texts suggest, or perhaps the Conquest and settlement broke down regional variation. Such was a further step, both practical and ideological, towards the fusion of various elements into a common law.

Common law is territorial, applying to people because they are within the realm, in contrast with a system of 'personal' law, where a person's nationality determines the type of law to which he or she is subject. Following Hastings, the conquerors might have chosen to maintain one law for themselves, another for the English. William I's reign did see legislation dealing with the relationship between conqueror and conquered, notably with regard to proof.[60] However, the Conquest did not result in any lasting strict and general division between laws for the conquerors and the conquered, as would later occur for example in Ireland. Rather, the Normans seem to have been happy to accept important elements of English custom, whilst imposing some of their own ideas and practices. Assimilation was doubtless eased by various factors, besides the gradual mingling of English and Norman. Norman lords were able to apply for themselves and their followers their own customs which most mattered

---

59. *LHP*, 6, Downer, p. 96; for local variation in the *Leges*, note also e.g. *LHP*, 64.1, Downer, p. 202. Cf. the aspiration to one law for the whole country expressed in *Consiliatio Cnuti*, Prooem. 2, Liebermann, i 618.

60. See Liebermann, i 483–4, also 487. For important comments, *inter alia*, on the problems of the texts, see G. S. Garnett, ' "Franci et Angli": the legal distinctions between peoples after the Conquest', *ANS* 7 (1985), 130–4. See also below, pp. 62–3 on the murder fine.

to them, concerning land-holding. Some of these came to be applied also to English tenants, as they received grants from Norman lords. Elements of English land law no doubt survived for those of lower status, but there is no sign that this body of custom was regarded as English. Besides this tendency to focus on status rather than nationality, assimilation was probably helped by the significant similarities between Norman and English custom. Both owed much to a Carolingian legacy. Attitudes as to which were the most serious offences were alike. Some elements of English law at least sounded peculiar to Normans, but when kings confirmed the *Laga Edwardi*, they were confirming something that may have been largely comprehensible to them and their followers. Again, therefore, the Conquest did not act as a barrier to the development of a common law.

What then of the phrase 'common law' itself? By the time of Innocent III (1198–1216), it was used by canonists to distinguish the ordinary law of the Church from any rules or privileges peculiar to particular provincial churches.[61] The English law book *Bracton* in the second quarter of the thirteenth century used it to indicate rights given to all men by the law of the land, rather than having their origin in some specially worded grant or contract. A writ of 1246 expressed the king's wish that all writs 'of the common law [*de communi iure*]' which run in England were similarly to run in Ireland.[62] At least by the middle of the thirteenth century, therefore, the phrase *ius commune* was being used to indicate the normal law of England, enforced by the king's court, above local custom. In the twelfth century, too, phrases were used to indicate some kind of law common to the whole of England. Courts were held 'as the custom is in England', cases were adjudged 'according to the custom of the land'.[63] Most significant of all is Richard fitzNigel's statement in the *Dialogue of the Exchequer, c.* 1179, that 'the forest has its own laws [*leges*] based, it is said, not

61. Pollock and Maitland, i 176–7.
62. Pollock and Maitland, i 177–8.
63. Note e.g. *Lawsuits*, nos 6 (Orderic's famous statements about English law and the laws of the Normans concerning treason), 183, 204, 381.

on the common law of the realm [*commune regni ius*], but on the arbitrary decree of the king'. The implicit emphasis on the justice, general applicability, and lack of arbitrariness of the common law is most striking.[64]

. . .

THE FORMATION OF THE ENGLISH COMMON LAW

Historians have given various accounts and explanations of the birth of the common law. F. W. Maitland, writing in the late nineteenth century, produced what is still the standard picture. He saw the common law as the product of the genius of Henry II and his advisers:

> the reign of Henry II is of supreme importance in the history of our law, and its importance is due to the action of the central power, to reforms ordained by the king. . . . He was for ever busy with new devices for enforcing the law. . . . The whole of English law is centralized and unified . . . .[65]

With regards to land law, there was not so much a change of substantive rules as a transfer of jurisdiction from local to royal courts; the latter offered swifter and more rational justice. In criminal law, on the other hand, there was a marked shift in the substance of the law during the twelfth century: the common law of crime, with its categorization of serious offences as felonies punishable by death, replaced an ancient system which laid far greater emphasis upon individual action aimed at compensation and other forms of payment.[66]

Most subsequent studies, notably those of Lady Stenton and R. C. van Caenegem, have been elaborations or qualifications of Maitland's picture, retaining his emphasis upon the Angevin period, and particularly Henry II and his genius.[67] However, since the 1960s S. F. C. Milsom has been producing a markedly different framework of development. From a focus upon land-holding, he argues that law before

---

64. *Dialogus*, pp. 59–60.
65. Pollock and Maitland, i 137–8.
66. Pollock and Maitland, ii 448ff.
67. See esp. Stenton, *English Justice*, R. C. van Caenegem, *The Birth of the English Common Law* (2nd edn, Cambridge, 1988), esp. p. 100.

the Angevin reforms was fundamentally different in nature from the common law.[68] The key unit – social, political, and legal – in Anglo-Norman England was the lordship, presided over by the lord in his honorial court. In such a context, law and land-holding rested on custom, not legal rules. Pressure for obedience came primarily from morals and habit, not from enforcement by a sovereign state. Tenants might, for example, commonly succeed to their fathers' lands, but they had no enforceable legal right to do so, since there was no superior authority to enforce such rights. The Angevin reforms transformed this situation, since they provided routine royal enforcement for tenants' customary claims against their lords. But this was an unintended effect. The reforms were restricted in intent and inspired not by genius but simply by a desire to make the old system work according to its own terms.

Maitland's picture is now also sustaining attack from a different direction. Patrick Wormald argues that key stages of the 'Making of English Law' took place in the Anglo-Saxon period. He emphasizes the power of Anglo-Saxon royal administration. England knew no great privileged areas from which the king was excluded, and lordship did not of itself involve significant powers of court-holding. Criminal law in particular had developed a considerable distance towards its common law form. The notion of serious offences being against the king, state, or community, and the general practice of punishing them by death, had emerged in the tenth and eleventh centuries. Practices were fairly uniform throughout the realm, and were determined and modified by royal law-making.[69]

The present book argues that, following very important developments after the Norman Conquest, key social,

---

68. See esp. Milsom, *Legal Framework*. Note J. G. H. Hudson, 'Milsom's legal structure: interpreting twelfth-century law', *Tijdschrift voor Rechtsgeschiedenis* 59 (1991), 47–66.

69. See e.g. P. Wormald, 'Maitland and Anglo-Saxon law: beyond Domesday Book', in Hudson, *Centenary Essays*; 'Charters, law and the settlement of disputes in Anglo-Saxon England', in W. Davies and P. Fouracre, eds, *The Settlement of Disputes in Early Medieval Europe* (Cambridge, 1986), pp. 149–68; his fullest statement will appear in *The Making of English Law* (Oxford, 1997). For the unity of Anglo-Saxon law, see also e.g. Stenton, *English Justice*, p. 54.

political and legal elements in the formation of the common law were in place by 1135: strong kingship; significant lordship; important inter-relations between rulers and local communities. These conditions underlie and are reflected in the development and standardization of custom in significant fields of law, such as land-holding. The existence of such customs, and the conditions underlying them, permitted the administrative and intellectual developments of the Angevin period which completed the formation of the common law. Thus the 'genius' of Henry II and his advisers receives less emphasis than in the Maitland tradition: Henry's servants applied their own notions and practices concerning administration to a body of existing customs and developing legal ideas which had deep roots in society. On the other hand, I argue that Milsom's view of these customs and legal ideas is flawed, and propose a markedly different picture of Anglo-Norman lordship and kingship. And finally, whilst the Anglo-Saxon legacy was considerable, the Norman, like the Angevin, was a very important creative period for legal development.

My purpose, therefore, is not to trace the origins of every element of the common law to its Anglo-Saxon, Norman, or other beginnings, but to analyse the processes whereby these elements were assembled in the century and a half after 1066. Some were derived from Anglo-Saxon England, most notably those which provided crucial administrative power, related to violence and theft, or concerned land-holding in the lower levels of society. Developments in these areas continued after 1066, in part because many Norman traditions and practices were not incompatible with those of Anglo-Saxon England.

Other elements were introduced by the Norman Conquest, or were a product of it. Norman legislation was limited,[70] and William I and his sons emphasized their position as legitimate rulers of England by confirming the *Laga Edwardi*, the 'Law of Edward', meaning the good old law of the Anglo-Saxon period. However, such confirma-

---

70. See below, pp. 48–9, 78; for further mention of Norman legislation, see Eadmer, *Historia Novorum in Anglia*, ed. M. Rule (London, 1884), p. 10.

tions did not lead to a simple continuation of Anglo-Saxon law. The confrontation of two sets of legal practices perhaps encouraged reflection upon custom. Certainly, the fact that England after 1066 was a colonial society, ruled by foreigners who had established themselves by conquest, itself had an effect on law. The strength of a conqueror, combined with the Anglo-Saxon legacy, produced a very powerful kingship. Anglo-Norman as opposed to Anglo-Saxon lordship seems to have combined more tightly elements of personal lordship, jurisdiction, and land-holding. The conquering Norman aristocracy, moreover, introduced ideas and customs concerning land-holding, particularly in the higher levels of society, which were to form the basis of common law property. Essential elements of the common law thus existed by 1135; however, royal power and judicial practice remained more *ad hoc*, less bureaucratized than they would be in the thirteenth century.

The restoration of royal authority after Stephen's reign involved reforms in the field of law and justice, reforms which continued throughout Henry II's reign and into his sons'. They were characterized by processes of categorization and routinization, in particular the routine royal treatment of a wide range of cases. In the field of land-holding, the period saw the emergence of the main common law actions, in that of violence and theft the appearance of the classification 'crime' and the terming of serious offences as 'felonies'. At the same time there started to emerge a specialist judiciary, a vital step towards an ever more specialized law, distanced from ordinary social life, and understood and practised primarily by professional lawyers. Considerable impetus for reform came from royal government, perhaps from royal officers more than the king himself. The reformers' great skill was not the invention of completely new measures but the cobbling together of successful devices from existing materials and their transformation by routine application. At the same time, it remains true to say that not even the most far-sighted amongst Henry II's administrators could have foreseen, let alone planned, the degree to which the business of royal courts grew. The impetus provided by the reformers was accelerated by the consumer demand for royal remedies. Together with the inheritances of custom and strong kingship from the Anglo-Saxon and Norman periods, these combined to form the common law.

Chapter 2

THE COURT FRAMEWORK IN ANGLO-NORMAN ENGLAND

In 1108 Henry I issued the following writ:

> Know that I grant and order that henceforth my shire courts and hundred courts shall meet in the same places and at the same terms as they met in the time of King Edward, and not otherwise. And I do not wish that my sheriff should make them assemble in different fashion because of his own needs or interests. For I myself, if ever I should wish it, will cause them to be summoned at my own pleasure, if it be necessary for my royal interests. And if in the future there should arise a dispute concerning the allotment of land, or concerning its seizure, let this be tried in my own court if it be between my tenants in chief [*dominicos barones meos*]. But if the dispute be between the vassals of any baron of my honour, let it be held in the court of their common lord. But if the dispute be between the vassals of two different lords let the plea be held in the shire court. . . . And I will and order that the men of the shire so attend the meetings of the shire courts and hundred courts as they did in the time of King Edward.[1]

Henry here named the most important lay courts in Anglo-Norman England: his own court, the shire and hundred, and the lord's honour court. There were others, notably manor and urban courts, and no doubt various *ad hoc* courts could also be held.[2] Henry's writ gives no impression of hostility to any of the courts mentioned. Rather it desires that they all function properly.

---

1. *EHD*, ii no. 43.
2. Note *LHP*, 57.1, Downer, p. 176 on courts at boundaries; *Lawsuits*, nos 66, 69–72, 74–6, 78–9, 172 on ridings.

This chapter concentrates upon preliminary answers to some basic questions: what sorts of court existed? who attended? with what business did they deal? The various types of court shared many features and functions. They could be not just judicial but also social meetings, places for making important decisions, giving and taking counsel, mediating in disputes, witnessing transactions, and reviewing and enforcing communal obligations; in general, places for the management of the affairs of those holding and attending the courts. Much of their legal business may have been routine, such as the investigation of excuses for non-appearance. They were composed of the court-holder, who presided in person or by representative, and of men who can be termed suitors, some of whom had a definite obligation to attend, others of whom did so for reasons of their own. Judgments and other decisions, for example concerning procedure, were to be made by the suitors, or at the very least with their counsel. Amongst the suitors, the most powerful, skilled, and experienced had particular authority.[3] In practice, of course, a strong court-holder was able to exercise considerable influence, for example over access to his court, the speed with which cases were heard, and over judgment itself. The court-holder received the income from penalties imposed. Still greater profit might come to him, and to a lesser extent to influential members of the court, from proffers made in the hope of swift or favourable justice or recognition of claims.[4] None of the courts seem to have maintained regular records of their hearings, although some may have kept note of income from cases.[5]

Distinctions between types of court were slightly less clear than some text-book accounts or indeed Henry I's writ might suggest. In terms of composition, for example, lords'

3. See e.g. G. T. Lapsley, 'Buzones', *EHR* 47 (1932), 177–93, 545–67. On men's peers, see Stenton, *First Century*, pp. 60–1.
4. For figures from the 1130 Pipe Roll, see J. A. Green, *The Government of England under Henry I* (Cambridge, 1986), pp. 78–87; note also the cautionary words in R. C. van Caenegem, *The Birth of the English Common Law* (2nd edn, Cambridge, 1988), p. 103.
5. H. G. Richardson and G. O. Sayles, *The Governance of Mediaeval England from the Conquest to Magna Carta* (Edinburgh, 1963), p. 185 on the eyre.

Nonfiction

Photographs & Illustration

Stacya Shepard Silverman is a Seattle-based writer and small business owner. She has written for the *Seattle Weekly* and the local shopping pages for *Seattle Met Magazine*.

Evelyn Tanner is a 24-year-old transgender woman currently dwelling somewhere within the confines of the state of Massachusetts. She creates various strange and unsettling writings, some of which find their way out into the world at large. She sleeps too little and dreams too much.

John Walters is an American writer who recently returned to the United States after spending thirty-five years abroad in Greece, Italy, India, and other countries. He writes novels, short stories, and memoirs of his wanderings around the world. His website is at johnwalterswriter.com. *Escape Strategies* is based upon his experiences with a loved one.

Susanne Wawre is a German visual artist based in Dublin. Upon graduating in Fine Art Painting at NCAD, she was awarded the Talbot Gallery and Studios Most Promising Graduate Award 2016. Further, she has received a Highly Commended in the Visual Arts from the global Undergraduate Awards and has been listed as one of the four artists of "50 People To Watch in 2017" in *The Irish Times*.

Her works connect parts of her life to sociopolitical and cultural history, particularly her growing up in East Germany before the fall of the wall.

courts might well include men other than their tenants. Lords could see the presence of a royal justice not as a threat to their jurisdiction but as a strength. Courts gained prestige not merely from their presidents but also from those attending. The presence of wise and powerful men increased the court's capacity to fulfil its functions.[6] In terms of business, too, the various courts had much in common. There were not strict rules of jurisdiction determining the court to which every dispute must come. The geographical location of the parties and the dispute could be important. Disputants may usually have brought cases, at least in the first instance, to the court they most commonly attended as suitors. Indeed, much may have rested on the choice of the parties; each would seek a court where they might obtain a favourable and lasting judgment.[7] At the same time, court-holders may have competed to settle disputes, since doing so could increase their authority and bring profit.

However, it would be wrong to hold that types of court were barely distinguishable, their business entirely negotiable. Disputes over jurisdiction did occur, and men could be sensitive as to which court did them justice. Early in the twelfth century, a dispute arose between Battle Abbey, currently controlled by a custodian during an abbatial vacancy, and the reeve of one of its manors. The reeve was summoned to the manor court, but there he resisted, 'backed by the force of the county nobles whom he had brought with him'. The custodian in the king's name then summoned Battle's opponents to appear in the abbey's court. When they eventually did so, they argued that they 'were bound to be subject to all justice done in their own county court', but not in the abbey court. The custodian asked if they would resist settlement in a royal court. ' "Not at all", they replied. "Well then", he said, "you cannot on that ground resist this court, for it is the king's." ' The custodian thus relied on the notion that Battle's court was not just any seignorial court – probably

6. See below, pp. 106, 114.
7. Note *Lawsuits*, nos 157, 233, 351; see below, p. 40, on shire and hundred. Note also settlements established in more than one court; e.g. *Lawsuits*, no. 209.

the view of the county knights – but rather one of a church and lordship so closely bound to the king that it was a royal court. The case very succinctly illustrates the capacity of parties to distinguish between types of court and their jurisdiction, despite the lack of generally accepted jurisdictional rules.[8] It also reveals, in the absence of such enforced rules, a strong political element in conflicts arising from differing perceptions of a court's customary business.

. . .

THE KING'S COURT

The doing of justice was a central role of the medieval ruler, prominent for example in the English coronation ritual with the kings' promises of peace and good judgment.[9] Kings and dukes had heard cases in England and Normandy before 1066. Such hearings could be very formal, in the presence of many important men, or could be royal responses to requests for justice in much less stately circumstances. Where the king was, there would men clamour for justice, there – in theory at least – might justice be obtained.[10] In this sense questions concerning the frequency, duration, or obligation to attend royal courts are beside the point. However, there certainly were some occasions of greater regularity, most famously crown-wearings. Writing in the early 1180s, Walter Map gave the following account of Henry I, which presents at least an ideal of royal accessibility:

> He arranged with great precision, and publicly gave notice of, the days of his travelling and of his stay, with the number of days and the names of the villages, so that everyone might know without the chance of a mistake the course of his living, month by month. . . . He would have no man feel the want of

8. *Lawsuits*, no. 174.
9. Note e.g. L. G. Wickham Legg, *English Coronation Rituals* (Westminster, 1901), pp. 30–1.
10. The medieval Latin *clamor* can have the sense of making a claim in a law case. Note Walter Map's praise of Henry II's patience, *De Nugis Curialium*, ed. and trans M. R. James, rev. C. N. L. Brooke and R. A. B. Mynors (Oxford, 1983), pp. 484–6.

justice or peace. To further the ease of everyone he arranged that on vacation days he would allow access to his presence, either in a great house or in the open, up to the sixth hour. At that time he would have with him the earls, barons, and noble vavassours. . . . And when this orderly method became known all over the world, his court was desired as much as others are shunned, and it was famous and frequented. Oppressors, whether lords or subordinates, were bridled.[11]

As the king was seen as the fount of justice, his court was potentially omnicompetent. He responded to personal requests for justice:

> When four great ships called canardes were on their way from Norway to England, Robert [de Mowbray] and his nephew Morel with their minions waylaid them and violently robbed the peaceful merchants of their goods. The merchants, having lost their property, went to the king in great distress and laid a complaint about their loss.[12]

There must also have been requests which the king refused to hear, or which never reached his ears. The criteria for accepting a request are unclear, but some people enjoyed preferential treatment: access to the king was a crucial source of success. Those personally favoured are hard to identify, but in various cases we see royal officials obtaining the king's help where justice might have favoured their opponents.[13] Others enjoyed a privileged position because of royal grants, for example that they were under the king's special protection or peace, or that they need not plead except before the king or his justices.[14] There were also cases in which the king was directly involved as lord, as in the land disputes between tenants in chief singled out by the 1108 writ. Further, the king was protector of the Church, sometimes hearing cases, for example, concerning the subordination of one church to another, more

---

11. *De Nugis*, pp. 470–2.
12. *Lawsuits*, no. 143C; also e.g. nos 146, 167; no. 1 shows a particularly confrontational approach.
13. E.g. *Lawsuits*, no. 222.
14. See A. Harding, *The Law Courts of Medieval England* (London, 1973), p. 39; Green, *Government*, p. 104.

frequently ones concerning ecclesiastical lands.[15] Such cases were particularly important because of the disruption following the Conquest, and also the increasing number of monastic foundations in the twelfth century.

In such instances the king heard the case because of the person involved; in others it was because of the nature of the plea itself, or a combination of plea and person. At least by Henry's reign, certain pleas were referred to as specially pertaining to the Crown.[16] The *Leges Henrici* list rights belonging to the king alone over all men in his land:

> breach of the king's peace given by hand or writ; Danegeld; plea of contempt of his writs or orders; about the killing or injuring anywhere of members of his household; unfaithfulness or treason; whoever despises or speaks badly of him; fortifications with three ditches; outlawry; theft punishable by death; murder; forgery of his money; arson; housebreaking; assault on the king's highway; fine concerning fyrd service; harbouring fugitives; premeditated assault; robbery; destruction of the highway; taking of the king's land or goods [*pecunie*]; treasure trove; wreck; things washed up by the sea; rape; abduction; forests; reliefs of his barons; whoever will fight in the king's house or household; whoever breaks the peace in the military host; whoever neglects borough or bridge work or military services; whoever has or keeps an excommunicate or outlaw; breach of the king's protection; whoever flees in land or sea battle; unjust judgment; default of justice; prevarication of the king's law.[17]

Clearly not all of these rights can be categorized as legal even in the widest sense. Of those that can, most may be assigned to certain, not necessarily mutually exclusive,

15. *Lawsuits* no. 276; see also below, p. 129.
16. Note G. S. Garnett, 'The origins of the Crown', in Hudson, *Centenary Essays*, pp. 171–214.
17. *LHP*, 10.1, Downer, p. 108 (my translation deliberately avoids tidying up the original phraseology); cf. e.g. *LHP*, 13, Downer, pp. 116–18, *Instituta Cnuti*, III.46–50, Liebermann, i 613–14. *RRAN*, ii no. 999; note the charter in Henry I's name in favour of London, *EHD*, ii no. 270, on which see C. W. Hollister, 'London's first charter of liberties: is it genuine?', in his *Monarchy, Magnates, and Institutions* (London, 1986), pp. 191–208. See also *RRAN*, ii no. 593; *Lawsuits*, no. 167.

categories: offences against the king's person or household; offences against royal authority or dignity; various serious offences against the person or against goods; failure to do proper justice. Other evidence supports the list, for instance concerning dishonest moneyers, and suggests further cases over which the king exercised control, for example disputes concerning tolls or jurisdiction.[18] In addition, all men over the age of twelve probably swore an oath of loyalty to the king, and promised not to be a thief or thief's accomplice. Serious offences could be seen as a breach of this oath, and hence a matter for royal justice.[19]

Having said that the king controlled this range of cases, it must be pointed out that royal courts could be held without the king's personal presence. Indeed, the Norman kings could not otherwise have exercised such wide-ranging justice. Provision had to be made during the king's absences on the Continent. Generally a member of his family was left in charge of the realm.[20] If no close relative was available, one or several royal officials served. However, even when the king was in England, his chief administrator or administrators heard cases. At least from early in Henry I's reign, the exchequer court met twice a year to receive sheriffs' accounts and to deal with financial disputes arising therefrom. Only two writs in the second half of Henry's reign, both involving the abbot of Westminster, suggest that the exchequer dealt with other kinds of disputes.[21] Nevertheless, key exchequer figures such as Roger of Salisbury were at the heart of the small group of men most closely approaching full-time justices at this period. They numbered a dozen or so, perhaps half of whom were active at any time. Although it is hard to tell whether they had any official title, a variety of sources refer to individuals as

18. Moneyers: *Lawsuits*, no. 239; tolls and jurisdiction, e.g. nos 15, 17, 189, 191, 254; see also *Leges Edwardi*, 13, Liebermann, i 640; Pollock and Maitland, ii 454–5 on Domesday lists of pleas.

19. P. Wormald, *The Making of English Law* (Oxford, 1977), ch. 9, and 'Maitland and Anglo-Saxon law: beyond Domesday Book', in Hudson, *Centenary Essays*, pp. 11, 14–15; also below, pp. 63, 162.

20. See e.g. *Lawsuits*, no. 189; D. Bates, 'The origins of the justiciarship', *ANS* 4 (1982), 1–12.

21. *RRAN*, ii no. 1538; *Lawsuits*, no. 277; Brand, *Legal Profession*, pp. 8–9, *Making*, pp. 86–7.

'justices of all England'.[22] This title indicates both their personal importance and their authority throughout the realm. It is interesting therefore to see Richard Basset enfeoffing a tenant by service 'of finding for the justice a messenger to go through the whole of England'.[23] The geographical problems for the regime were considerable, for royal justice had to be taken to the localities.

. . .

LOCAL AND ITINERANT JUSTICES

Anglo-Saxon kings had sent their officials to deal with business in local courts, and Norman dukes had no doubt done likewise.[24] How frequent such activities were, and whether there were any royal justices permanently based in the localities, is not known. The Norman period certainly saw innovations, but these are somewhat obscure, in part because writers at the time referred to very different types of men simply as 'justices'. Four main categories can be distinguished. First there were resident justices having a certain jurisdiction throughout one or more shires. Secondly, there were minor local officials responsible for attending to the king's pleas. Thirdly, individuals were appointed to hear particular cases as royal justices. And fourthly, there were 'itinerant justices' sent on a circuit of counties to hear a wide variety of cases.

The evidence for justices resident in the localities is very sparse before 1100. *Ad hoc* arrangements existed, such as that in the Conqueror's reign giving Aethelwig of Evesham wide jurisdiction in western Mercia. An early twelfth-century Ramsey document refers to Ralph Passelew as justice of Norfolk and Suffolk in Rufus's time.[25] Under Henry I there

---

22. Richardson and Sayles, *Governance*, pp. 174–6; W. T. Reedy, 'The origin of the general eyre in the reign of Henry I', *Speculum* 41 (1966), 694–7; F. West, *The Justiciarship in England, 1066–1232* (Cambridge, 1966), ch. 1. For one expression of the ideals of one member of this group, see the Basset seal, on the cover of Hudson, *Land, Law, and Lordship*, discussed by Stenton, *English Justice*, p. 61.
23. C. F. Slade, ed., *The Leicestershire Survey c. A.D. 1130* (Leicester, 1956), p. 15.
24. See e.g. *EHD*, i no. 135.
25. H. A. Cronne, 'The office of local justiciar in England under the Norman kings', *Univ. of Birmingham Historical Journal* 6 (1958),

are various references to justices, notably in the addresses of writs, sometimes in accounts of court proceedings. However, these do not establish that there was an office of shire justice, instituted in every shire. Unlike references in writ addresses to the sheriff, those to justices are often in the plural. This could mean that there was more than one shire justice in the relevant county, but might also refer to a variety of resident officials exercising justice, or to justices visiting the shire. These uncertainties apply equally to mentions of justices before whom cases were heard in the shire court. Even references to the 'justice of shire N.' do not indicate that every shire had its own shire justice, just as references to the 'earl of shire N.' do not mean that every shire had an earl. Rather, holders of such titles were particularly honoured men. The title and position of shire justice seems to have been increasingly attractive under Stephen, with, for example, Geoffrey de Mandeville referring to himself in a charter as 'earl of Essex and justice of London'.[26]

What seems most likely is that a variety of men were responsible for justice in the localities, and that on occasion one might be singled out by the extent of his authority. A document of the Empress Matilda refers to Geoffrey de Mandeville as 'chief justice' of Essex, perhaps implying the existence of lesser justices.[27] These lesser men's appointments may have varied in scope and formality. A case of Henry I's reign mentions a justice of a village, a writ of Stephen is addressed to the justices of two hundreds. Other men were referred to as 'king's sergeants', as was a certain Benjamin whose payment 'to keep the pleas which pertain to the Crown of the king' is recorded in the 1130 Pipe Roll.[28] The keeping of the crown pleas

---

18–38 argued strongly for a general office of shire justice; note also R. F. Hunnisett, 'The origins of the office of coroner', *TRHS* 5th Ser. 8 (1958), esp. 91–2, 101–2; cf. Green, *Government*, pp. 107–8; *EHD*, ii no. 218; *Lawsuits*, nos 151–2.

26. Cronne, 'Local justiciar', 22; see also e.g. *RRAN*, ii no. 1714, iii nos 201, 490.

27. *RRAN*, iii no. 274.

28. *Lawsuits*, no. 251, *RRAN*, iii no. 105; *PR31HI*, p. 91; below, p. 53 on Robert Malarteis. Most of the references to justices in the *Leges Edwardi* point to fairly minor men; see esp. cc. 28–9, Liebermann, i 651–2, where headmen of tithings and hundredmen are referred to as *justiciarii*.

probably involved, for example, the viewing of wounds and of victims of unnatural death, duties later taken on by coroners.[29] Moreover, ordeals generally had to be performed in the presence of a royal official, and this would often have been a royal sergeant or minor justice.[30] For the majority of the population, such men provided one of their main contacts with royal justice.

The sending of individuals to act as justices in specified cases must have been limited to altogether weightier matters. Probably such delegations of authority occurred throughout the Anglo-Norman period, although evidence before 1100 is poor. Hearings before them might constitute special meetings of the shire or several shires for business of particular interest to the king, with the royal delegate presiding.[31] If such delegations were sent to hear a group of cases in several places, they start to resemble itinerant justices. The Domesday Inquest shows groups of commissioners being used for diverse business including the settlement of disputes, but it remains likely that the events of 1085–86 were unique, at least in their scale.[32] The 1130 Pipe Roll's record of considerable activity over several years by itinerant justices may reflect an upturn of royal activity, but may simply for the first time reveal a longer-standing pattern of activity. The justices named in the Pipe Roll include men such as Ralph and Richard Basset who were also prominent elsewhere in the royal administration of justice. They heard a wide range of pleas, including land disputes, false judgment, murder, breach of the peace, treasure trove, and wreck. Henry I's eyres were in some ways limited compared with those of his grandson, apparently lacking, for example, the later efforts to cover the entire realm within a set time. Yet certainly by 1130

29. Hunnisett, 'Origins', 92–6, Hurnard, *Pardon*, p. 24, *Lincs.*, p. xlv; the vocabulary is sufficiently vague that Hunnisett perhaps exaggerated the significance of the shift from local justices to sergeants. For differences from coroners, see Hunnisett, 'Origins', 96–9; and on coroners themselves, see below, p. 138.
30. Hyams, 'Ordeal', p. 113; on ordeal, see also below, pp. 72–5.
31. See e.g. *Lawsuits*, nos 15, 18G; Brand, *Legal Profession*, p. 7; below, p. 78 on the hangings at 'Hundehoge'.
32. *Lawsuits*, no. 144 is not satisfactory evidence for itinerant justices under William Rufus; see Reedy, 'Origins', 693.

they were a very important element of justice in the localities and a major means of carrying royal authority to the broadest possible public.[33]

. . .

SHIRE COURTS

Despite the activities of eyres and local justices, sheriffs, the shire, and the hundred remained vital to local administration. Their courts provided a meeting place for the major figures of the district and for lesser men. These courts were also in a sense royal courts; Henry I's writ of 1108 referred to '*my* shires and hundreds'. They had been regularized during the tenth century in the growing area of authority of the kings of Wessex and England, and together with the king's own court they were the key judicial meetings in Anglo-Saxon England. They seem to have survived the Conquest reasonably well. The large numbers of suitors of English descent must have provided pressure for continuity of custom, particularly with regard to procedure.[34] The problem mentioned by Henry I concerning men avoiding attendance need not have been new, and the *Leges Henrici* suggests that Henry had to insist on the regularity of meetings not because too few but because too many were being summoned.[35]

Shire courts sometimes met outdoors, but might also take place in a house, the hall of a castle, or a monastery.[36] A few counties always held joint sessions, but in addition there were occasional extraordinary meetings of more than one shire, sometimes by royal order, sometimes perhaps because the sheriff presiding had charge of more than one shire.[37] By the thirteenth century, standard shire meetings

33. For the limits of Henry I's eyres, see Reedy, 'Origins'; also Brand, *Legal Profession*, p. 8; *Surrey*, pp. 7–8. See Reedy, 'Origins', 698ff. for eyre personnel.
34. See e.g. *Lawsuits*, nos 5B, 18G, 31; also below, p. 54.
35. *LHP*, 7.1, Downer, p. 98. Note the shire and hundred bringing testimony especially before the Domesday commissioners: *Lawsuits*, nos 15, 22–127 *passim*.
36. Pollock and Maitland, i 555–6; J. R. West, ed., *Register of the Abbey of St Benet of Holme* (2 vols, 1932), i nos 178, 217 (both from the second half of the twelfth century).
37. R. C. Palmer, *The County Courts of Medieval England* (Princeton, NJ, 1982), p. 29; *Lawsuits*, nos 10, 18, 185.

were every four weeks, except in a few counties with local customs, like Lincolnshire where they were held every forty days. Before the Conquest, however, there seem to have been only two meetings a year, and the *Leges Henrici* have the same basic requirement. How did the frequency increase? The holding of extra sessions between the two regular courts, followed by the regularization of such extra meetings, seems the most likely explanation. The extra sessions may have been held by royal summons for necessary royal interests, as laid down in the 1108 writ, or by sheriffs to deal with a variety of business.[38]

According to the *Leges Henrici*, the court was summoned seven days in advance. It heard pleas for just one day, and exceptions merited particular comment.[39] The size of court obviously varied from shire to shire, and there is little upon which to base estimates of numbers present in the twelfth century. However, it has been suggested that most county courts in the thirteenth to fifteenth centuries would be gatherings of 'at least 150 men, and occasionally very many more'.[40] The sheriff presided, and his influence must have been considerable, particularly in the Conqueror's reign when many sheriffs were also barons. Still, it was the suitors of the court, particularly the more important of them, who made judgments.[41] No doubt there was much variation in the obligation to attend, but generally it seems to have rested on status as indicated by land-holding. A writ of William Rufus to Bury ordered that no tenants were to be forced to attend the hundred or shire except those 'who hold so much land that they were worthy in the time of King Edward to go to the shires or hundreds'.[42] This evidence is supported by the *Leges Henrici*, which specified

---

38. Pollock and Maitland, i 538–9. Neighbouring counties sought to avoid meeting on the same days, in case suitors had to attend both; W. A. Morris, *The Early English County Court* (Berkeley, CA, 1926), p. 90.

39. *LHP*, 7.4, 51.2a, Downer, pp. 100, 166; *Lawsuits*, no. 5; see also Pollock and Maitland, i 549, Palmer, *County*, p. 17.

40. J. R. Maddicott, 'The county community and the making of public opinion in fourteenth-century England', *TRHS* 28 (1978), 30; note also Pollock and Maitland, i 542–3.

41. *LHP*, 29, Downer, pp. 130–2; J. A. Green, *English Sheriffs to 1154* (HMSO, 1990), pp. 9–18; *Lawsuits*, no. 340.

42. *RRAN*, i no. 393.

The Gunpowder Review and *The Airgonaut*. When not writing, she is the Book Reviews Editor for the magazine *Bewildering Stories*, and a regular contributor to and website manager for the international literary collective *Reader's Abode*. In her spare time, she blogs about local author events and interviews writers at www.alisonmcbain.com.

Aneeta Mitha is a queer muslim photographer.

They use the intersections of their identities to create work that subverts the invisibility and hypervisibility used against the marginalized. Their aim is to counter the hegemonic narratives that mask the other as lifeless victims, angry savages, or entirely nonexistent. You can find them online at www.IJIPhotography.com.

Sue Paterson is a writer, psychiatric nurse, world traveler and shaman. She lives in the Northwest with her husband, two llamas, fourteen chickens, two dogs and four cats.

Kristina V. Ramos is a student from Sacramento, California. She believes it's important to talk about controversial issues, like imprisonment and immigration. She also believes we can change the world one story at a time.

Anna Schott is the author of *The End by Fanny Middleton*. She's also been a dog-walker, record store owner, and musician. She lives in Brooklyn with her family.

Alex Shvartsman is a writer, translator and game designer from Brooklyn, New York. Over one hundred of his short stories have appeared in *Nature, Galaxy's Edge, InterGalactic Medicine Show*, and other magazines and anthologies. His website is www.alexshvartsman.com.

Susan Silberman has a Ph.D. in Human Development and Child Psychology and has practiced as an attorney in California for the past twenty years. She has written fiction her entire life but chose to pursue safe careers instead. She is now dedicating herself fully to writing.

that the following should attend: 'bishops, earls, sheriffs, deputies [*uicarii*], hundredmen, aldermen, stewards, reeves, barons, vavassours, village reeves, and other lords of lands'. Not all these need have attended in person. Stewards might often represent the men of the highest status, and the presence of a baron or his steward might acquit lesser men of his lands of any obligation to attend. In the absence of the baron or his steward, the *Leges Henrici* suggest, the reeve, priest and four of the most important men of the village had to attend, whilst further evidence points to the presence of manor reeves and other men not of the first rank in county society.[43] Later, perhaps as sessions of the court became more frequent, the obligation to attend became attached to specific tenements.

Attendance at courts could be a considerable burden:

> let us try to picture to ourselves the position of some petty freeholder whose lands lie on the north coast of Devon. Once a month he must attend the county court; once a month, that is, he must toil to get to Exeter, and we can not always allow him a horse. Even if the court gets through its business in one day, he will be away from home for a week at least and his journeyings and sojournings will be at his own cost.[44]

Yet the formality of obligation which lay behind attendance, and indeed the desire to avoid attendance, must not be assumed. An account of a mid-twelfth-century court has Hervey de Glanville 'truly declare, attest, and demonstrate that fifty years have passed since I first took to frequenting hundreds and shires with my father, before I was a householder and afterward up until now'.[45] Some enjoyed being at the centre of affairs, watching and participating in the drama of pleas, whilst others were present in order to pursue their own business or to support friends and kin.

The shire dealt with a very wide range of business, far from all of which concerned legal matters. As for disputes,

---

43. *LHP*, 7.2, 7.7–7b, Downer, pp. 98–100; see also 29, 31.3, pp. 130–4; but note 30.1, p. 132 which suggests that both a baron and his tenants might be present; *Lawsuits*, no. 172; Pollock and Maitland, i 546.
44. Pollock and Maitland, i 538.
45. *Lawsuits*, no. 331.

the county heard land claims, offences involving violence or theft, and probably certain ecclesiastical cases.[46] Some of the cases, particularly the less serious, could no doubt be heard in any county court. The more serious offences, in particular those involving breach of the king's peace, may increasingly have required the presence of a royal representative, either in a standard shire court or a session specially summoned by royal order.[47] Similarly, certain county courts to which land cases were referred by writ may have been special sessions, some meeting on the disputed land itself.[48] Even taking into account the changing rates of documentary survival, evidence such as writs, the presence of itinerant justices, and the transfer of cases all point to an increasing integration of the county into the royal administration of justice by 1135.[49]

· · ·

HUNDRED COURTS

In the 1270s there were 628 hundreds or wapentakes (the Danelaw equivalent) in England, and it is unlikely that the figure in the Anglo-Norman period was much lower. The number of hundreds in each shire varied; there were thirty-five in Devon, fourteen in Oxfordshire in the 1270s. So, too, did the size of individual hundreds; a hundred reeve might well have ten to twenty villages in his hundred, but some in Kent had only two.[50] Some hundreds

---

46. Note *LHP*, 7.3, Downer, p. 100; on cases involving Christianity, see below, p. 49; on land cases, see e.g. *Lawsuits*, nos 160, 267, the 1108 writ, cited above, and also below, pp. 113–14; Green, *Sheriffs*, p. 10; W. L. Warren, *The Governance of Norman and Angevin England* (London, 1987), p. 197; see also *Leges Edwardi*, 12.9–13.1, Liebermann, i 639–40; the later remaining importance of the shire court particularly in the initial stages of criminal prosecution, (see below, p. 168), may well survive from an earlier still fuller authority. See below, p. 69 on outlawry.

47. On the king's peace, see below, p. 82–3.

48. See below, pp. 113–14; e.g. *Lawsuits*, nos 132, 245, *Royal Writs*, no. 1, *CMA*, ii 93, *RRAN*, ii no. 957.

49. See below, p. 51, on the transfer of cases.

50. H. M. Cam, *The Hundred and the Hundred Rolls* (London, 1930), pp. 137, 153; for hundred courts generally, ibid., esp. chs 2 and 10, Pollock and Maitland, i 556–60. On hundredal rearrangement in some shires during the twelfth century, see Cam, *Hundred*, p. 9.

customarily met as groups, others did so on occasion by royal order.[51] In 1066 lords held possibly about 100 wapentakes or hundreds from the king, and the number had increased markedly by the early thirteenth century, doubling or trebling in Wiltshire. Such hundreds were not evenly spread throughout the realm, being far more common, for example, in the south-west than in the east.[52] Hundreds were important sources of revenue, and indeed lords may have desired them primarily for financial rather than judicial benefits.

The Anglo-Saxon evidence and the *Leges Henrici* point to hundred courts being held once every month or four weeks, unless there was more pressing royal or public business. However, by the early thirteenth century hundreds were apparently held every fortnight. This may have been a recent change, or, as with the county, may reflect gradual development through the holding of courts between the main sessions.[53] Each session seems to have lasted a single day. Courts met in a variety of places, for example in churchyards or at thorn trees. Judgments rested with the suitors, generally presided over by a bailiff, appointed by the sheriff or by the lord in the case of hundreds in seignorial hands.[54] The obligation to attend again rested on the larger land-holders of the hundred, as specified in William II's writ to Bury cited above. Likewise, a writ of Henry I opens: 'Henry, king of the English, to all barons and vavassours and all lords who hold lands in the wapentake of Well, greeting. I order you all to come to the pleas and wapentake of the bishop of Lincoln.'[55] What of the overall size of the courts? Sixty-four sokemen, who probably owed suit to the court, were said to belong to Clacklose hundred when Edward the Confessor granted it

---

51. E.g. *Lawsuits*, nos 232, 287, and below, p. 46; N. D. Hurnard, 'The Anglo-Norman franchises', *EHR* 64 (1949), 446; note also *LHP*, 7.5, Downer, p. 100.
52. Cam, *Hundred*, p. 138; *Victoria County History, Wiltshire*, v 44–9.
53. *EHD*, i no. 39; *LHP*, 7.4, Downer, p. 100; *Calendar of the Close Rolls, 1231–4*, pp. 588–9.
54. Cam, *Hundred*, pp. 170, 172; Brand, *Legal Profession*, p. 6.
55. See above, p. 35, *Lawsuits*, no. 279; on suit becoming tied to particular tenements by the thirteenth century, see Cam, *Hundred*, p. 172, Pollock and Maitland, i 557.

to Ramsey, whilst later evidence suggests that suitors generally numbered between a dozen and seventy or eighty. Some speculative calculation is in order. If we take a reasonably conservative figure of thirty as the average number of suitors at a hundred court, and multiply it by the 628 hundreds, we get a figure of about 20,000. Some of these would be the same person attending more than one hundred, and some owing suit would fail to attend, but we must add those bringing their own business or simply attending the courts although they did not owe suit. If we accept an estimate of a population of 1.5 million in 1086, we can be reasonably sure that at least one per cent of the population attended hundred courts, and the proportion of adult males doing so might easily be one in twenty.[56] Moreover, there were each year two particularly large sessions, to be attended by all freemen. These sessions, amongst other duties, checked the functioning of the system of peace-keeping and policing known as frankpledge, to be discussed in chapter 3.

Besides this special business, the hundred court dealt with an extensive variety of affairs. Royal officials may have concentrated their attention primarily on the shire, leaving the hundred to deal with fewer of the serious cases which were considered to pertain to the king.[57] Yet the jurisdiction of the hundred and the shire had many similarities. A case might be dealt with at different stages by the shire and the hundred courts. Royal writs sometimes treat shire and hundred as equally suitable locations for land disputes, whilst others specified just the hundred.[58] For many of the population, in a large proportion of the

---

56. Cam, *Hundred*, pp. 173–5; H. C. Darby, *Domesday England* (Cambridge, 1977), pp. 87–91; for a note of caution, see *LHP*, 7.5, Downer, p. 100, on proceedings transferred because of a shortage of 'judges', presumably suitors.
57. On the ordinary business of the thirteenth-century hundred court, see Cam, *Hundred*, p. 181, although at p. 179 she notes that even in the second half of the thirteenth century appeals of felony could occur there. Note also Hurnard, 'Franchises', 445.
58. See e.g. *Lawsuits*, nos 185, 157, *RRAN*, ii no. 1185. For land cases in the hundred court, note also *Lawsuits*, no. 334, cf. Pollock and Maitland, i 557 on the thirteenth-century situation. See below, p. 49 on ecclesiastical cases.

cases in which they could become involved, the hundred would be their court of first resort. Indeed, the main difference of business between the hundred and the shire may have arisen from the hundred concentrating on cases between men who lived within its bounds, or involving offences committed therein. For this reason, rather than because of jurisdictional rules, the disputes heard there may have been lesser in scale than those in the shire court. The latter's business might concern more extensive lands or men of higher status who lived in the same county, but not in the same hundred.

The survival of the shire and most hundred courts under royal control was a vital legacy from Anglo-Saxon England. Their crucial importance in the development of common law is re-emphasized when compared with the loss of control of the equivalent courts by the kings and most of the great counts and dukes of post-Carolingian France.[59] Certainly in England, lords might exercise considerable influence over suitors of shire or hundred courts. However, the pattern of Norman settlement, the restricted significance of compact lordships, the scattering of lords' lands, the presence in almost every shire of at least some royal demesne, limited lordly influence and ensured the continuing importance of non-seignorial courts. Moreover, a man's influence in his county need not have been in direct proportion to his national importance. Amongst the leading figures of these courts were the predecessors of those knights who were to be essential to the running of the common law.[60]

. . .

SEIGNORIAL COURTS

Lords had more than one type of court. In particular the courts for the greater men of their lordship or 'honour' must be distinguished from those for the minor, and often

---

59. The classic treatment remains G. Duby, 'The evolution of judicial institutions', in *The Chivalrous Society*, trans C. Postan (London, 1977). See also below, p. 122, on Stephen's reign.
60. See esp. R. V. Lennard, *Rural England, 1086–1135* (Oxford, 1959), pp. 61–2; note also Stenton, *English Justice*, pp. 57–8, and below, p. 221.

unfree, men, which are best referred to as hallmoots. The latter, presided over by a reeve, dealt with the concerns of the inhabitants of one or more manors. Most of the surviving evidence concerns their witnessing of the lord's grants, but they no doubt treated local agricultural affairs and disputes.[61] Much more central to our concerns is the honorial court. There is no indication of such courts in Anglo-Saxon England, and although early evidence from Normandy is sparse, such courts must surely arise from imported Norman practice.[62]

Like the king, a lord must always have been hearing his men's requests, and in this sense he was always holding court. However, there were also specially summoned meetings, some referred to as the lord's pleas (*placita*), emphasizing their judicial aspect. It is uncertain how frequent were such meetings, or how often they were for the entirety of the honour, how often only for part of it. Their duration might depend upon the amount of business, far from all of which would be judicial. The obvious place to hold a court was in a hall or castle, particularly the castle which was the 'head' of the lord's honour.[63]

Cases were decided by the court composed of the suitors with the lord, or on occasion his representative, acting as president. The lord must have been very influential, but in claims between him and a tenant, his court was surely not irretrievably biased in his favour. The suitors of the court were concerned not only to cultivate seignorial favour, but to maintain their own honour and interests and this might involve opposing their lord. Claimants did bring cases

---

61. On the hallmoot bringing testimony in a land dispute, see *Lawsuits*, no. 332. See also *Lawsuits*, no. 219; *LHP*, 56.1, Downer, p. 174. See above, p. 38, and below, p. 45 on private hundreds.

62. D. Bates, *Normandy before 1066* (London, 1982), p. 127. The examples of suit of court in E. Z. Tabuteau, *Transfers of Property in Eleventh-Century Norman Law* (Chapel Hill, NC, 1988), pp. 58–9 are all from after 1066. See also below, p. 88, for land-holding, lordship, and conquest.

63. See e.g. H. E. Salter, ed., *Facsimiles of Early Charters in Oxford Muniment Rooms* (Oxford, 1929), no. 9. For a minimalist view of the importance of lords' courts, see S. M. G. Reynolds, *Fiefs and Vassals* (Oxford, 1994), pp. 375–9.

against their lord in the lord's own court, something they would surely not have done had they known that defeat was inevitable.[64] That records of claimants successful in these cases are rare may well reflect the court president's influence, but also the nature of the evidence: lords were responsible for the production of most of the relevant charters, and did not wish to record their defeats.

The tenant's obligation to attend his lord's court is spelt out in an unusual mid-twelfth-century grant to the abbot of Ramsey of land to be held like a lay fief:

> And if the lord, Walter of Bolbec, shall hold a plea in his court and shall desire the abbot to attend, the abbot shall come if he can, or send worthy representatives of his men in the aforesaid shires, and this by the usual summons and without dispute.[65]

Others, not obliged to do suit, also attended, and analyses of witness lists demonstrate that honour courts quite often included men who were not the lord's tenants.[66] As for those against whom claims were brought, the *Leges Henrici* reflect contemporary custom in stating that 'every lord is permitted to summon his man that he may impose justice on him in his court. Even if the man resides at a very distant manor of the honour of which he holds, he shall go to a plea if his lord summons him.'[67] Nor was it just the lord's immediate tenants and their business which came to his court. Cases involving his sub-tenants might be brought there, and indeed even the king sent to overlords' courts cases in which a man's lord had failed to do justice.[68] Occasionally, disputants may have sought justice in the

---

64. See e.g. *Lawsuits*, nos 214, 226 (below, pp. 105–8), both unsuccessful claims; note also no. 340 for a sheriff losing a case in his own county court.

65. *EHD*, ii no. 253. See also J. H. Round, 'The Burton Abbey surveys', *EHR* 20 (1905), 282, a Burton grant to Ralph son of Orm: Ralph should come to the abbot's court to judge a thief if he is caught and to judge trial by battle.

66. E.g. *Lawsuits*, nos 164, 266, and see below, p. 106.

67. *LHP*, 55.1, 1a, Downer, p. 172; on summonses, see 41.3–4, p. 146. Note also the obligation to answer specified in *EHD*, ii no. 257, with reference to William of Aunay.

68. See below, pp. 113, 128; note also e.g. *CMA*, ii 85.

court of a regionally dominant lord, even if they had no tenurial connection to him.[69]

Honorial courts were the key venue for the management of seignorial resources and personal relations. The lord received advice from his vassals and negotiated with them, and they no doubt participated in similar activities amongst themselves. Particularly important is the variety of business concerning land-holding. The lord's barons witnessed and occasionally were said to have consented to his grants, and their own grants were sometimes made in his court. Enquiries might be held to clarify whether a predecessor had granted away lands.[70] Quitclaims and agreements could be made or publicized, and, as Henry I's writ of 1108 specified, land disputes involving men of honour were decided.[71]

Seignorial courts of various types also dealt with various offences against the person or goods. The origins of such jurisdiction are not entirely clear now, and may have been somewhat confused at the time. Besides the lord's rights over the unfree, there was a general belief that great men should keep their households in order and take the necessary judicial and retributive actions, especially concerning minor offences against the person like beatings and insults.[72] Lords may have been tempted to extend such authority to their men generally and perhaps to anyone's offences committed on their lands.[73] Such authority would then coincide with the form of jurisdiction called 'sake and soke'.[74]

Most twelfth-century descriptions of sake and soke are

69. See below, p. 113 n. 66.
70. See e.g. *Oxford Charters*, no. 6; C. W. Foster and K. Major, eds, *The Registrum Antiquissimum of the Cathedral Church of Lincoln* (10 vols, Lincoln Record Soc., 1931–73), i nos 130–1; see below, p. 88 on charter addresses and enquiries.
71. Lords' courts also heard disputes over other types of rights; see e.g. *Lawsuits*, no. 198 concerning a parish church.
72. See below, p. 164–6.
73. Note e.g. *LHP*, 27, Downer, p. 128.
74. Sake and soke in the Anglo-Saxon period are highly controversial, notably as to whether lords held courts as a result of such rights; see e.g. F. W. Maitland, *Domesday Book and Beyond* (Cambridge, 1897), H. M. Cam, 'The evolution of the medieval English franchise', *Speculum* 32 (1957), 427–42.

imprecise, and doubtless different perceptions of the extent of jurisdiction allowed lords to seek to extend the business of their courts. In general, however, sake and soke jurisdiction seems to have been similar to the hundred's, with the exception perhaps of any jurisdiction the hundred enjoyed involving capital punishment, notably of thieves. Neither hundredal jurisdiction nor sake and soke would encompass the pleas pertaining to the Crown, and the limits of sake and soke are further demonstrated by many such grants including the privilege of infangentheof, the right summarily to execute thieves caught red-handed.[75]

Some Normans inherited rights of sake and soke from their Anglo-Saxon predecessors, and the Anglo-Norman kings made further grants, to the financial and judicial benefit of lords. No doubt kings emphasized that all such rights derived from royal grant, either specifically of sake and soke or perhaps as a concomitant of office. Another view, however, saw lords as deriving sake and soke from their very status. For example, men regarded as barons may generally have been taken to exercise sake and soke.[76] The development possibly took the following form: grants of sake and soke gave a court for certain types of case; then it was found that all significant lords had courts, and perhaps were exercising a jurisdiction similar to those who had received grants of sake and soke; finally such lords were described as having sake and soke even though they had received no special grant. Late twelfth-century definitions could reflect such a development: 'sake means jurisdiction, that is court and justice'.[77]

If the honorial court was meeting in the relevant locality,

---

75. J. Goebel, *Felony and Misdemeanor* (New York, 1937), pp. 391–9; Hurnard, 'Franchises', 294–5, 300, 445; D. Roffe, 'From thegnage to barony', *ANS* 12 (1990), 157–8; and note *Glanvill*, i 2, Hall, p. 4. For soke involving some jurisdiction over theft, see *Leges Edwardi*, 22, Liebermann, i 647.

76. Stenton, *First Century*, pp. 103–4, esp. 103 n. 2 remains convincing, despite recent criticisms. Note also *LHP*, 20.2, 25, Downer, pp. 122, 128. The king could grant land without granting the soke; *LHP*, 19.2–3, Downer, p. 122.

77. Howden, ii 242; see also Pollock and Maitland, i 579–80; *Bracton*, f. 154 b, Thorne, ii 436; other definitions were completely misguided, e.g. *CMA*, ii 282.

it might hear cases arising from sake and soke jurisdiction. Other cases may have gone before hallmoots. In addition, particularly if the lord's right of sake and soke extended over a considerable area, seignorial officials may have held court sessions to hear the resultant business. On occasion, the lord or his official had to claim his rights over a case taking place in a shire or hundred court. Then he might hear the dispute at a special meeting on the fringe of the main gathering,[78] or choose simply to take the financial reward, rather than insist on hearing the case in his own court.

Sake and soke and infangentheof were the most common judicial franchises enjoyed by lords, but there were more extensive grants. Some involved the right to deal with specific pleas, for example *hamsocn*, or assault on a person within a house. Others were of hundreds or the right to hold ordeals.[79] Lords, in turn, could pass such grants, like those of sake and soke, on to their own men or to churches.[80] In addition, there were a few holders of even greater franchises. Clauses in royal writs or charters forbade royal officials to interfere in privileged lands of churches such as Durham, Chertsey, and Battle, and similar grants may have been made for laymen, for example the lords of Cheshire, Shropshire, Herefordshire, Holderness, Cornwall, and Wallingford.[81] However, even with these grants, the lords probably only had jurisdiction over serious cases of violence and theft if they also controlled the relevant shire court or group of hundreds.[82] Such extensive liberties were enjoyed in particular by a few major pre-Conquest abbeys – Bury, Ramsey, Ely and Glastonbury – not within all their estates, but concentrated on specific areas, for example the

---

78. As suggested by *Lawsuits*, no. 169 and Maitland, *Domesday Book and Beyond*, p. 97.
79. See above, p. 38; Hyams, 'Ordeal', p. 113; Green, *Government*, p. 116; R. B. Patterson, ed., *Earldom of Gloucester Charters* (Oxford, 1973), no. 171; Hurnard, 'Franchises', 436–7. On barons without the right of ordeal, see *Leges Edwardi*, 9.3, Liebermann, i 633.
80. E.g. F. M. Stenton, *Types of Manorial Structure in the Northern Danelaw* (Oxford, 1910), pp. 92–3; Stenton, *First Century*, p. 104.
81. E.g. *RRAN*, i nos 235, 294, 306, 311, 344; ii nos 767, 774, 859, 1651; S. Painter, *Studies in the History of the English Feudal Barony* (Baltimore, MD, 1943), pp. 110–11, 117; Warren, *Governance*, p. 51. On greater franchises in Anglo-Saxon England, see Hurnard, 'Franchises'.
82. Hurnard, 'Franchises', 444, also 448–9.

a winner of The Charlotte Newberger Poetry Prize and is a Pushcart nominee. She has work forthcoming in *Pantheon Magazine, Redactions Poetry & Poetics, Mizmor L'David Anthology, Lines+Stars, Origins,* and *dreams&nightmares.* She can be reached at babokamel.com.

Jen Karetnick is the author of three full-length poetry collections, including *American Sentencing* (Winter Goose Publishing, May 2016), a finalist for the 2017 Julie Suk Award from Jacar Press, and *The Treasures That Prevail* (Whitepoint Press, September 2016), a finalist for the 2017 Poetry Society of Virginia Book Award. She has also published four poetry chapbooks and edited two anthologies of South Florida poets and writers. She is currently writing a full-length spoken word play set in Everglades National Park.

Joy Kennedy-O'Neill holds a Ph.D. in Literature and teaches English at a small college on the Texas Gulf Coast. She's been published in *Strange Horizons, Nature,* F*lash Fiction Online, Daily Science Fiction,* and *New Orleans Review.* More stories are forthcoming in *Galaxy's Edge* and *The Cimarron Review.* Find her at Joykennedyoneill.com.

Laurinda Lind lives and teaches in New York's North Country near the St. Lawrence River. Her poetry has been in *Comstock Review, The Cortland Review, Ekphrasis, Main Street Rag, Off the Coast,* and *Paterson Literary Review.*

A. G. Lopes is a jack of all trades, who makes time in her life to be a writer. She uses her brother as a bouncing board for her plots, which he endures because he loves her and not because she bakes him yummy treats. At the moment, she's working on several other short stories, as well as two novel-length stories, and a small series.

Ligang Luo is a visual artist based in Beijing. He observes, wonders, paints, draws, teaches, reads, designs, and sometimes writes.

Alison McBain is an award-winning author with over sixty short stories/poems published, including work in *Litro, FLAPPERHOUSE,*

eight and a half hundreds held by Bury.[83] To these were added a very few, specially privileged monasteries after the Conquest: Henry I's foundation at Reading and his father's at Battle. Notably, however, the king carefully preserved his right to deal with cases the abbots were unable or unwilling to hear:

> The abbot and monks of Reading are to have throughout their possession all justice concerning assault and thefts and murders, about shedding of blood and breach of peace, as much as pertains to royal power, and about all wrongs. If the abbot and monks neglect to do such justice, the king is to compel it to be done, in such a way that it does not at all diminish the liberty of the church of Reading.[84]

Other great churchmen, particularly archbishops, also enjoyed special privileges.[85]

As for laymen, in the south-east the boroughs of Colchester and Maldon and the castles of Tunbridge and Pevensey each were surrounded by a specially privileged area or 'banleuca'. More extensive privileged areas were the Sussex Rapes, granted by William I to loyal followers in order to secure his Conquest. However, there is evidence that their independence decreased under Henry I, probably because Sussex no longer represented a threatened frontier. In the north and west there is more evidence for continuing liberties. Much of the material is late, but it does seem likely that these lords enjoyed wide powers during the Anglo-Norman period. Most independent of all were the earls of the border counties of

---

83. Hurnard, 'Franchises', 316; for Ely's privileges in the Norman period, see E. Miller, *The Abbey and Bishopric of Ely* (Cambridge, 1951), chs 2, 7.

84. *RRAN*, iii no. 675; on Battle Abbey, see *RRAN*, ii no. 529 and Hurnard, 'Franchises', 434–6. See also Hurnard, 'Franchises', 455 on the possibility of a special court resulting from the extended sanctuary of Tynemouth, and its possible link to the rights enjoyed by Robert de Mowbray, earl of Northumbria. On possible grants of immunities by lords to their foundations, see D. Crouch, 'The foundation of Leicester Abbey, and other problems', *Midland History* 12 (1987), 7.

85. Canterbury: *Lawsuits*, no. 5, Hurnard, 'Franchises', 456; see also 457–9 on Lincoln. York: *RRAN*, ii no. 518; *Lawsuits*, no. 172; Hurnard, 'Franchises', 315–16, note also 438.

Shrewsbury and Chester, and the bishop of Durham. The earls enjoyed not merely territorial domination of the counties but also control of their shire courts, and hence might exercise a full range of royal powers. However, the special powers of the earls of Shrewsbury did not survive the breaking of the Bellême family early in Henry I's reign. This left Chester and Durham, whose peculiarly independent status continued to develop until they were distinguished in the thirteenth century by the title of palatinates.[86]

Lords' courts therefore were significant throughout Anglo-Norman England. They need not be seen to conflict necessarily with royal or other local courts, but rather to be one of the means whereby the conquerors ruled England. Besides the activities of their honorial courts, lords brought effective authority to disputes on a very local level through their hallmoots. Similarly, privileges acknowledged the local power of lords and also allowed the effective exercise of Norman authority in areas which royal government found hard to reach.

. . .

URBAN COURTS

Two other types of court remain, even though they will not be central to this book: urban and church courts. Information on town courts in the Anglo-Norman period is very sparse, particularly before 1100. Whilst the Anglo-Saxon law codes mention the 'borough court', it is uncertain whether this was a court for the *burgh* or a court held in the *burgh* for the surrounding area. Domesday Book mentions lawmen in Cambridge, Stamford, Lincoln, and York, and these were presumably leading members of a borough court. It also provides some evidence for the court of Chester.[87] Other post-Conquest mentions of town courts

86. Hurnard, 'Franchises', 314, Green, *Government*, pp. 113–15. On the Marcher lords of South Wales, see R. R. Davies, 'Kings, lords and liberties in the March of Wales, 1066–1277', *TRHS* 5th Ser. 29 (1979), 41–61.
87. J. Tait, *The Medieval English Borough* (Manchester, 1936), pp. 43–4, S. M. G. Reynolds, 'Towns in Domesday Book', in J. C. Holt, ed., *Domesday Studies* (Woodbridge, 1987), pp. 307–8. On the relationship of the borough court to the hundred court, see Tait, *Borough*, p. 60.

appear in charters for boroughs or very occasionally in case records. For example, a charter of Abbot Anselm of Bury St Edmunds in favour of the burgesses of Bury laid down that 'they shall not . . . need to go outside the town of St Edmund to the hundred court or to the shire court, nor may they be impleaded in any plea except at their port-moot'.[88] In London there may at first have been a large folk-moot, together with landowners' courts for their tenants, but in the twelfth century the most important gathering came to be the Husting which met weekly. This may originally have been a commercial court, but took on much wider duties.

The urban courts shared many of the functions of other courts, for example the witnessing of transactions. Their business naturally reflected urban circumstances, and in addition to cases concerning land-holding, we see others, for example, over the payment of tolls.[89] By the end of Henry I's reign London may have had control of all pleas, including those pertaining to the Crown, but other towns were not so privileged. A survey of Henry II's time, purporting to record the customs of Newcastle in his grandfather Henry I's reign, states that 'pleas which arise in the borough shall be held and concluded there, except those which belong to the king's crown'.[90] Nevertheless, the autonomy enjoyed by towns allowed the growth or maintenance of various local customs both procedural and substantive, for example concerning the inheritance and alienation of land.[91]

· · ·

ECCLESIASTICAL COURTS

Moves towards the existence of separate ecclesiastical courts, with their own procedure, areas of jurisdiction, and largely clerical personnel, started soon after the Norman Conquest as part of more general Church reform.[92] In the early or mid-1070s William I ordered that

88. *EHD*, ii no. 287.
89. E.g. *Lawsuits*, nos 270, 191.
90. *EHD*, ii no. 298.
91. See Reynolds, 'Towns in Domesday'; *Borough Customs*; Pollock and Maitland, i 644, 647–8.
92. For a good introduction to ecclesiastical justice in this period, see F. Barlow, *The English Church, 1066–1154* (London, 1979), ch. 4.

no bishop or archdeacon shall henceforth hold pleas relating to the episcopal laws in the hundred court; nor shall they bring to the judgment of secular men any case which concerns the rule of souls. But anyone cited under the episcopal laws in respect of any case or wrong shall come to the place which the bishop chooses and names, and there he shall answer concerning his case or wrong. Let him do what is just for God and his bishop not according to the law of the hundred, but according to the canons and episcopal laws.[93]

The writ's probable concern is a not very clearly defined category of offences against moral law and the rights of the Church, rather than, for example, cases involving church lands. As far as can be told, it continued to allow 'pleas relating to the episcopal laws' to be heard in the shire, where the bishop might be present. Indeed, Wulfstan of Worcester reputedly 'applied his mind vigilantly' to religious affairs in the shire court, but slept 'disdainfully' through the mass of secular business.[94] However, the writ did move cases to the bishops' own courts. These courts included an annual or biennial synod of the diocese, but also additional hearings.[95] By Stephen's reign, the pressure of judicial business on the bishop was reduced by archdeacons' courts taking much of the burden. These heard accusations brought by individuals, but also cases prosecuted *ex officio* by the archdeacons.[96] Above all others remained the pope's court, which by the mid-twelfth century was receiving an ever increasing number of appeals from England.

Ecclesiastical courts heard disputes involving lay people, cases of marriage and bastardy, of the bequest of moveables after death, and – although the surviving evidence is sparse – of lay sin.[97] They also heard accusations of clerical

---

93. *EHD*, ii no. 79.
94. C. Morris, 'William I and the church courts', *EHR* 82 (1967), 451, 458, 460–1. See *Lawsuits*, no. 442 for a tithe case in the shire court early in Henry II's reign.
95. Barlow, *English Church*, pp. 154–5.
96. Barlow, *English Church*, pp. 155–6, R. C. van Caenegem, 'Public prosecution of crime in twelfth-century England', in his *Legal History: a European Perspective* (London, 1991), pp. 1–36.
97. Barlow, *English Church*, pp. 166–71.

offences, although many of these would have been settled out of court, for example in the monastery. In the Anglo-Norman period the punishment of clerical offenders seems often to have involved co-operation with lay powers, perhaps after the cleric had been deprived of his orders. Cases between great ecclesiastics, for example over the relationship of two churches, were often heard by the king, or by a combination of royal and ecclesiastical courts.[98] Likewise, a wide range of cases involving ecclesiastical lands or other rights took place either in royal courts or those of ecclesiastics in their role as lords. Certainly, in the latter there might be a large ecclesiastical element, but they must still be distinguished from, for example, diocesan courts.[99] Conflicts of jurisdiction did occasionally arise, and tended to be decided by the king and his court. However, overall before 1154 there is little evidence of conflict, much more of co-operation between ecclesiastical and lay courts.[100]

· · ·

CONCLUSIONS

Thus Anglo-Norman England combined new courts and those which survived from Anglo-Saxon England. There must have been variation of practice between courts, particularly with regard to procedure, but there are also signs of shared procedure and of shared custom on substantive matters.[101] The diffuse settlement pattern of Anglo-Norman England again helps to explain such shared practice, with men attending several honorial, shire, or hundred courts. It can also be explained by royal control and the inter-relationship of the courts. Cases could be transferred from one to another. Overlords may have heard

98. Barlow, *English Church*, pp. 166, 172–3.
99. See e.g. *Lawsuits*, nos 178, 180, 197 for cases in the king's court involving prebends, burials and tithes; no. 226 (below, p. 106) for a court with a large ecclesiastical element. On cases involving land, see Barlow, *English Church*, pp. 173–6, and on free alms, below, p. 129.
100. Barlow, *English Church*, p. 171; note also the combination of ecclesiastical and lay courts used e.g. in *Lawsuits*, no. 223.
101. Variation: e.g. *Glanvill*, ix 10, xiv 8, Hall, pp. 113, 177; also below, p. 132, on the Assize of Essoiners. Shared substantive customs: see below, p. 116.

complaints of default of justice from sub-vassals against the intermediate lord. However, as noted earlier, default of justice and false judgment were royal rights, and the capacity to transfer cases was primarily a royal one. Failure of the hundred court to do justice might lead to a hearing in the county.[102] Similarly, cases might be removed from seignorial courts to the county once default of justice had been proved. And from there, cases could be taken to the king's own court. The impression of integration is reinforced by the use of royal writs and the evidence for the presence of royal justices in shire and seignorial courts, most notably when serious pleas were being heard.[103] Doubtless many factors, notably of geography, meant that some courts, be they shire, hundred or seignorial, were more independent than others, but the impression remains that the courts could combine effectively.

There is little sign of a confusion of courts in Anglo-Norman England, although certainly there was not the precision nor the rules of jurisdiction which existed in the developed common law. The immediate post-Conquest period must have required some adjustment of assumptions. Yet, if the 1108 writ designating land cases to various courts may signify that clarification was needed, there is very little other evidence that at least by Henry I's reign people felt confused by the court system. The lack of rigid jurisdictional rules need not have been a disadvantage for disputants. The availability of a variety of regular courts, some within easy reach, may have been beneficial, and may indeed have encouraged men to bring their disputes into court.[104]

---

102. *LHP*, 7.6, Downer, p. 100.
103. See below, p. 70; also p. 114; Palmer, *County*, pp. 144–7; *Lawsuits*, no. 19; also *Leges Edwardi*, 9.2, Liebermann, i 633.
104. Cf. e.g. below, p. 168, on the problem of increasingly lengthy gaps between eyres after Henry II's reign.

Chapter 3

VIOLENCE AND THEFT IN ANGLO-NORMAN ENGLAND

As with the holding of various courts, law and associated activities relating to wrongdoing showed notable continuities from at least the tenth century to the twelfth and even beyond. Types of offence did not change markedly. The capture of offenders remained a major problem. Local action continued to be essential to any effective prevention, policing, and prosecuting of wrongs, and royal administration had to work through the local.[1]

The elements of co-operation and of balancing of interests within local communities no doubt brought benefits, but the system's successes rested in part on peer pressure, on informing – secretly or in a formalized manner[2] – with all its opportunities of persecution and rumour-mongering, on the threat of financial penalties, and on the presence in, or close to, the communities of local, ever-watchful Big Brothers.[3] Even the preference for out-of-court settlements, idealized as 'Love' being preferred to 'Law', gave considerable scope for domination by the powerful.

Moreover, potential tensions persisted between the aims of the various parties involved. An accuser might, above all, want vengeance. This might conflict with the king's aim of

1. See above, p. 33, on the part played, for example, by royal sergeants in preliminaries such as the investigation of corpses. This chapter owes much to years of help from, and conversation with, Patrick Wormald. His ideas appear in his *Making of English Law* (Oxford, 1997), ch. 9; also his 'Maitland and Anglo-Saxon law: beyond Domesday Book', in Hudson, *Centenary Essays*, pp. 1–20.
2. See below, p. 65, on presentment.
3. See below, p. 53, for Robert Malarteis.

maintaining the peace, obtaining revenue, and increasing his prestige. On other occasions, the king might desire that the offender be punished whereas the victim desired compensation for the injury and dishonour sustained. Such problems and such conflicting aims underlie the functioning and development of law relating to theft and violence during the Anglo-Norman and Angevin periods.

. . .

BRICSTAN'S CASE

A letter of the bishop of Ely, preserved by the chronicler Orderic Vitalis, records an unusual event in 1115 or 1116:

A certain man named Bricstan lived in an estate of our church, in a village called Chatteris. This man, as his neighbours bear witness, did wrong to no man but was peacefully content with his own goods, sparing those of others. For he was neither very rich nor very poor, but managed his affairs and those of his family respectably after the fashion of a layman with a modest competence. He lent money to his needy neighbours, but not at usury; only, because so many men are untrustworthy, he retained securities from his debtors. So he kept between the two extremes, being considered neither better than other good men nor worse than bad ones. Believing he was at peace with all men and without a single enemy, he was inspired by divine grace ... to seek to be bound by the rule of St Benedict and clothed in the habit. ... He came to our monastery, which was built in honour of St Peter the apostle and St Etheldreda, and sought admission from the monks, promising to put himself and all that he had under their government. But, sad to relate, the evil one through whose envy Adam fell from Paradise will never cease to vex with envy his descendants up to the very last generation. ... A certain minister of King Henry, who was more particularly a servant of the devil with wolf-like fangs, appeared on the scene. ... His name was Robert and he was nick-named 'Malarteis', from the Latin meaning 'ill-doer'. The name was deserved. For he seemed to have no function except to catch men out. ... He accused all equally whenever he could, striving with all his might to harm everyone. ... If he could find no valid reason for condemning them, he became an inventor of falsehood and father of lies through the devil who spoke in him. ...

When it was rumoured that Bricstan wished to put on the

habit of religion, Robert, following the teaching of his master who always lies and deceives, appeared on the scene. He, beginning to heap falsehood upon falsehood, said to us: 'Know that this man, Bricstan, is a thief, who has seized the king's money by larceny and hidden it, and is trying to take the habit to escape judgment and punishment for his crime [*crimen*], not for any other kind of salvation. For he found hidden treasure, and by secretly stealing from it has become a usurer. Since he is guilty of the great crimes of larceny and usury, he fears to come before the king or his justices. Therefore I have been sent here to you at the king's command, and I forbid you to receive him into your community.' We therefore, hearing the king's prohibition and fearing to incur his wrath, refused to receive the man among us. . . . He was sent under surety to trial. With Ralph Basset presiding, all the men of the county were assembled at Huntingdon, according to English custom, and I Hervey was present with Reginald abbot of Ramsey, Robert abbot of Thorney, and a number of clerks and monks. To cut a long story short, the accused was charged together with his wife, and the crimes falsely attributed to him were repeated. He denied the charge; he could not confess what he had not done. The opposing party charged him with lying and made fun of him, for he was somewhat corpulent, short of stature, and had what one might call a homely face. After many undeserved contumelies had been heaped upon him, he was unjustly condemned . . . and sentenced to be handed over with all his goods to the king's custody. [He and his wife handed over all their goods, and his wife offered to carry the hot iron in order to support his oath that he had held nothing back.] Then he was bound and taken into custody, and taken to London where he was thrown into a dark prison. There, unjustly laden with iron fetters of excessive weight, he suffered the torment of daily hunger and cold for a considerable time. But finding himself in such a plight, he cried out as well as he knew how for divine aid to come to him in his great need. . . . He called incessantly with a sorrowful heart and all the voice he could raise on St Benedict, under whose rule he had vowed in all sincerity to live . . . and on the holy virgin Etheldreda, in whose monastery he had proposed to do so.

[After five wretched months], one night, when the bells were ringing for the night office throughout the city, and he in his prison had been without food of any kind for three days, in addition to his other sufferings, and was almost despairing of bodily recovery, he was repeating the names of the saints in feeble voice. ... [whereupon, in a blaze of light] St Benedict and St Etheldreda, with her sister St Sexburga, appeared to the suppliant. ... The venerable Benedict placed his hand on the ring fetters and broke them on both sides, drawing them from the feet of the prisoner in such a way that he felt nothing at all and the saint seemed to have broken them more by his command than by force. When he had pulled them off he tossed them aside almost contemptuously and struck the beam which supported the room above the dungeon with such violence that he made a great crack in it. At the sound of the impact the guards who were sleeping in the room above, were all awakened in terror. Fearing that the prisoners had fled they lit torches and rushed to the prison. Finding the doors undamaged and locked, they turned the keys and entered. When they saw that the man they had thrown into fetters was freed, they marvelled greatly.

The events were reported to the queen, who sent Ralph Basset to investigate. He checked that there had been no witchcraft, realized that a miracle had occurred, and then, 'rejoicing and weeping', brought Bricstan to the queen and barons.[4]

Here we have an unusually full, if sometimes problematic, account of an offence, trial, and preparation for punishment. Bricstan is accused of a combination of theft, failure to hand over treasure trove, and usury. The degree of distinction between the first two is not entirely clear. Perhaps the account did not need to be more specific, perhaps court proceedings did not require any greater precision. Nor is the degree of Bricstan's guilt certain. The letter presents him as unjustly accused, although the statement that, while no usurer, 'he retained securities from his debtors, because so many men are untrustworthy' sounds like special pleading. However, a closely related account states that when Bricstan reached adulthood, 'he was caught up more and more in the wickedness of the world to the point that he obtained his livelihood from unhappy usury and nothing else'.[5] What is clear is the form of accusation. It is brought by a royal official, who resembles the royal sergeants we met in the

4. *Lawsuits*, no. 204A.
5. *Lawsuits*, no. 204B, from the *Liber Eliensis*.

Samara Golabuk is a Pushcart nominee whose work has appeared or is forthcoming in *Inklette, Eyedrum Periodically, Peacock Journal, Memoryhouse* and others. She has two children, works in marketing and design, and has returned to university to complete her BA in Poetry. More at www.samarawords.com.

Christy Hartman is a monkey-wrencher at heart who currently co-produces the podcast, *State of the Human.*

Ingrid Jendrzejewski has been published in places like *Passages North, The Los Angeles Review, The Conium Review, Jellyfish Review,* and *Rattle,* and her novella-in-flash, *Things I Dream About When I'm Not Sleeping,* is available in the anthology *How to Make a Window Snake,* published by Ad Hoc Fiction.

She has been nominated for a Pushcart Prize, Vestal Review's VERA Award, and twice for Best Small Fictions. Links to her work can be found at her website, www.ingridj.com and you can find her on Twitter @LunchOnTuesday.

Becca Borawski Jenkins holds an MFA in Cinema-Television Production from USC and has short stories appearing or forthcoming in *Menacing Hedge, The Forge, The Journal of Compressed Creative Arts, Syntax & Salt, Corium,* and *Jellyfish Review.* She is also an Associate Flash Fiction Editor at *jmww.* She and her husband spent the last year living off-grid in a remote part of North Idaho, and now roam North America in their RV.

Emily Joynton is currently a textile designer and freelance illustrator living in Philadelphia. She graduated with an MFA in Illustration Practice from Maryland Institute College of Art in May of 2017. She has since self-published two personal narrative comics,

Babo Kamel has appeared in literary reviews in the US, Australia, and Canada. Some of these include *Painted Bride Quarterly, Abyss & Apex, The Greensboro Review, Alligator Juniper,* and others. She was

last chapter 'keeping the king's pleas'. The case was heard in the shire court, presided over by a royal justice, Ralph Basset, but apparently a regular meeting rather than one specially summoned for the king's business. Procedure as described consists of accusation and denial, followed by debate on issues including the general character and appearance of the accused. Flexibility is also apparent when the question of the confiscation of Bricstan's goods arises, for then his wife offers to undergo ordeal, with no suggestion that the court was demanding it of her. Bricstan was sentenced, presumably to a physical penalty; despite its long duration, his imprisonment does not seem to have been regarded as the punishment. In this case, however, divine and saintly intervention freed the prisoner before he could be punished.

Bricstan's case is of the type which we, and thirteenth-century writers, would call criminal. However, the familiar distinction between civil and criminal pleas only began to enter into English law in the late twelfth century, under the influence of Roman and canon law.[6] The word *crimen* was familiar in the Anglo-Norman period, but its meaning was more flexible, often more extensive, than the modern notion of crime. In particular, it was employed to mean 'sin'.[7] Nor were the other words used to describe offences which we would call crimes solely applicable to a clearly defined category of acts. We have therefore a terminological problem: the need to avoid using the handy term 'crime', for fear of projecting back a later categorization. I instead take as the area of investigation offences committed by individuals or small groups primarily against the victim's person or his moveable goods. Often the more serious offences involved force, sometimes violence; in the terms of the time, they threatened the peace. Such a threat might make them of concern to the king, as would the notion that they were breaches of the general oath of loyalty and good behaviour sworn to him by men over the age of twelve.[8]

6. See below, pp. 160–1.
7. See e.g. Orderic, i, *index verborum*, under *crimen*, and also e.g. *reatus*. See also Downer, *LHP*, pp. 427–30.
8. See above, p. 30.

Faced with very limited case material, writers on the Anglo-Norman period have been lured by the mirage of plenty offered by the *Leges*. However, these are archaicizing texts, and I prefer to use them only when they are congruous with other contemporary material, or with the general pattern of legal development revealed by the more plentiful later sources.[9] Setting aside the *Leges*, we are left mainly with anecdotal material from ecclesiastical narrative sources. These have obvious disadvantages, including an ecclesiastical bias, and a preference for the unusual. They resemble newspaper stories rather than law reports. However, since it is unlikely that any great shift in the nature of offences occurred, conclusions can be tested against the much more plentiful sources emerging from *c.* 1200. Moreover, reliance on anecdotal evidence can have some positive advantages. It discourages concentration on the royal administration of justice or the genealogy of certain common law actions, compelling instead an interest in the setting of individual disputes, the relationship of offence and offenders to society.

.   .   .

OFFENCES, OFFENDERS, AND MOTIVES

In Anglo-Norman accounts, homicide and theft predominate. There are no contemporary indications of homicide rates, but thirteenth-century records may suggest a rough annual average of one killing per twenty villages. This was a knife-carrying society, in which potentially fatal fights could easily arise. If knives were not available, other weapons such as sticks or axes were readily at hand.[10] Poor medicine meant that even minor wounds could prove fatal. Nevertheless, the earliest surviving royal court rolls from the decades around 1200 show that many sustained non-fatal wounds, and the absence of wounding from anecdotal sources reflects their preference for the most dramatic. Other serious offences included rape, forgery, and arson. As well as its impact on highly combustible buildings, arson was particularly hated as an offence

9. See also below, p. 249–50.
10. See J. B. Given, *Society and Homicide in Thirteenth-Century England* (Stanford, CA, 1977), pp. 40, 189.

involving stealth. Such offences were very hard to prosecute and also considered dishonourable, unmanly.

Killing might occur in the context of theft, or the associated offences of robbery and burglary.[11] The type of theft would vary with the social context. A severe problem, particularly in the more pastoral areas of the west and north, was cattle theft, for animals were a major element of agricultural capital. No doubt there was much minor larceny, and we hear of a pick-pocket taking advantage of a large and absorbed crowd:

> As [some monks of Evesham] arrived in Oxford and preached the word of God to the people, a man of great faith ... humbly approached the reliquary of Saint Ecgwin among the others, very devoutly completed his prayers three times and during these prayers put his hand into his purse and produced a threefold donation which he faithfully offered to God's saint. But the old enemy was not prepared to let this happen and with ardent greed instigated one of his followers ... to cause damage to the faithful man, who was concentrating on his prayers. Remarkable madness! While almost everybody was thinking of higher things, this unhappy creature, as a member of the devil, approaches the man and stealthily takes from his purse as many pennies as he can; he repeats his wicked work and commits this same act for a third time.[12]

There must also have been a mass of minor wrongs, assaults, insults and so on, which never appears in the sources. Numerous petty conflicts must simply have been an accepted part of village life. Many would never reach a court.

The majority of offenders were lowly men of whom we would otherwise know nothing – vagabonds, villagers, or men of slightly higher status like Bricstan. Not surprisingly in a population with a large clerical element, some churchmen committed offences, whilst others had acts of horrific barbarity attributed to them. According to Orderic, David of Scotland and Countess Judith's first-born child

---

11. See Given, *Homicide*, pp. 106, 110.
12. *Lawsuits*, no. 14; see below, p. 67 for the outcome of this incident. See also above, p. 13 n. 51, for charms against theft.

was cruelly murdered by the iron fingers of a certain wretched clerk. This man was punished for an appalling crime which he had committed in Norway by having his eyes put out and his hands and feet cut off. ... Afterwards Earl David took him into his care in England for the love of God, and provided him and his small daughter with food and clothing. Using the iron fingers with which he was fitted, being maimed, he cruelly stabbed his benefactor's two-year-old son while pretending to caress him, and so at the prompting of the devil he suddenly tore out the bowels of the suckling in his nurse's arms. ... The murderer was bound to the tails of four wild horses and torn to pieces by them, as a terrible warning to evil-doers.[13]

Occasionally, particularly in Stephen's reign, higher-status laymen were accused of homicide or theft, but instances are fairly rare. This may reflect not only patterns of activity, but also contemporary classification. The same deed might be categorized by different people as theft if committed by a villager, as oppression or distraint if carried out by a lord or royal official, as youthful exuberance if perpetrated by loutish young aristocrats.[14]

Contemporaries had various explanations for offenders' activities. Not surprisingly, the predominantly ecclesiastical sources emphasized sin, the devil, or diabolically inspired madness, as in the case of the Oxford pick-pocket. Other more practical reasons were also given. Drunkenness was a particular problem, as we shall see again in the Angevin period.[15] Inspiration could also come from greed, revenge, jealousy or passion, as in the following tale of entrapment told of the mother of Hugh de Morville, one of Becket's murderers:

His mother, so it is said, was ardently in love with a young man called Litulf, who rejected adultery. She asked by some extraordinary female trickery that, with drawn sword, he should bring her horse forward, as if playing a game. As he did this, she in the language of the country, exclaimed to her husband who was in front of her: 'Hugh de Morville, beware,

13. Orderic, iv 274–6; for more probable clerical crime, see *Lawsuits*, no. 169.
14. See e.g. *Lawsuits*, no. 143, and below, pp. 160, 191; for offences by officials, see e.g. *Lawsuits*, no. 12.
15. See below, p. 159.

beware, beware, Litulf has drawn his sword.' Therefore the innocent young man was condemned to death, boiled in hot water and underwent martyrdom as if he had stretched out his hand to spill the blood of his lord.[16]

If contemporaries concentrated mainly on moral and personal causes of offences, the sources also give some sense of their geographical and social setting. Some areas, notably thick forest, were particularly dangerous, and roads along which wealth was carried made a sensible focus for robbers.[17] Towns, with their markets and crowds, could also provide happy grounds for thieves, and the concentration of population increased the chance of riots.[18] In addition, there occasionally surfaces the poverty which must have forced men to turn to theft. Of Ralph Basset's mass execution of thieves in 1124, the *Anglo-Saxon Chronicle* commented that

> a large number of trustworthy men said that many were destroyed very unjustly there, but our Lord God Almighty that sees and knows all secrets – he sees the wretched people are treated with complete injustice. First they are robbed of their property and then they are killed. It was a very troublous year. The man who had property was deprived of it by severe taxes and severe courts; the man who had none died of hunger.[19]

Few may have been excused their offences on the grounds of compulsion by poverty, but particularly in respect of homicide, notions of liability were quite sophisticated. It was recognized that killing might be in self-defence, although in the developed common law such a killer was unlikely to be acquitted but rather had to obtain a royal pardon.[20] Alternatively, killing might be accidental. However, it was one thing to have fairly sophisticated notions of liability, another to bring them to bear in settling a dispute. A particular danger was that the victim's

16. *Lawsuits*, no. 330. Note also *LHP*, 72.1a, Downer, p. 226; for greed, see *Lawsuits*, no. 688.
17. See e.g. *Lawsuits*, no. 8.
18. *Lawsuits*, no. 173.
19. *Lawsuits*, no. 237.
20. *LHP*, 72.1b, 72.2, Downer, pp. 226–8; Hurnard, *Pardon*, pp. 108, 299–302.

kin would see as intentional and malicious a homicide which the killer regarded as accidental or self-defence. Such a clash of views may well underlie the following conflict:

> William, nicknamed the bald, lacked the confidence to bring his quarrels into the open. He had killed a man but not on purpose, and he could in no way buy the friendship of the relations of the killed man nor at any price obtain their forgiveness. . . . There were five brothers who were so furious and uttered such threats for the death of their brother that they could frighten away anyone.

Regular procedures appear to have been unable to deal with this dispute, and we shall see that it required the dramatic intervention of Wulfstan of Worcester and of still higher powers to bring a solution.[21]

.   .   .

PREVENTION AND POLICE

Medieval societies, with no police forces, had great difficulty apprehending offenders who were allowed any time to escape. They had either to prevent offences being committed, or to catch the perpetrators red-handed. Effective action therefore had to be locally based. Measures such as an insistence that cattle sales be publicly witnessed might help to prevent theft or ease its prosecution.[22] Much else would be *ad hoc*, the individual seeking to break up a fight, a group of senior figures discussing local problems. Activity could be aggressive, deterring outsiders from attacking members of the community; such protection was one of the functions of lordship. Or action could be defensive, as in the provision of watchmen, or more extensive protection for towns. Thus a grant of the customs of the burgesses of Bury states:

> it is their custom to find eight men per year for the four wards to guard the town at night and on the feast of St Edmund sixteen men for the four gates, two during the day and two during the night and similarly during the twelve days following

21. *Lawsuits*, no. 139; see below, p. 66.
22. See 'Ten Articles of William I', c. 5, *EHD*, ii no. 18; *Leges Willelmi*, 45, *Leges Edwardi*, 38–9, Liebermann, i 517–18, 668–70.

the birth of the Lord. They shall also find four gatekeepers per year for the four gates, the fifth gate being the east gate and in the abbot's hand. If need be, the sacrist shall find the necessary material for the gates and the burgesses shall repair them . . .[23]

There was a considerable fear of outsiders, of those for whom no one would answer. They had either to be prevented from entering the community for any length of time, or to find people to answer for them.[24]

Concern with the activities of a community's own members is apparent in a lord's responsibility for his household. According to the *Leges Edwardi*, c. 21, here significantly expanding a brief law of Cnut to fit the contemporary context,

> barons had their knights and their own servants, namely stewards, butlers, chamberlains, cooks, and bakers under their own frankpledge, and these men had their esquires and other servants under their frankpledge [*sub suo friborgo*; see below, p. 63]. So that if they did wrong and the complaint of their neighbours arises against them, [their lords] had them to right in their own courts, if they had sake and soke and toll and team and infangentheof. . . . And those who do not possess these customs shall do right before the king's justice in the hundred or wapentake or shire courts.[25]

The effectiveness of communal responsibility could be sharpened by the threat of monetary penalty. Most famous of these is the *murdrum* fine, a penalty exacted by the Conqueror and his successors for failure to produce the secret killer of a Norman. In such circumstances, a fine was imposed on the hundred or perhaps the village or the lord of the land in which the killing had happened. According to some sources the fine could be as much as £44 but

23. *Lawsuits*, no. 295. Note also obligations for the protection of roads, e.g. *Lawsuits*, no. 8.
24. See e.g. *LHP*, 8.5, Downer, pp. 102–4, *Leges Willelmi*, 48, *Leges Edwardi*, 23, Liebermann, i 519, 648, Assize of Clarendon, c. 10, *EHD*, ii no. 24; see also W. A. Morris, *The Frankpledge System* (New York, 1910), pp. 71–2.
25. Stenton, *First Century*, p. 142; see also *LHP*, 8.2a, 41.6–7, Downer, pp. 102, 148.

according to the 1130 Pipe Roll amounts were often between £10 and £20.[26] Such penalties gave an incentive not only to produce murderers but to prevent killings. Thus a combination of pressure from above and from peers was the main recipe for the maintenance of order, be it in a village, a hundred, a lordship, or a seignorial household.

All of these were communities with a variety of functions, but one grouping was particularly formed for purposes of good order: the frankpledge. This was a group of ten or twelve men, or sometimes of all the men of the village, acting as mutual sureties that they would not commit offences, and bound to produce the guilty party if an offence were committed. If they failed to do so, they were amerced, that is they made a payment for the king's mercy.[27] The group was referred to as a tithing, reflecting its basic number of ten members. Entry to tithing was probably marked by swearing to be faithful to the king and neither to commit nor to consent to theft. The village had an incentive for ensuring full membership of tithing, for if an offence were committed and the offender was not in tithing, the village was amerced.[28]

The term frankpledge first appears between 1114 and 1118 when the *Leges Henrici* use the Latin form *plegium liberale* (free pledge). The English term of the same meaning, *friborg*, is probably older, raising the possibility that frankpledge was Anglo-Saxon in origin. Many of the conditions making frankpledge desirable existed before 1066, but the pre-Conquest laws leave uncertainty. Certainly by Cnut's reign, there were tithings, men had to have sureties, and all over twelve years of age took an oath not to be a thief or a thief's accomplice.[29] The question remains

26. See *Leges Edwardi*, 15, Liebermann, i 641–2; *LHP*, 91, Downer, pp. 284–6; *Dialogus*, pp. 52–3; *Surrey*, p. 107. £10–20 is roughly equal to the annual income from a reasonably sized knight's fee in the mid-twelfth century; Stenton, *First Century*, pp. 167–9.

27. *Lincs.*, e.g. nos 1038, 1040, 1043, 1045 suggest that by 1202 half a mark or a mark was the appropriate amercement for a frankpledge which allowed one of its members to flee.

28. *Leges Edwardi*, 20, Liebermann, i 645–6; Morris, *Frankpledge*, pp. 86–9, 130 citing thirteenth-century texts; Pollock and Maitland, i 568–9.

29. See above, pp. 30, 56.

whether these related practices were separate or were united as in frankpledge. Arguments, but not conclusive ones, exist for both positions. However, a twelfth-century opinion is highly suggestive. William of Malmesbury believed that a system of tithings acting as mutual sureties, effectively frankpledge, was created in Alfred's reign, and whilst the precise attribution may be doubted, it seems very unlikely that William would have so predated a Norman innovation. The evidence for frankpledge existing before the Norman Conquest is as strong as can reasonably be expected.[30]

Certain areas and groups of men were not included in frankpledge: inhabitants of forests, of some boroughs, clerics, and those under the control of their lords. Similarly, those of a status above ordinary freemen seem to have been exempt. Perhaps compulsory membership of a tithing composed of lesser men was seen as demeaning to their honour, and anyway they could be brought to justice by other methods, notably by distraining upon their land.[31] In addition, there appears to have been no frankpledge in the northern or western border counties. This may stem from Anglo-Saxon arrangements, or from the limited control exercised there by the first Norman kings.[32] Aside from these exceptions, all men over the age of twelve were to participate in the frankpledge system.

The tithings' duties were various: to maintain a general watch on local affairs; to raise the hue and cry and make arrests; to keep captured offenders in custody; to act as surety that their members would appear in court to answer

30. Wormald, *Making*, ch. 9, 'Maitland', pp. 14–15; II *Cnut*, 20, 21, *EHD*, i 50, *Liebermann*, i 322–4. William of Malmesbury, *Gesta Regum*, ed. W. Stubbs (2 vols, London, 1887–9), i 129–30. Cf. Morris, *Frankpledge*, pp. 2, 5–35, who argues that before the Conquest tithing's only purpose was the capture of thieves. Suretyship was separate, only one surety being required for people of good repute, and parties not having to enter into mutual surety relationships. Moreover, suretyship was temporary and voluntary in that the surety could withdraw from the arrangement.
31. Morris, *Frankpledge*, pp. 61–4, 72–85. By the thirteenth century even some ordinary freemen were excused membership, but this may well have been a later development, perhaps linked to an increasingly rigid law of status.
32. Morris, *Frankpledge*, pp. 44–59.

charges; and perhaps to make good damage that was done. Failure to produce the member who had committed an offence resulted in amercement for the whole tithing.[33] Underlying such duties there was a further function, to ensure that their members did not commit offences. This obviously was the best method of avoiding amercements. It was prevention through peer pressure backed by financial interest.

Each tithing had a head-man, but the general regulation of frankpledge was the business of the sheriff in the hundred court. Other evidence supports the *Leges Henrici*'s statement that

> If a specially full session is needed, all freemen, both house-holders in the own right and those in the service of others, shall assemble twice a year in their hundred to determine, among other things, whether tithings are complete, or what persons have withdrawn or have been added, and how and for what reason.

In order to hold such sessions, the sheriff made a biennial tour of his county, and hence the sessions were referred to as the sheriff's tourn.[34] These sessions could also deal with infractions of the peace, and with presentments by the tithings. Although evidence for such presentments only becomes clear from 1166, it is very hard to see how the frankpledge system could otherwise have worked. If the offender had not fled, but the tithing knew his identity, the only way for its members to fulfil their oath taken on entry to frankpledge and to avoid amercement was to give him up, in effect to present him. This might happen at any time, but the most likely regular occasion was when the sheriff was checking the proper working of frankpledge at his tourn. In this case, Henry II's supposed introduction of

---

33. Morris, *Frankpledge*, pp. 90–100; on restoration for damage, *Leges Edwardi*, 20.4, Liebermann, i 646. *Consiliatio Cnuti*, II.19.2d, Liebermann, i 618 states that tithing was popularly referred to as 'ward' or 'watch'.
34. *LHP*, 8.1, Downer, p. 102; see also Morris, *Frankpledge*, esp. pp. 127–30, H. M. Cam, *The Hundred and the Hundred Rolls* (London, 1930), pp. 185–7. Profit emphasized by Morris, *Frankpledge*, p. 115. On privileged boroughs, see Morris, *Frankpledge*, pp. 147–50.

Tracy Davidson lives in Warwickshire, England, and writes poetry and flash fiction. Her work has appeared in various publications and anthologies, including *Poet's Market, Mslexia, Atlas Poetica, Writing Magazine, Modern Haiku, The Binnacle*, and more.

Alex DiFrancesco is a writer of fiction, creative non-fiction, and journalism. Their first novel, *The Devils That Have Come to Stay*, was published in 2015, and their second book, *Psychopomps*, is due out from Civil Coping Mechanisms Press in 2018. They have recently moved from Brooklyn to Cleveland, where they attend the NEOMFA program and think a lot about "Sweetest Day."

Elizabeth Fernandez is an educator, writer, and longtime activist, fighting for LGBTQ rights, domestic violence survivors, and increased political engagement, among many other things. She's a member of the board of Engage Miami, an alumni of the New Leaders Council Miami, and a Big Sister with Big Brothers, Big Sisters. A South Florida native, she loves comics and always finds her way back to the beach again.

Joaquin Fernandez is a recovering filmmaker and South Florida native perpetually on his way back to the West Coast. He's been featured in *Thought Catalog* and *Rebelle Society* and is currently at work on a novel.

Jennifer L. Freed writes, raises her children, and leads writing programs for retirees in Massachusetts. Her recent work appears in *Zone 3, The Worcester Review*, and *Connecticut River Review* (for which she received a Pushcart nomination). Her chapbook, *These Hands Still Holding* (Finishing Line Press), was a finalist in the 2013 New Women's Voices contest.

María José Giménez is a Venezuelan-Canadian poet, translator, and editor working in English, Spanish, and French. Assistant Translation Editor of *Anomaly* (formerly known as *Drunken Boat*), María José is co-founder of Mass Collaborative (dba Easthampton Co.Lab) and serves on the board of the American Literary Translators' Organization. Learn more at mariajosetranslates.com.

the procedure looks more like a restoration, perhaps involving greater regulation and standardization.[35]

Even with the frankpledge system, the major problem remained that of capturing wrongdoers. Occasionally the offender might make no attempt either to conceal his deed or to flee. He might feel sufficiently confident in his own strength and that of his supporters to deter accusation or to win a trial by combat. Alternatively, a man might remain if he believed that he had committed no serious wrong, but then find himself accused of a major offence: this was most likely to occur in cases of killing, where the killer felt his action had been self-defence or an accident. Let us return to the case of William the bald, whose plea that he had killed accidentally was unacceptable to the victim's brothers. Bishop Wulfstan of Worcester was at Gloucester, consecrating a church, in the presence of a vast crowd.

> His preaching filled a good part of the day, as he told them abundantly what he knew to be the most important thing to hold. I mean peace. . . . Many who had previously resisted all efforts at reconciliation were on that day persuaded to consent to pacification. People encouraged each other and if anyone thought he had to resist, the bishop was consulted. [The five brothers did not respond to the general mood.] They were brought before the bishop who asked them to forgive the wrong, but they refused utterly and violently. They added . . . that they would rather be altogether excommunicated than not avenge the death of their brother. Thereupon the bishop wearing his episcopal insignia threw himself before their feet hoping to obtain full satisfaction. As he was lying on the ground, he repeated his prayers promising to the dead man the benefit of masses and other advantages, in Worcester, as well as Gloucester. In no way influenced by such humility, they rejected all conciliation. . . . Hence as the bishop made little headway by using blandishments, he fought the sickness of their stubborn attitude with a more severe remedy. [He drew upon the crowd's support for his view that just as peace-makers are the children of God, so those who resist peace are the sons of the devil.] The malediction of the people was

35. Cf. N. D. Hurnard, 'The jury of presentment and the Assize of Clarendon', *EHR* 56 (1941), 379–83, Morris, *Frankpledge*, p. 117; Pollock and Maitland, i 558–60. Note that some control could pass into private hands, with or without royal permission; Assize of Clarendon, c. 9, *EHD*, ii no. 24; Morris, *Frankpledge*, pp. 134–5.

followed immediately by divine vengeance, for one of the brothers, the most violent, went mad. The wretch rolled around on the ground, biting the soil and scratching it with his fingers, foaming abundantly at the mouth and as his limbs were steaming in an unheard of manner he infested the air with a horrible stench. . . . [The brothers'] pride left them, their insolence disappeared, their arrogance withered away. You should also have seen them cherish what they had spurned, offer peace, implore mercy. . . . The sight of these events moved the bishop to clemency and immediately after mass he restored health to the sufferer and security to the others and established peace among them all.

This clearly is an extreme case which required considerable outside intervention, but later evidence also suggests that many serious cases were brought to agreement, sometimes in court, generally outside. This must have been still more true of minor offences, where even a court judgment might concentrate on the paying of compensation.[36] Such offenders might well choose to remain rather than flee.

Generally, however, if a serious offender were to be successfully brought to judgment, he had to be caught red-handed, or, in the case of our Oxford pick-pocket, shrivel-handed:

Saint Ecgwin did not wait long to punish the hands of this thief, for when this unfortunate man put his hand into the purse for the third time, it suddenly dried up and was retained inside that space as if it were closed. You should have seen this thief tremble, turn pale, wildly look around as if he had gone mad and fearing all sorts of deaths! The onlookers understood how it had all come about and proceeded to catch the thief, to marvel at the event and to praise God's saint aloud.

Without such saintly intervention, the victim or witnesses had to take a more active part, alerting their neighbours by raising the hue and cry, and then all were obliged to pursue the offender.[37] If he resisted, he might be killed.

36. *Lawsuits*, no. 139, also see above, p. 61; for out-of-court intervention, between sentence and punishment, see *Lawsuits*, no. 210, below, p. 79; for compensation, see below, pp. 80–3; for later evidence, see, pp. 165–6.
37. On pursuit in cases of cattle theft, see Pollock and Maitland, ii 157–8; also on offenders caught in the act, see the Penenden Heath reports, *Lawsuits*, no. 5B, 5K.

Such a pursuit not only helped to capture offenders but also allowed the victim to vent his own pain and fury. Indeed, the presence of neighbours may sometimes have been necessary to ensure that he did not take justice into his own hands.

Many perpetrators, however, were not caught in this way. Sometimes their identity was a mystery. On other occasions, everyone knew their identity, and then the threat of a communal penalty such as the *murdrum* fine may have helped to flush out the name.[38] However, it was not all a matter of penalties. Desire to fill, as well as protect, one's purse could encourage co-operation, and the *Leges Henrici* state that if a murder is discovered 'announcements shall be made all about with liberal promises of rewards, and if anyone can help . . . rewards shall be provided in great quantity'.[39] Once caught, the accused had to be securely detained until a final judgment was reached and any punishment carried out. Security was provided either through the accused's tithing, or through his obtaining special sureties – men who pledged for his appearance in court – or through imprisonment, as in Bricstan's case.[40]

Still, if the offender was not caught rapidly, he was unlikely to be caught at all. Sometimes he had fled too far to be easily pursued, partly because of the sheer distance, partly because of difficulties in continuing the pursuit beyond one's own hundred or shire. Later evidence suggests that only a very small proportion of crimes were actually brought to trial.[41] Look at matters from the offender's point of view. If you had committed a serious offence, capture might lead to the death penalty. Therefore, unless you were particularly confident, were friendly with important local figures, or could bribe them,[42] there was little joy in staying put. One alternative was to seek sanctuary. A few privileged sanctuaries gave protection for life, but in addition every consecrated monastery,

38. See above, pp. 62–3.
39. *LHP*, 92.8a, Downer, p. 288.
40. See above, pp. 54, 64–5; also Pollock and Maitland, ii 582–4, 589–90, 593.
41. See below, pp. 176, 180–3.
42. See below, p. 181 on corruption.

church or chapel with a graveyard gave sanctuary for a limited period, generally thirty to forty days. Once there, you should not be extracted by force. The period of respite might allow a settlement to be made with your victim or his/her kin, or an agreement that you should leave the realm for ever.[43] Your most common option, however, must have been to flee. You would then be repeatedly summoned to appear in court, and failure to comply resulted in outlawry. In the Anglo-Norman period the county may have been the usual forum for such proceedings – it was later to enjoy a monopoly of the process – but contemporaries emphasized that proclaiming outlawry was a royal right. You were placed outside the normal workings of the law, in the phrase of the time you wore 'the wolf's head'.[44] If captured, you might be executed immediately outlawry had been proved. If you resisted arrest, you might be slain. Retribution had in this case merely been delayed; however, at best – and this must often have been the outcome – flight and outlawry ended any possibility of punishment.

. . .

TRIAL

If the offender was seized red-handed, his trial was likely to be perfunctory. The case of our pick-pocket is untypical only in its ending:

> to general applause, the thief is condemned to death according to the law and they prepare the execution. However, the monks, carrying the relics of the saint, did not stop praying until, with the help of Saint Ecgwin, they overcame the decision of the judges. Thus the Almighty twice

43. See *Lawsuits*, no. 172; most evidence is late, see e.g. R. F. Hunnisett, *The Medieval Coroner* (Cambridge, 1961), ch. 3, but note *Leges Willelmi*, 1, *Leges Edwardi*, 5, Liebermann, i 492–3, 630, and D. Hall, 'The Sanctuary of St Cuthbert', in G. Bonner, D. W. Rollason and C. Stancliffe, eds, *St Cuthbert, His Cult and His Community* (Woodbridge, 1989), pp. 425–36. Some offenders might seek escape by becoming a monk; see above, p. 53, on Bricstan, and Assize of Clarendon, c. 20 (*EHD*, ii no. 24).

44. M. M. Bigelow, *History of Procedure in England* (London, 1880), pp. 348–9, Pollock and Maitland, ii 449–50, 580–2; J. Goebel, *Felony and Misdemeanor* (New York, 1937), pp. 419–23.

showed his benignity through his saint . . . by saving his servant from theft and mercifully saving the thief from death.[45]

'The law' seems to allow very swift condemnation before a very *ad hoc* court. It was these types of case, involving theft, that lords held by the right of infangentheof. Local action, bordering on self-help, was the most effective means of police and punishment.

What if the case came to a more formal trial? The relevant courts were discussed in chapter 2: those of the lord with sake and soke, the hundred, and the county, the most important cases being heard in the presence of a royal justice. Most prosecutions were brought by victims or their kin, and these will be discussed shortly. However, there were two further important methods, presentment by a group or accusation by an individual royal official. Both methods had existed in Anglo-Saxon England, and both were known in the Anglo-Norman period.[46] Given the basis of both methods in the localities, the royal here again merges with the communal. A major target of such prosecutions must have been those offenders whom no individual would or could prosecute but who were a menace to the community, for example the recalcitrant robber whose power scared individual accusers. We have already seen that tithings were probably obliged to make presentments. In cases of murder, the hundred could make a communal accusation in order to avoid the *murdrum* fine.[47] On some occasions, specially constituted bodies of sworn men may have been used to make presentments. The holders of shire and hundred courts may also have required lords or their stewards, representatives of villages, and priests to present their knowledge of local wrongdoing. This may have extended to making presentments of offenders, but given the limited sources, there is

45. *Lawsuits*, no. 14; the final fate of the thief is uncertain. For measures following unjust execution, see *LHP*, 74, Downer, pp. 230–2, *Leges Edwardi*, 36, Liebermann, i 666–8.
46. See III *Ethelred*, c. 3, *EHD*, i no. 43; Wormald, *Making*, ch. 9; see also Hurnard, 'Presentment', R. C. van Caenegem, 'Public prosecution of crime in twelfth-century England', in his *Legal History: a European Perspective* (London, 1991), pp. 4–9.
47. Hurnard, 'Presentment', 385–90.

unsurprisingly no direct evidence for such being a general obligation.[48]

A supplement to presentment was prosecution by royal officials, especially of pleas of the crown. Such prosecution was one of the roles of local justices or sergeants, as we saw so vividly in the case of Robert Malarteis. The *Leges Henrici* mention that 'if anyone is lawfully impleaded by the sheriff or a justice of the king about theft, arson, robbery, or similar offences, he is to be subjected by law to a threefold oath to clear himself'. Prosecution by officials may have been especially important in the border regions which lacked frankpledge. The effectiveness of such activities, as well as the potential for rapacity, is reflected in the unpopularity of *ex officio* prosecution.[49]

Most commonly, however, the accusation was brought by an individual, through a process called appeal.[50] Yet despite this being the main form of procedure concerning homicide, wounding and the like, recorded instances are singularly scarce in the Anglo-Norman period, and I only give a summary here, leaving more detailed description until chapter 6. If both parties appeared on the appointed day, the accuser would formally state his charge, and offer to prove it; the defendant would make a formal denial. Less formal, wider-ranging pleading and debate might then follow, involving the parties, who might have recourse to counsellors, and the suitors of the court. Specific evidence might be brought, alibis stated, claims made that a deed was done in self-defence. Facing an accusation of cattle theft, the accused might accept a challenge to battle, or he might produce the person from whom he had bought the goods or witnesses to the sale; if he was successful in producing the seller, the latter would have to make similar proof of his right to the goods.[51] The accuser might well struggle if he could find no one to back his claim. Quite

---

48. Hurnard, 'Presentment', 383–5.
49. See van Caenegem, 'Public prosecution'; R. Stewart-Brown, *The Serjeants of the Peace in Medieval England and Wales* (Manchester, 1936), pp. 76–80; *LHP*, 63.1, 66.9 (quoted), Downer, pp. 200, 212; see above, pp. 29–30 on pleas of the crown.
50. On women and appeals, see below, pp. 173, 235–6.
51. Pollock and Maitland, i 57–8, ii 158, 162–5; see also *Leges Willelmi*, 21, Liebermann, i 506–9.

technical arguments might be raised, no doubt by men who were proud of their experience in the courts.[52] Additionally, factors such as the repute of the parties might also be considered. The defendant who was notorious or had often been accused was in a particularly weak position; even if he was not swiftly condemned he might be faced with an especially tough form of proof, for example carrying a red-hot iron three times the weight of the usual ordeal iron. The hope must often have been to obtain a confession or a compromise.[53] Failing this, if guilt was not obvious – and in many cases within small communities it would have been – the court had to settle upon a form of proof, generally to be undertaken by the accused, and announced in a 'mesne [i.e. intermediate] judgment'. The accused then gave sureties that he would undertake the proof on the appointed day.[54] If he was successful in this proof or through his earlier pleading, not only was he cleared but the accuser faced a penalty. This probably took the form of a monetary payment to the king, perhaps a loss of capacity to make future accusations, and in addition he might have to come to some arrangement with the wrongly accused.[55]

Three main methods were used to decide hard cases which had defied other forms of decision or settlement: ordeal, battle, oath. All three introduced God and the supernatural into the centre of proceedings. Ordeal, the *judicium Dei*, was a ritualized appeal to God for judgment. It revealed the guilt of the party in the specific case, rather than merely their general sinfulness or purity. Ecclesiastical participation was vital, and it was stated that ordeals should only be held at an episcopal see, at a place designated by a bishop, or at the very least in the presence of the bishop's

---

52. See e.g. *LHP*, 22.1 (technicality), 45.1a (unsupported accusations), Downer, pp. 124, 154. *LHP*, 31.5, 48.4, Downer, pp. 134, 160 suggest at least one man's concern with over-reliance on witnesses.
53. See e.g. *Lawsuits*, no. 192, and Bricstan's case, above, p. 54; also *LHP*, 57.7, 61.18a, Downer, pp. 178, 198. On triple ordeal, see *LHP*, 65.3, Downer, p. 208, based on II *Cnut*, 30; note also Liebermann, i 429.
54. Pollock and Maitland, ii 602–3.
55. Evidence is very scarce, but see *LHP*, 24.2, 59.28, Downer, pp. 126, 190; *Glanvill*, ii 3, xiv 1, Hall, pp. 25, 172.

minister and his clerks.[56] In Anglo-Norman England, ordeal took two main forms. In trial by cold water, according to the recorded rites, the accused was taken to church at Vespers on the Tuesday preceding the ordeal, dressed in penitent's clothes, and made to fast for three days, hearing matins and mass with the appropriate liturgy. On the Saturday, the priest again started mass, and then addressed the accused, telling him that he was not to receive the body of Christ if he had committed, consented to, or known of the offence. The accused was being given plenty of opportunity to admit his guilt. If he did not, the mass continued, and he was led from the church, stripped, and given only a loin-cloth lest he be shamed. Then with due ceremony he was led to the ordeal. The pit for trial by water was to be twenty feet wide and twelve deep and filled to the top. A third of the pit was covered with a platform to bear the priest, the judging members of the court (*iudices*), the accused, and two or three men to place him in the water. Then – at what must have seemed great length to the accused – the priest blessed the water, addressing God, 'the just judge . . . that you judge what is just and your right judgment'. God was to order the water that it receive the man if he was innocent, reject him if guilty. The man was bound, and then lowered by a rope which was knotted a 'long hair's length' from where it was tied to the man. If he sank that far, his innocence was proved, if he floated, he was guilty.[57] In trial by iron, following a similar preparation, the accused had to carry a piece of red-hot iron for three paces. His hand was then bound, and examined on the third day after the trial. If it was infected, guilt was established; if clean, the person was cleared.

Ordeal was offered more often than it actually took place. The offer could be used tactically, to back one's word, as when Bricstan of Chatteris's wife offered to carry

56. See William I's writ concerning 'episcopal laws', *EHD*, ii no. 79; also *Leges Edwardi*, 9.3, Liebermann, i 633; F. Barlow, *The English Church, 1066–1154* (London, 1979), pp. 159–64. Note also John of Worcester, *Chronicle*, ed. J. R. H. Weaver (Oxford, 1908), p. 30. See above, p. 33 on royal control of ordeals.

57. For ordeal rituals, see Liebermann, i 401–29, esp. 417–18 for my account here. On ordeal generally, see Hyams, 'Ordeal', and Bartlett, *Trial*.

the hot iron in order to support his oath that he had surrendered all his goods.[58] Most ordeals which actually took place seem to have been in disputes where other methods of investigation had failed to establish guilt; there was no headlong rush for the supernatural. Hence ordeal was often used to settle charges based on general suspicion rather than detailed and supported accusation.[59] Part of the purpose was no doubt to scare the accused into confession. Fear of God, the elaborate ritual build-up, the certainty of physical pain in trial by hot iron, the potential for execution following failure, could all encourage submission in the hope of a settlement which would at least leave one alive and unburnt.

Contrary to popular modern opinion, ordeal was not irretrievably weighted against those undergoing it, and medieval evidence suggests that they had a better than even chance of passing the test.[60] One man whom such successes reputedly worried was William Rufus, and interpretation of a story concerning him recounted by his enemy the Canterbury monk Eadmer, is central to the question of how widespread was a thorough-going scepticism about ordeal. Fifty Englishmen were taken for forest offences and put to trial by ordeal:

> When the king was told that on the third day after the ordeal these men who had been condemned all presented themselves together with their hands unburnt, he is said to have exclaimed in disgust: 'What is this? Is God a just judge? Perish the man who after this believes so. For the future, by this and this I swear it, answer shall be made to my judgment, not to God's, which inclines to one side or the other in answer to each man's prayer.'[61]

The instance is almost unique, even in a European context in this period, and Eadmer's use of the words 'is said to have exclaimed' strike a warning note that William may not

58. See above, p. 54.
59. Bartlett, *Trial*, pp. 29–33.
60. Note M. H. Kerr, R. D. Forsyth and M. J. Plyley, 'Cold water and hot iron: trial by ordeal in England', *Journal of Interdisciplinary History* 22 (1992), 573–95.
61. *Lawsuits*, no. 150.

actually have uttered these words. It is nevertheless significant that Eadmer may have been identifying an area of belief which was more regularly questioned than our sources allow.

However, recorded instances of doubt were much more often confined to specific instances, and tended to focus on the honesty of those responsible for the procedure. Such specific doubts are not surprising, since ordeal was used in cases which were already problematic. Overall, the use of ordeal seems to have been acceptable, even if it was far from a matter of blind faith. It was a means whereby superior authority and local communities could settle difficult disputes. Problems in deciding the actual outcome of the ordeal, for example whether a hand actually was clean, might lead to the perpetuation of strife.[62] Ideally, though, the preceding ritual, the drama of the ordeal itself, the participation of the clergy, suitors, and court president, and the belief that God had judged, should bring an end to a dispute. They cauterized a potentially dangerous local malaise which might otherwise have festered, grown inflamed, and thereby threatened the peace.

By the later twelfth century the preferred method of proof in appeals concerning serious offences was trial by battle. Indeed, from soon after the Conquest a preference for battle may have contributed to the decline of the use of oaths and ordeals; ordeals, particularly by water, were possibly associated with lowly status. Generally, the accuser was the victim or his surviving kinsman, but on occasion it was an 'approver', an offender who had been caught and agreed to bring accusations against his fellows in return for his own life and limbs.[63] Battle again could be preceded by religious ritual, particularly important since victory in combat represented God's just judgment, but overall the sacral and clerical elements were less important than in ordeal by iron or water.[64] The battle was fought between the accuser and the accused, if both were fit. They

62. See esp. Bartlett, *Trial*, pp. 39–41.
63. F. C. Hamil, 'The king's approver', *Speculum* 11 (1936), 238–58. On battle being reserved for serious cases, see *LHP*, 59.16a, Downer, p. 188.
64. Bartlett, *Trial*, pp. 116, 121–2; *Duellum*, Liebermann, i 430–1.

CONTRIBUTORS

Matthew Barron was born in Tampa, Florida, but grew up in the upstate of South Carolina. In recent years he has worked as a naturalist, camp counselor, and trip leader in the Blue Ridge Mountains, a construction worker for Habitat in Washington DC, and a school counselor and teacher in North Carolina and South Carolina. He lives in Travelers Rest, SC with his wife and their seven children (pets).

He was recently exhibited in the Theatre Art Galleries in High Point, NC and is currently showing at the White Rabbit Fine Arts Gallery in Travelers Rest, SC. Find him at www.lookingglassphotos.me.

Zella Christensen received a BFA in Creative Writing from George Mason University in 2017. At the time of this publication, she works as a housekeeper on a cruise ship. Her poetry has appeared at *Strange Horizons*, *Star*Line*, and elsewhere.

Adrienne Christian is the author of two poetry collections, *12023 Woodmont Avenue* (Willow Books, 2013) and *A Proper Lover* (Main Street Rag, 2017). She has received fellowships from Callaloo and Cave Canem, and was a finalist for the 2016 Rita Dove International Poetry Award. Adrienne's poems have been The Editor's Choice in *The Los Angeles Review*, and have been featured in *Concis, Obsidian, frogpond*, and other journals and anthologies. Adrienne is currently pursuing her Ph.D. in English/Creative Writing at the University of Nebraska at Lincoln.

Andy Connor is a writer, drummer, and philosophy postgrad who lives in Melbourne, Australia. They've been published in *Going Down Swinging, The Lifted Brow*, and V*oiceworks*, and blogs at becausegoodbye.tumblr.com.

Summer Cowley is a graphic novel artist, writer, and education researcher who focuses her work on moments of emotional struggle and discomfort.

employed hammers or staffs with sharpened and reinforced ends, rather than the swords used in trials concerning land.[65] Unfortunately, we lack English anecdotes from this period, but near contemporary evidence suggests that 'fight' would be a better term than the rather chivalric sounding 'duel'. The following story from the late twelfth century was preserved because of the intervention of St Thomas Becket:

> Two men who had been adjudged to a duel came together, one being much bigger and stronger than the other. The stronger man catches the weaker one, lifts him high above his head ready to throw him hard on the ground. The smaller man hanging thus in the air lifts up his mind to heaven and says a short prayer: 'Help, holy Thomas martyr'. The danger was great and sudden and the time for prayer short. There are witnesses who were present: the stronger man, as if oppressed by the weight of the holy name, suddenly collapsed under the one he held and was vanquished.[66]

As well as illustrating the rough-and-tumble nature of such trials, the anecdote perfectly illustrates the tension that existed in men's minds between the obvious fact that stronger men had an advantage and the conviction that battle brought the supernatural into the doing of justice.

Oaths of exculpation might be undertaken by the party alone, or together with other 'oath-helpers'.[67] Unfortunately, we have no case material on the subject, and must look to the Anglo-Saxon laws and to the post-Conquest *Leges* which rely heavily on Anglo-Saxon precedent. In general, they suggest that the party bearing

---

65. M. T. Clanchy, 'Highway robbery and trial by battle in the Hampshire eyre of 1249', in R. F. Hunnisett and J. B. Post, eds, *Medieval Legal Records* (London, 1978), pp. 33–4.

66. *Lawsuits*, no. 502; also below, p. 172. On weapons, see Pollock and Maitland, ii 34.

67. On oaths, see e.g. *LHP*, 18.1, 65, Downer, pp. 120, 208, *Leges Willelmi*, 3, Liebermann, i 494–5; Bigelow, *Procedure*, pp. 297–8, 301–8, Pollock and Maitland, i 91 n. 3, ii 600–1, 634–7; for later uses, see e.g. F. W. Maitland and W. P. Baildon, eds, *The Court Baron* (Selden Soc., 4, 1891), *passim*. Oaths remained more important in towns, see e.g. *Borough Customs*, i 34, 37. See above, p. 12 on the importance of one's word.

proof often had to make an oath, by himself or with others, and that support from others was particularly necessary for men of ill-repute. The groups upon whom the accused could draw for such 'compurgation' would include his kin, friends and neighbours, and his tithing. Alternatively, the court or his opponent might impose swearers upon him. The oath was a re-affirmation of the defendant's original denial, in words such as 'by the Lord, the oath which N. has sworn is clean and unperjured'. Again the supernatural is being drawn into procedure, but again the workings of the procedure can also be seen in more functional terms. In particular, men might be unwilling to swear in support of one who had become a liability to their interests, and denial of whose ill-doing would call into question their own position as lawful men of honour. Hence self-interest as well as fear of God might ensure that justice was done in cases of compurgation. Oaths seem to have been of decreasing importance for serious offences, but may have continued to be vital for matters arising from procedure and also for lesser offences.

.   .   .

PUNISHMENT AND COMPENSATION

If the accused failed in his proof, he was condemned to the appropriate penalty. For serious offences, he would face the death penalty, although he might escape with mutilation. In addition, as in the case of Bricstan, his goods would normally be forfeited to the king.[68] His land, if he had any, might pass to his lord. Anglo-Saxon England was familiar with the death penalty, sometimes when the offender could not make the very high payments appropriate, but also for offences too serious for pecuniary emendation, for example

---

68. See above, p. 54; *Lawsuits*, no. 192 specifies loss of life and goods as proper practice 'according to the judicial usage of England'; however, the text may have been written in Henry II's reign. It does not specify to whom the goods were to pass, although the king becomes involved in the settlement. Assize of Clarendon, c. 5, *EHD*, ii no. 24, allows chattels of those convicted other than by presentment under the assize to be distributed as customary. This, of course, does not preclude them from going to the king in crown pleas; others might receive chattels if they were specially privileged in relation to serious cases, or more generally for lesser cases.

murder, treason, arson, manifest theft, and assaults upon houses.[69] One of the documents purportedly recording legislation of William the Conqueror has him abolish the death penalty, replacing it with blinding and castration. However, the text has no official status, and may be a partial version of a real decree, a statement of goodwill rather than real intent, or a garbled version of pre-Conquest legislation prohibiting the death penalty for minor offences or for young offenders.[70] Domesday customs mention the use of the death penalty. We have already heard from a slightly later source the story of the Oxford pick-pocket's narrow escape from execution during William's reign, and William of Malmesbury noted that Rufus loosed the noose from robbers' necks in return for money. Henry I's initiatives against thieves, for example in 1108, were not a reintroduction of the death penalty but its re-affirmation or extension. William of Malmesbury commented that Henry I in the early years of his reign favoured the cutting of limbs in order to deter offenders by example, but later preferred to take payment from them. However, in 1124 use of the death penalty was in full swing as Ralph Basset hanged forty-four thieves at *Hundehoge*. If the figure can be trusted it is exceptionally large compared with the number who would be executed at a single sitting of the eyre in the later twelfth or thirteenth centuries.[71]

The death penalty was generally carried out by hanging, although in a few circumstances and certain areas beheading took place. The condemned was denied the sacraments before his execution and Christian burial after it.[72] Mutilation in cases where death was appropriate was a form of clemency, leaving the punished in a better position

69. See e.g. Hurnard, *Pardon*, p. 1.
70. *EHD*, ii no. 18, c. 10 (and see comments in Liebermann, iii 278, 281); note e.g. II *Cnut*, 2.1, Liebermann, i 308–11; Hurnard, *Pardon*, p. 5 n. 3; *Leges Willelmi*, 40, Liebermann, i 516.
71. Pollock and Maitland, ii 456–7; above, p. 69; *Gesta Regum*, ii 369, 487; *SSC*, p. 113 from 'Florence' of Worcester; *RRAN*, ii no. 518; *Lawsuits*, nos 167 (on the 'bodily punishment of thieves'), 237; note also Suger, *The Deeds of Louis the Fat*, trans R. C. Cusimano and J. Moorhead (Washington DC, 1992), p. 70.
72. See Gerald of Wales, *The Jewel of the Church*, trans J. J. Hagen (Leiden, 1979), pp. 89–90.

to save their souls after their short sharp shock. Why six men at *Hundehoge* escaped with blinding and castrating is unclear, but the offender's youth may explain the case of a boy who, until he was saved by the bishop of Winchester, was to be deprived of his eyes for committing theft.[73] Such a penalty seems to us all the more savage because it could be the accuser, not some dispassionate public executioner, who carried out the sentence – as the gore-hungry reader will see in chapter 6.[74]

Severe retribution was considered appropriate, both because the convicted deserved it and also to deter others, a very important element in a society where few offenders were caught. The impact could be increased through rhetoric and ritual accompanying the process of punishment, re-affirming what those in authority considered good order. A priest might also impose penance for the deed, reinforcing the association between the offence and sin which was already manifest, for example in trial by ordeal.[75] Alternatively, if the convicted begged for and was granted mercy, this too might emphasize the power of the giver of mercy, the wrongfulness of the original offence, the baseness of the offender.[76]

Physical punishments for serious offences coexisted with payments to the king, and official or unofficial compensation to the victim or kin. We saw above that those convicted at least of pleas of the crown might forfeit their possessions as well as their lives. Punishment and forfeiture are seen as underlying payments by those in the king's mercy, which came to be called amercements. This practice existed in Normandy before 1066 and on both sides of the Channel thereafter. In return for a payment, the duke or king would show his mercy by not exacting the full penalty.[77]

73. *Lawsuits*, no. 210.
74. See below, p. 160, and further Pollock and Maitland, ii 496 n. 7, which also notes some peculiar local punishments.
75. See T. F. T. Plucknett, *Edward I and Criminal Law* (Cambridge, 1960), ch. 3.
76. For supplication, see e.g. *Lawsuits*, nos 143 (throwing self at king's feet), 192 (notably involving the queen as well as the king).
77. J. Yver, 'Les premières institutions du duché du Normandie', *Settimane di Spoleto* 16 (1969), 350–3; Goebel, *Felony*, esp. pp. 238–48, 266–7, 381–5; J. P. Collas, ed., *Year Book 12 Edward II* (Selden Soc., 81, 1964), pp. xxii-xxxiii; see above, p. 77 on forfeiture.

This combination of punishment and amercement is often contrasted with the Anglo-Saxon system of fixed *wites*, payments made to the king, or some delegate, for an offence.[78] As far as we can tell – and we cannot tell much – there was no such pattern of fixed payments in Normandy before 1066. This may partly be a matter of the sources: there are no Norman parallels to the laws which have determined our picture of Anglo-Saxon practice. Moreover, the Anglo-Saxon laws and the *Leges*, and indeed the Domesday Book lists of customs with their local variations,[79] may be misleading in the precision with which they define *wites*, both before and certainly after the Conquest. Their lists may be indications of what was considered by some to be good practice, an equivalent of post-Conquest statements that emendations or amercements should be proportionate to the offence.[80] Outside the *Leges*, evidence for payments of fixed *wites* is very scarce.[81] The 1130 Pipe Roll suggests that there was no such system of rigidly fixed *wites*; rather the payments resemble those in later Pipe Rolls which everyone takes as amercements. Anglo-Saxon kings, too, no doubt exacted payments for mercy. Entries in an Anglo-Saxon royal account might have resembled those in the 1130 Pipe Roll, and have contrasted with the impression of fixed *wites* given by the Laws. And if *wites* were more flexible than the laws suggest, twelfth-century records show that amercements, in particular for minor wrongs such as breaches of procedure, became quite standardized. The difference between *wite* and amercement in practice disappears.

As for compensations, there is very little case evidence in the Anglo-Norman period, less even than for punish-

---

78. See Wormald, *Making*, ch. 9, 'Maitland', p. 14, on the relationship of *wite* and *bót* in late Anglo-Saxon England.
79. Pollock and Maitland, ii 456–7.
80. See e.g. Henry I, *Coronation Charter*, c. 8, *EHD*, ii no. 19; *Magna Carta*, c. 20; note also the specificity of II *Cnut* on amounts of heriots and the *Leges* on *murdrum*, which other evidence shows were not precisely paid in practice.
81. *EHD*, ii no. 270, Henry I's charter to London (on which see above, p. 29 n. 17), limits amercements to the Londoner's *wer* of 100s.; note also *Borough Customs*, i 23 (London), and ii 47 from early fourteenth-century Manchester; Holt, *Magna Carta*, p. 58.

ment.[82] It is therefore uncertain when the arrangement of compensations ceased to be central to court decisions concerning serious offences. The homicide case in which Wulfstan intervened so dramatically was an out-of-court settlement involving an accidental killing, a type of dispute to which compensation was peculiarly suited. One is left struggling with the *Leges*.[83] The *Leges Edwardi*, probably dating from between the 1130s and 1150s, give a very perfunctory account, but the *Leges Willelmi* and in particular the *Leges Henrici* from the 1110s present a complicated system of fixed compensations. Yet these are very closely based on Anglo-Saxon texts, notably Alfred's laws and a tract called *Wer*. Should their treatment of compensations be taken as the letter of the law, when their presentation of *wites* has just been rejected? The *Leges* may be best treated as guides to good thinking about law, as encouragement of compensations permitting settlements. Even if any formal compensation system of fixed monetary payments, enforced in court for serious crimes, had functioned in the late Anglo-Saxon period, it seems likely that it was disappearing during Henry I's reign at the latest.[84]

Why did this happen? There was surely no single royal decree abolishing compensation for serious offences. Rather a more complex pattern such as the following seems plausible. Compensations seem to have been less prominent in Normandy than in Anglo-Saxon England. Dudo of St Quentin's story that the first count of Normandy, Rollo, issued a law that robbers should be hanged may signify a preference for punishment in early eleventh even if not in early tenth-century Normandy. Post-Conquest sources refer explicitly to English words and proverbs concerning compensations, reinforcing the association with the Anglo-Saxon, not the Norman past.[85] Moreover, the role of

---

82. Note, however, the appeal of larceny where not only did the thief get hanged but the victim received his goods back: Plucknett, *Criminal Law*, pp. 80–2.

83. See esp. *LHP*, 49.7, 68, 70, 76–9, 93–4, Downer, pp. 164, 214–22, 236–48, 292–302; *Leges Willelmi*, 7–11, 18–19, *Leges Edwardi*, 12.4–6, Liebermann, i 498–501, 504–5, 638–9; note the comments of Goebel, *Felony*, pp. 381–2 n. 155.

84. See also Wormald, *Making*, ch. 9.

85. See Goebel, *Felony*, pp. 187–206; *Leges Edwardi*, 12.6, Liebermann, i 638–9; note also *Lawsuits*, no. 172 on 'botless' offences.

compensations – fixed or negotiated – may have been declining even in late Anglo-Saxon England, with royal efforts to enforce peace, with the high level of compensations making payment difficult, and perhaps with the sheer complexity of the system; punishments and amercements had a simplicity which might well attract royal servants and others. Some of the methods which may once have ensured that compensations were paid, notably feud, were decreasingly available, and even enslavement for failure to pay disappeared after the Conquest.

Thus in the Anglo-Norman period, if not before, punishment fixed by the court came to be increasingly disconnected from compensations settled by the parties. Indeed, kings and their officials may have sought to control the type of out-of-court settlement which would avoid punishment, and perhaps deprive the king of profit.[86] Such developments were linked to other aspects of increasing royal control, the developing notion of crown pleas discussed in chapter 2, and an emphasis upon the king's peace. The development of a general king's peace extending throughout the realm is clear in Henry I's Coronation Charter, although it may have begun well before 1100 or even 1066.[87] When Henry stated that 'I place strong peace on all my kingdom and order it to be held henceforth', he was deliberately invoking something more than general peacefulness, and something different from his protection specially given to individuals. Rather he was placing his power behind a strong peace closely associated with kingship.[88]

---

86. *LHP*, 59.27, Downer, p. 190 on justices controlling settlements; see also below, pp. 169–70.
87. See Wormald, *Making*.
88. *EHD*, ii no. 19 c. 12. For the Anglo-Saxon period, see Wormald, *Making*. Cf. Goebel, *Felony*, pp. 423–40; Hurnard, *Pardon*, p. 8. See Eadmer, *Historia Novorum*, ed. M. Rule (London, 1884), p. 184 on Henry bringing Normandy after 1106 'under royal peace'; also Orderic, vi 92 and William of Malmesbury, *Historia Novella*, ed. and trans K. R. Potter (Edinburgh, 1955), p. 17. For the king's special protection, see e.g. 'Ten Articles of William I', c. 3, *EHD*, ii no. 18; *LHP*, 10.1, 16, 79.3–4, Downer, pp. 108, 120, 246, *Leges Edwardi*, 12, 27, Liebermann, i 637–8, 651; *Lawsuits*, no. 134 (p. 93). The custom that an appeal of felony must include mention of a breach of the king's peace (see below, pp. 161, 165) may have developed more slowly, and have led to a refinement of notions of that peace.

This was in part an ideological assertion, and the concern of Henry I and his father with 'Peace' is clearest in Normandy with their involvement in, and control of, the Peace and Truce of God. However, the assertion of the strong peace was also practical. The king and his officials were intent on enforcing peace, and peace hence came to be associated with them. One of their methods was to use the death penalty, or at the very least the example of punishment by life or limb. Another was prosecution by royal officials.[89] Offenders, most notably culpable killers and thieves were subjected to a persecuting regime.

However, the move from compensation to punishment was not complete, particularly since much out-of-court activity coexisted with the judicial. First, some use of compensation continued even for serious offences. Sometimes the king exacted the death penalty but allowed compensation to the victim or kin. Royal efforts which had the effect of reducing the role of compensation may have met with resistance.[90] Also, courts still might help the parties arrange settlements involving compensation. Secondly, compensations probably maintained great importance in areas outside regular royal jurisdiction, for example towns. Thirdly, compensations continued for lesser offences, probably the circumstances where they had always been most important, before merging into payments for damages under common law actions such as trespass.[91] They were the most satisfactory way of settling such disputes which did not threaten the wider peace.

. . .

CONCLUSIONS

The Norman kings ordered that the *Laga Edwardi* be observed. During this chapter, we have seen much continuity, and, indeed, with regard to frankpledge and amercements more continuity than some historians would

---

89. See above, p. 71; also Hurnard, *Pardon*, esp. p. 18.
90. Hurnard, *Pardon*, ch. 1.
91. See below, pp. 164–6. See *Borough Customs*, i 30–1 on a twelfth-century Preston custom, which fixed the amount payable per inch of a wound, if both parties could be made to agree to such a settlement.

allow. As suggested earlier, pre-1066 England and Normandy probably shared many important characteristics, for example in some classifications of serious offences. Continuity also existed in particular with regard to lesser offences, where, indeed, elements of procedure and settlement practices survived beyond the period of this book. No doubt this continuity was helped by the fact that most of the population using such procedures, or composing courts which heard such cases, would have been of English descent. Moreover, certain features linked to social and administrative organization remained unchanged: the small proportion of serious offenders ever punished; the necessity for local activity, influenced by considerable royal involvement; the essential responsibilities of lords and of communities for any efficient attempt to prevent or prosecute offences.

We have also seen continuing development, for example in use of the death penalty, in forms of presentment, and perhaps in notions of the king's peace. Clear Norman innovations are fewer, the most notable being trial by battle. It is difficult to tell how far an apparent increase in royal activity is real, how far a product of more extensive sources; however, the level of activity at the time of the first surviving Pipe Roll, in 1130, was probably not matched until a decade into Henry II's reign. Inspired by a desire both for peace and profit, royal activity involved administrative action, legislation, and more general developments, for example in thinking about crown pleas. Such developments may have brought increased standardization. However, whilst the statements of the *Leges Henrici* and the *Leges Willelmi* about the differences of Mercian, Wessex and Danelaw may be treated with considerable doubt, and are not very prominent in the *Leges Edwardi*, much room remained for local variations in procedure and perhaps in penalties, particularly for lesser offences.[92] Frankpledge was absent from extensive northern and western areas, and so too probably was the *murdrum* fine.[93] There were also, as we

92. See above, p. 80 on Domesday customs; also e.g. *LHP*, 39, Downer, p. 144.
93. F. C. Hamil, 'Presentment of Englishry and the murder fine', *Speculum* 12 (1937), 290.

saw in chapter 2, some particularly privileged areas where royal control was especially restricted. Such local powers would increase, the development of royal authority be reversed, under Stephen. The renewal of royal authority under Henry II would bring it a rather different form.

ACKNOWLEDGMENTS

There are many people without whom this book could not be possible. Many thanks are in order to:

Charles Overbeck at Eberhardt Press, for providing his mentorship and inspiring printed matter, Lucas Hunt for his advice and good will, Casandra Johns at House of Hands for her editing expertise, and Cheston Knapp at *Tin House Magazine* for his unending support and wisdom.

The biggest thanks go to our contributors and to everyone who felt compelled to submit their words and images to this project. There were almost a thousand of you, and while it was not possible to get back to everyone, we see you and appreciate you.

Thank you.

Chapter 4

LAW AND LAND-HOLDING IN ANGLO-NORMAN ENGLAND

I have done this at the advice and with the approval of many wise men, moved especially by the exhortation, the prayers, and the counsel of the lord Theobald archbishop of Canterbury and primate of all England, who showed me by reasonable and most truthful arguments that a noble gentleman [*vir nobilis et liberalis*] who has a fief of six knights should most justly give not only the third part of a knight's land to God and the holy Church for the salvation of himself and his kin, but the whole of a knight's land or more than that. He added also that if this man's heir should try to take away the alms which are interposed as a bridge between his father and Paradise, by which his father may be able to pass over, the heir, so far as he may, is disinheriting his father from the kingdom of heaven, and therefore should not obtain the inheritance which remains, since he who has killed his father has proved himself no son.

> Confirmation charter of Roger of Valognes for Binham Priory, *c.* 1145[1]

Discussion of land law has been central to the writing of legal history. 'Tenure' sits proudly at the start of Maitland's thematic analysis in his *History of English Law*. Such prominence reflects in part the concerns of post-medieval lawyers, and also political thinkers' interest in the nature of 'property'. But it also stems from medieval evidence and interests. Because land was fundamental to the power of the aristocracy, and more locally to lesser men as well, the customs and procedures which can be referred to as land

---

1. Stenton, *First Century*, pp. 39, 260–1.

law were of great importance. Land cases feature prominently in the records. *Glanvill*, writing at the end of the 1180s, devoted most of his *Treatise* to land law, leaving criminal pleas to a brief final book.

Analysis of land-holding has been vital both to writings on the functioning of law and lordship within the Anglo-Norman period and to those on the formation of common law. Debate has focused upon the similarities or differences between Anglo-Norman practices and those of the thirteenth century; upon the strength of the tenant's control of his land in relation to his lord; and upon the extent of royal intervention in the hearing of land disputes.[2] I shall argue that the Normans introduced important new land-holding practices, that by end of Henry I's reign much of the vocabulary and many of the customs of common law land-holding were emerging, and that there was also by then significant, if not routine, royal involvement in land-holding cases.

.   .   .

LAND, LORDSHIP, AND LAW

It was largely through their lands, their lordships, their 'honours' as they were called at the time, that great men obtained their wealth, their prestige, their honour. Land was used in the negotiation and maintenance of the relationships whereby men achieved or sustained eminence. It is little wonder that some aristocrats developed reputations for litigiousness.[3] Yet, as was argued in chapter 1, law concerns much more than disputes. It has other important functions, such as enabling certain actions. For example, one way in which men rose to prominence in our period was by marriage to aristocratic women, in particular heiresses. The heiress differed from the male heir in that, whilst she might inherit land, she did not hold it herself.

---

2. See above, p. 20; and S. E. Thorne, 'English feudalism and estates in land', *Cambridge Law Journal* (1959), 193–209; Milsom, *Legal Framework*; J. C. Holt, 'Politics and property in early medieval England', *Past and Present* 57 (1972), 3–52, 'Feudal society and the family in early medieval England', *TRHS* 5th Ser. 32–5 (1982–5); Hudson, *Land, Law, and Lordship*.
3. See above, p. 5.

Rather, if she was married, control of the land rested with her husband. If she was unmarried, it rested with her lord, who might give her to a husband he wished to favour; hence the value of heiresses for patronage and for the binding of alliances. However, the heiress is not a universal feature of all aristocratic societies. Rather she seems to have risen to prominence in western Europe through developments in inheritance practices during the later eleventh and early twelfth centuries.[4]

In Anglo-Norman society, land-holding was closely linked to lordship. Those to whom a lord gave lands 'in fee' would have done homage to him. At least if lord and man had no previous relationship, the ceremonies of 'seising', that is transferring land, and of doing homage might be very closely connected.[5] This connection to lordship reflects partly practices imported from Normandy, but also the impact of Conquest. To the king who saw the new realm as his, those to whom he gave lands as reward for their services were his men, holding from him. This perception was repeated as the king's followers distributed lands to their own men. In such circumstances it is not surprising that the majority of charters from the period recording land grants are addressed to the lord's barons and men, that is, to those who made up the honour and its court. However, there was much more to a tenant holding land than merely having been seised of it by his lord. People spoke of land as theirs by right even if they were not seised of it.[6] Moreover, once lands had remained in tenant families for an extended period, the effect of lordship diminished. Provided services were performed, the impact of lordship would be immediate only at certain weak points in the family history, such as succession, particularly of a minor or an heiress. It is at these weak points that lords enjoyed the rights which historians group as 'feudal incidents', relief payable by an heir wishing to succeed,

4. See e.g. J. Martindale, 'Succession and politics in the Romance-speaking world, c. 1000–1140', in M. Jones and M. Vale, eds, *England and her Neighbours* (London, 1989), esp. pp. 32–40.
5. See Hudson, *Land, Law, and Lordship*, pp. 16–21; also S. M. G. Reynolds, *Fiefs and Vassals* (Oxford, 1994), pp. 370–3. On holding in fee, see below, pp. 90, 94ff.
6. See e.g. *Lawsuits*, no. 294; also below, p. 115.

wardship of the lands of heirs who were minors, supervision of marriages.

In this chapter, rather than laying down a monolithic set of customs concerning land, I sketch a variety of perceptions. Perceptions might vary according to the position the party held in any land-holding relationship. From the lord's point of view, land law provided him with a way of controlling key resources, his wealth, and his followers. From the tenant's point of view, land and the customs relating to it enabled him to provide for himself, his family, and his followers, in his life-time and beyond. However, each party might also vary in his own perceptions, or statements of his – or her – position. A tenant might try to put forward a justification of his own position which he would condemn when propounded by another. Yet the picture is not entirely one of diversity. For example, self-interest might ensure that the tenant emphasized the lord-ship element in land-holding.[7] There is, indeed, much evidence for lords and tenants sharing perceptions, not least because the same person would be lord in one situation, tenant in another. The way in which various perceptions of land-holding competed with or complemented one another will be a central theme of this chapter.[8]

·   ·   ·

THE FORMS OF LAND-HOLDING

During the period 1066–1216 different forms of land-holding were increasingly rigorously classified. Admittedly, no one at the time seems to have drawn up a written scheme of tenures. Terms continued to have more than one meaning, and some distinctions remained blurred.[9] Even so, a process of distinguishing between

7. See below, p. 110, on warranty.
8. For arguments emphasizing the close relationship of lordship and land-holding, see Thorne, 'Estates in land' and Milsom, *Legal Framework*; for an opposing point of view, Reynolds, *Fiefs and Vassals*. For ideas underlying the approach taken here see J. G. H. Hudson, 'Anglo-Norman land law and the origins of property' and S. D. White, 'The discourse of inheritance', in Garnett and Hudson, *Law and Government*, pp. 173–97, 198–222.
9. For classification according to later schemes of tenures, differing in some ways from the categorizations here, see e.g. A. W. B. Simpson, *A History of the Land Law* (Oxford, 1986), ch. 1.

forms of land-holding influenced legal development. Although I here consider other types of land-holding briefly, this chapter and chapter 7 on the Angevin period will concentrate primarily upon land which was described as held 'in fee'. This concentration reflects the surviving evidence, the links between such tenure and common law property, and also the wide extent of holding in fee. A charter of the earl of Lincoln in 1142 divided his tenants into just two categories, those holding 'in fee and inheritance', and rustics.[10]

The Norman conquerors imported in their heads the word 'fee' and other ideas upon which would rest vital customs concerning lay land-holding. This need not mean that Norman and Anglo-Saxon land-holding practices before 1066 were vastly dissimilar. However, the almost complete replacement of the English aristocracy by 1086 ensured that their customary perceptions were also replaced. This conclusion is supported by a change in the vocabulary of land-holding, not absolute proof, but as good evidence as one can expect. The Anglo-Saxon word *bocland* – bookland – all but disappears. *Feudum* – fief or fee – comes to predominate. This was a matter of substantive change, not merely translation. Indeed, in the twelfth century, men who were seeking to understand the Anglo-Saxon laws adopted a variety of translations of *bocland*; no generally agreed form was available. Meanwhile, in the last four decades of the eleventh century Norman and English charters had come to use the word 'fee' not only to describe an actual tenement, but also to classify a form of land-holding by the phrase 'in fee'. Such were lands held heritably by honourable secular service, often, but not necessarily, military.[11]

10. F. M. Stenton, ed., *Facsimiles of Early Charters from Northamptonshire Collections* (Northants. Record Soc., 4, 1930), Frontispiece; see also Reynolds, *Fiefs and Vassals*, p. 394.
11. On fee, see Hudson, *Land, Law, and Lordship*, pp. 94–7; on Normandy, E. Z. Tabuteau, *Transfers of Property in Eleventh-Century Norman Law* (Chapel Hill, NC, 1988), pp. 51–65, 297–8. For arguments for greater continuity across the Conquest, see Reynolds, *Fiefs and Vassals*, ch. 8; D. Roffe, 'From thegnage to barony', *ANS* 12 (1990), 157–76. Change in the ways in which laymen held lands from churches may have been slower, partly because of the use of

In the Anglo-Saxon period, charters had usually described ecclesiastical land-holding in language based on the notion of inheritance. In the Anglo-Norman period, doubtless under the influence of Church reform, this was replaced by the vocabulary of alms. Such language could describe gifts to, or holdings of, individual clerics, but increasingly frequently the phrase 'in alms' referred to the fashion in which churches held lands. It emphasized in particular that the land had been given primarily in the hope of salvation, not of secular services. As early as the 1080s in Normandy a terse and explicit contrast was made between holding 'in alms' and 'in fee'. In England, the phrase 'in alms' becomes common in royal charters in the reign of William Rufus, particularly from c. 1093.[12] In the twelfth century, adjectives stressed the freedom, purity and perpetuity of such grants, in contrast to those made to laymen, but both royal and private charters show that the basic categorization had taken place by the early 1100s.

Socage came to be the great residuary tenure of the developed common law, covering various forms of free land-holding which fitted no other category. Not surprisingly, given this residuary nature and the restricted evidence, the characteristics of socage are difficult to classify even in the later twelfth century. Such land did not owe knight service, but money or other dues. In this it could resemble 'fee farm', heritable lands owing a fixed money rent. Variation existed in socage custom, for example as to whether the tenement should pass to just one heir or be partible.[13] Given that many of those later described as holding 'in socage' were of English descent,

---

leases on both sides of the Channel, partly because of the initial survival of English abbots. On 'fee-farms', lands held for a fixed money rent, which were generally but initially not invariably heritable, see Hudson, *Land, Law, and Lordship*, pp. 95–6.

12. Hudson, *Land, Law, and Lordship*, pp. 91, 96; very rare instances of grants 'in fee and alms' reveal the limits of classification. See generally, B. Thompson, 'Free alms tenure in the twelfth century', *ANS* 16 (1994), 221–43.

13. See *Glanvill*, vii 3, Hall, p. 75; Pollock and Maitland, i 291–5. There were some villein sokemen, most notably on the royal demesne; see e.g. P. R. Hyams, *King, Lords, and Peasants in Medieval England* (Oxford, 1980), pp. 26, 186, 194–5.

socage may have perpetuated some characteristics of tenures which Domesday Book simply described as 'holding freely'. Socage probably started as a fairly specific word, associated with holding by sokemen ('soc-men'), and was later employed more generally for lands held freely. Early instances of the phrase 'in socage' are very rare, perhaps because of the scarcity of documents treating the relevant levels of society. More likely, however, the phrase only became widely used once it was felt that all types of land-holding should be classifiable by some such simple term, perhaps in the later twelfth century.

Also likely to reflect pre-Conquest arrangements are some forms of land-holding which came to be categorized as sergeanties. Such arrangements continued to be made after the Conquest. A Peterborough Abbey survey in the later 1120s records that Abbot Thorold (d. 1098) gave a sixth of a hide in Oundle and a quarter of a hide in Warmington to a certain Vivian 'in sergeanty'. The service owed was a knight in the army with his own weapons and two horses, the abbot providing him with everything else necessary. This grant reveals both the use of the category 'in sergeanty' and also the limits of its distinctiveness, at least to our eyes: here we have a grant apparently for military service described as 'in sergeanty'.[14]

Certain other forms of land-holding existed only in particular regions. Notable amongst these are the gavelkind of Kent and the thanage and drengage of the far north of England. G. W. S. Barrow has written that

> Typically, the thane is a man of substance, holding a village or in some cases as much as a 'shire', i.e. a group of settlements

---

14. E. King, 'The Peterborough "Descriptio militum" (Henry I)', *EHR* 84 (1969), 87, 101; see generally E. G. Kimball, *Serjeanty Tenure in Medieval England* (New Haven, CT, 1936), A. L. Poole, *Obligations of Society in the XII and XIII Centuries* (Oxford, 1946), ch. 4; on the Anglo-Saxon background, J. Campbell, 'Some agents and agencies of the late Anglo-Saxon state', in J. C. Holt, ed., *Domesday Studies* (Woodbridge, 1987), pp. 210–12. Distinct rules, for example prohibiting alienation and division between heiresses, came to be seen as distinctive of all sergeanties. They may well have developed only in the later twelfth century, yet by the thirteenth such rules were on occasion disregarded.

consisting of a nucleus with outliers. He is liable for cornage [a levy on cattle], he holds heritably, and he will usually pay a rent in money and/or kind; in other words, he is a tenant in fee farm . . . . Drengs . . . must be considered part of the noble order yet are clearly on its borderline. Like the thane, the dreng held by a ministerial tenure, but his services were markedly more agricultural, more personal, even menial.[15]

Again, the arrangements must closely resemble practices before 1066.

All such land-holding would have been categorized as free. What of the lands held by the large proportion of the population who could be classified as 'unfree'? Freedom and unfreedom were relative. The weight and types of service, openness to arbitrary demands, a tie to the land excluding the possibility of leaving, all contributed to classification as unfree. The forms of burden no doubt varied locally. Yet the emphasis is on status not tenure. Domesday Book and early estate surveys contain little indication that there were villeinage lands. Rather they reveal lands held by *villani*, best translated as peasants. References to lands held 'in villeinage' only appear in the second half of the twelfth century. Certainly, earlier documents are scarce, but some do survive which might have used such language. The association of unfreedom with tenure seems to be the product of various forces: the increasing classification of land-holding generally; the confusion as to whether services were a burden on the person or the land; and the emphasis in Angevin legal remedies that they applied only to free tenements.[16]

So far I have been dealing with long-term arrangements. However, there were also grants for limited terms. Most obviously there were leases, some for as long as three lives, some for one life, some for a term of years. A contrast was drawn between such leases paying a fixed rent or farm and the generally heritable tenements called fee farms.[17] In

15. G. W. S. Barrow, 'Northern English society in the twelfth and thirteenth centuries', *Northern History* 4 (1969), 10–11. On gavelkind, see e.g. Pollock and Maitland, ii 271–3.
16. See also below, p. 122. On the north, see Barrow, 'Northern society', 12–14.
17. See above, n. 11.

addition, there were temporary states into which lands could fall because of circumstances. These included the wardship of a minor's lands, and dower, the allocation to a widow.[18]

This survey brings two main conclusions. First, changes in the form of land-holding at the top level of lay society were accompanied by greater continuity lower down. Indeed, some of the lesser tenures of common law probably contain elements of practices proper to the Anglo-Saxon aristocracy, practices forced downwards by Norman colonization. Secondly, the classification of land-holding developed significantly in the Anglo-Norman period. Some such developments were already occurring in Normandy before 1066, but there were also other causes. Broad changes in thought may have been influential, and in particular Church reform compelled distinctions to be drawn between ecclesiastical and lay land-holding. The process of settlement, and the meeting with unfamiliar forms of land-holding, may have encouraged reflection, whilst the Domesday Inquest must often have raised the question 'how are the lands held?' At the same time, in the processes of negotiation, grant, and dispute, similar question must also have arisen and the categorizations been refined. Certainly, the distinctions were not as clear as, and in some cases were markedly different from, those of the thirteenth century. Yet by 1135 much of the vocabulary and conceptualization of common law land-holding was in place.

. . .

THE CUSTOMARY FRAMEWORK: CONTROL OF LAND HELD IN FEE

Perceptions and practices of holding land 'in fee' are best considered under three headings: security of tenure in

18. On dower, see e.g. J. Biancalana, 'Widows at common law: the development of common law dower', *Irish Jurist* ns 23 (1988), 255–329; note e.g. uncertainties concerning allocation even in the early thirteenth century, on which see also below, p. 218 n. 121. On the land the wife brought to her marriage, the *maritagium*, and on the husband's enjoyment of his wife's lands after her death, 'curtesy', see e.g. Pollock and Maitland, ii 15–16, 414–20, Simpson, *Land Law*, pp. 63–5, 69–70.

relation to the lord; heritability; alienability, the capacity to give away the holding. These categories reflect a land-holder's concerns: he would wish to be safe in his own position, to be sure that his family would continue to enjoy his lands after his death, but also to be able to grant or sell his lands to a church or to a person who was not his heir. The three elements are intimately connected, indeed can be seen as differing perspectives on the same problems. For example, what for a donor was his capacity to make alienations lasting beyond his death was from the donee's point of view his security of tenure against the donor's successor.

The following analysis will show that by 1135 the position of the tenant in fee was strong. His hold on his land was secure, so long as he performed due services and refrained from any great act of disobedience. Even if he did fall out with his lord, he might avoid forfeiture and end any disciplinary action with a negotiated settlement. He could rest assured that his heirs would, in general, succeed to his lands, particularly if there were close relatives available at each succession. He was free to alienate lands, so long as he did so reasonably and preferably made other parties feel as if their interests had been taken into account. No doubt each party in the lord–tenant relationship attempted to strengthen his own position. Yet lords' main concern seems to have been that they receive the due services. Such was the essential background for *Bracton*'s statement in the thirteenth century that the tenant held a fee 'in demesne', the lord a fee 'in service'.[19]

(i) Security of tenure

A newly established lord, to whom perhaps the king had given lands which another lord had forfeited, might take very aggressive action. His natural desire to establish himself and his own followers could involve ejecting existing tenants. Such evictions may underlie the

---

19. E.g. *Bracton*, f. 46b, Thorne, ii 143; see also Hudson, 'Origins of property', p. 211, and e.g. W. Farrer and C. T. Clay, eds, *Early Yorkshire Charters* (12 vols, Edinburgh/Yorks. Archaeological Soc., 1914–65), iii no. 1332.

disinheritances made by one of Henry I's new men, Nigel d'Aubigny. Significantly, these earlier acts worried Nigel when he believed himself to be dying.[20] It is indeed notable that in Anglo-Norman England security of tenure may have been greater amongst sub-tenants rather than tenants in chief, whose position was most affected by political conflict in the royal house. Perhaps in part through royal protection, sitting sub-tenants often survived the fall of their lords.[21]

In relation to an existing lord, or even when a lord was succeeded by his heir, the tenant's security was considerable.[22] For the lord, especially one who had made the initial gift, the proper performance of services was fundamental to his man's continuing enjoyment of the land. Failure to perform service, especially if accompanied by a denial that the land was even held of the lord, demanded that the lord act if he was not to lose both prestige and dues. His response would be to 'distrain'. This took the form of seizing moveable goods belonging to the tenant, and on some occasions repossessing the land.[23] The action should not be excessively violent, but could certainly involve a display of force, aimed at cowing the tenant into submission. Customary pressure that the distraint be carried out 'reasonably' might still leave the lord with considerable leeway, particularly if he had obtained his court's backing or if the tenant's disobedience had been flagrant. The removal of the tenant's goods or land was, in the first instance, to be temporary. They were not to be given away and should be restored to the vassal in return for security that he would answer the lord's claim.[24] However, continuing failure to perform services could lead to the tenant forfeiting his holding. That we know of very

20. D. E. Greenway, ed., *Charters of the Honour of Mowbray, 1107–91* (London, 1972), no. 3; the incident reveals that a lord at one point in his life may have believed an act right, at another wrong.
21. Holt, 'Politics and property', 30–6.
22. On security of tenure, see Hudson, *Land, Law, and Lordship*, ch. 2.
23. On the absence of a strict order in which land and chattels should be taken, but the utility of taking chattels first, see Hudson, *Land, Law, and Lordship*, pp. 29–31.
24. However, for late twelfth-century evidence to the contrary, see below, p. 191.

few instances of such forfeitures within honours may stem simply from the limits of the evidence, but may also reflect reality.[25] Perhaps in contrast to distraint, the enforcement of forfeiture was a very weighty matter. A court hearing would usually have preceded any forfeiture; otherwise the lord might be seen to act unreasonably, not showing due respect to his man. The hearing itself provided an opportunity for compromise, when the shared interest of lord and man in the maintenance of their relationship might reassert itself. Misbehaviour by the tenant need not lead to his permanent loss of the land, his lasting 'disseisin'.

What then of the tenant's attitude to his security of tenure? In Normandy before 1066, tenants enjoyed considerable security, and such no doubt was their desire in their newly acquired English lands.[26] Some tenants may have aspired to independence of their lords, but in general they seem to have admitted, if sometimes grudgingly, that they owed services. Nevertheless, a tenant could still regard his hold on the land as less intimately related to these services than did his lord. Rather he might see the land as a reward for his past good service. Indeed, receipt of land could mark not the creation of his relationship with the lord, but a distancing of it, as he moved from the lord's household on to his own tenement. The feeling that the land, although burdened by service, was the tenant's own to enjoy securely would grow the longer the land was held by him and his heirs.[27]

(ii) Heritability

The Normans came to England accustomed to the notion that sons succeeded to their fathers' fiefs.[28] This expectation is reflected in England after the Conquest, and strengthened during the Anglo-Norman period. As soon as relevant charters survive in any number, they record gifts made to the donee and his heirs to hold of the donor and

25. See e.g. *Lawsuits*, no. 317; also *Glanvill*, ix 1, Hall, p. 105; Hudson, *Land, Law, and Lordship*, pp. 33–4.
26. Tabuteau, *Transfers of Property*.
27. On royal protection, see below, p. 115; security in relation to a third party, below, p. 111.
28. On heritability, see Hudson, *Land, Law, and Lordship*, chs 3 and 4.

his heirs. Such wording surely reflects that of the many unwritten grants about which we now know nothing. Moreover, charters recording gifts from churches to laymen often specify that the grantee hold only for life, the land then to return to the church and the heir to have no claim. These charters reinforce the notion that inheritance was customary, the Church employing writing to counter customary lay assumptions. A survey of inheritance in practice suggests that if the genealogically closest heir were the son, daughter, grandchild, brother or sister of the deceased, he or she was rarely denied the inheritance. With male heirs the eldest received the whole inheritance. With female heirs this may have been the case until the early 1130s, but thereafter by royal decree inheritances were divided between heiresses of the same genealogical proximity to the decedent, that is between daughters, or between sisters, and so on.

The above evidence suggests a set of shared assumptions between lords and tenants. However, there were circumstances in which disputes could arise, implying conflicts of perception. Very occasionally the closest heir was rejected for reasons of personal unsuitability or incapacity.[29] Succession by minors might be threatened, particularly if their kinship to the deceased tenant was not very close; even sons who were minors might be in danger, particularly during times of political disruption. The lord might want an adult vassal, other claimants may have seen the heir's temporary weakness as an opportunity to pursue their own ends.[30] Divisions between heiresses could cause particular problems.[31] Likewise, lords may have been more discriminating in their acceptance of claims by more distant heirs, for example nephews and nieces, uncles and aunts, or their descendants.[32]

29. Ibid., p. 126 suggests that the form of incapacity might have to be quite severe, except in cases where there was some other complication in the inheritance, as in the Marshwood case, below, p. 99.
30. E.g. *Lawsuits*, no. 145; also Hudson, *Land, Law, and Lordship*, p. 116, and for a later instance, Holt, *Magna Carta*, p. 103.
31. S. L. Waugh, 'Women's inheritance and the growth of bureaucratic monarchy in twelfth- and thirteenth-century England', *Nottingham Medieval Studies* 34 (1990), 71–92; also below, p. 216.
32. Hudson, *Land, Law, and Lordship*, pp. 114–15.

Additionally, in certain circumstances there might be uncertainty as to who was the closest heir. One example is particularly famous since it affected the royal house in 1199. On one side was John, younger brother of Richard the deceased; on the other was their nephew Arthur, son of an intermediate brother, Geoffrey, who had predeceased Richard.[33]

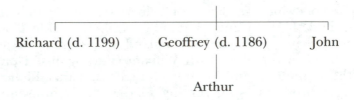

Richard (d. 1199)   Geoffrey (d. 1186)   John

Arthur

Disputes also frequently arose when the recently deceased had married more than once: what was the relative claim of his sons by each marriage? In such complicated circumstances the lord might choose not to regrant the land to an heir, either waiting to settle the dispute or exploiting the confusion to retain the land for as long as possible. Or he might use his discretion to choose which party he favour with the land. The 1208 Pipe Roll recorded that Henry I had 'by will' enfeoffed the son of a second marriage with the barony of Marshwood as he was a better knight than the son of the first.[34]

Again, it is in such difficult cases that lords may have most greatly exploited their right to take relief. The weaker the hereditary claim, the more the lord might charge the claimant, or the more likely the lord might in effect sell the land to the highest bidder amongst the claimants. Henry I's Coronation Charter indicates both that some lords, notably Henry's brother William Rufus, had exploited reliefs in arbitrary fashion, and that in certain circumstances lords would admit that such action was wrong: 'if any of my barons, earls or any other who holds of

33. This is the 'king's case', which arose on the death of Richard I; see J. C. Holt, 'The *Casus Regis*, the law of politics and succession in the Plantagenet dominions 1185–1247', in E. B. King and S. J. Ridyard, eds, *Law in Mediaeval Life and Thought* (Sewanee, TN, 1990), pp. 21–42.
34. *PR10J*, p. 113 n. 8.

me should die, his heir will not buy back his land as he did in my brother's time, but will relieve it with a just and lawful relief. Similarly, too, the men of my barons will relieve their lands from their lords by just and lawful relief.'

Particularly when the genealogically closest heir was hard to identify, was a distant relative, or had somehow made himself undesirable to his potential lord, rivals sometimes made claims on other grounds than being the closest heir.[35] Following the death of Gilbert de l'Aigle between 1114 and 1118, Henry I denied Gilbert's eldest son Richer's claim to his land in England. Richer may already have been in rebellion with William Clito against Henry on the Continent, and Henry reputedly said that Richer's younger brothers 'were serving in the king's household and confidently expecting the same honour by hereditary right'. Henry refused repeated claims from Richer who eventually turned for support to the king of France. Yet despite this disloyalty, his uncle succeeded in reconciling Richer with Henry who granted him all he had claimed, and Richer eventually obtained all his father's lands in England and Normandy. Here even an apparently strong claim not based on being the closest heir was in the end rejected. The lord was unwilling to exercise his discretion and the customary claims of the closest heir were re-affirmed.[36]

(iii) Alienability

There were two main ways in which lands could be granted away, be 'alienated'. The first is generally referred to as enfeoffment or subinfeudation. The land was given to the new tenant, who henceforth held it of the donor and performed services to him. This was the most common form of grant, and gifts to the Church were generally in similar fashion, although the services owed might be spiritual and there was less emphasis upon the land being held from the donor. The alternative was substitution, whereby the current tenant returned the land to his lord

35. On such claims, see Hudson, *Land, Law, and Lordship*, pp. 122–31.
36. Orderic, vi 188, 196–8, 250.

who gave it to the new tenant to hold from him for service.[37]

How did a man decide which and how much of his lands he might alienate? A first significant distinction was between inheritance and acquisition. The potential donor's family generally preferred that inherited lands should pass to the heir, leaving the current holder with greater freedom to dispose of lands he had acquired himself. However, lords appear to have felt a particular claim to control lands which tenants had recently acquired from them, leaving the tenants greater freedom to dispose of their inheritances. Next, a variety of non-legal factors, such as the position of the estates in relation to the centre of the man's power might determine which he alienated; often there was a preference for the alienation of distant estates. Thirdly, there was no clear indication that a fixed proportion of lands was alienable, in contrast with the custom which was to exist, for example, in early thirteenth-century Normandy.[38] Rather, the grantor was to act reasonably, and perceptions of what was reasonable might well differ according to circumstances and between parties. Negotiation – as in the quotation which began this chapter – or court discussion, perhaps even court judgment, might be required.

Both donor and donee would normally desire that the gift be as secure as possible, and the means by which gifts were secured are very illuminating.[39] Giving land was not simply a legal or economic transaction but involved a wide variety of interests and purposes. Gifts were public events, conducted before witnesses, often in the donor's court or the recipient church. Sometimes an elaborate ritual was involved, as when a donor and other interested parties placed a symbol of the gift upon the church's altar. Ceremonies of seising, of transferring land, also no doubt

37. See e.g. *EHD*, ii no. 249, an instance typical of many substitutions in concerning land acquired rather than inherited by the donor, and also a family arrangement. For a more extensive treatment of alienability, see Hudson, *Land, Law, and Lordship*, chs 5–7; ibid., ch. 8 deals with a topic largely omitted here, the alienability of church lands.
38. *TAC*, lxxxix, Tardif, pp. 99–100.
39. See further Hudson, *Land, Law, and Lordship*, ch. 5.

occurred in gifts to laymen. A beneficiary might also acknowledge a donation by presenting counter-gifts to the donor and sometimes to others as well. Such counter-gifts could later act as evidence, and also symbolized the mutuality of the relationship of the parties involved. Likewise, a charter acted as lasting testimony to a gift, and occasionally might set down the penalty for those who harmed the gift, the blessing or favour for those who supported it.

Most telling of all are the records, particularly in charters, of consents by interested parties.[40] Mention of, say, an heir or a lord consenting to a gift need not indicate that without their consent the gift was invalid or unsustainable. Rather, such people may have desired mention in the grant in order to share in the donee's gratitude, or, in the case of gifts to monasteries, the prayers for salvation offered up by the favoured monks. Even so, patterns of consenting remain significant with regard to perceptions of alienability, and can reveal potential conflicts of interest. Family members sometimes appear, in particular heirs, and also wives, especially when their own inheritances or marriage portions were being given. No doubt one of the concerns was that the current holder of the land grant away so much that he damage their own or the family's fortunes. However, such consents seem to have been less frequent than in various areas of France for which equivalent studies have been made, suggesting that land was relatively more freely alienable in Anglo-Norman England.

Lords surely assumed that their tenants might alienate their lands just as they themselves had. There is little sign that a lord's consent had to be obtained before every single grant was made. He might have no objection to gifts which would strengthen the retinue of his follower, and hence strengthen his own position. Other grants were less acceptable, although unfortunately we are likely to be left no evidence of a planned gift so objectionable to the donor's lord that he prevented it. Obviously, a lord would object to gifts to his enemies. Concern was also expressed

---

40. See ibid., chs 6 and 7; also S. D. White, 'Maitland on family and kinship', in Hudson, *Centenary Essays*, pp. 106–10.

about grants at reduced services, often to the donor's family and in particular to churches. Whilst lords could supposedly still exact full service, grants to religious houses might bring problems for distraint and jurisdiction, and thus limit his capacity to exact his dues.[41]

Overall, the tenant was free to alienate a reasonable proportion of his land, provided there was no threat to the services which he owed. The amount considered reasonable would depend on his powers, not least of persuasion. The strength of his position in relation to his family, although not his lord, may be linked to the considerable proportion of lands in post-Conquest England that were acquisitions. In general, the donor and his family's interests were usually sufficiently compatible to ensure that major conflict did not arise; for example, a father as much as an heir might desire the perpetuation of the inheritance. However, when a man lay dying, surrounded perhaps by clerics reminding him of the dangers to his soul, he might forget his obligation to his kin, and act unreasonably. For such death-bed gifts, Anglo-Norman charters support the testimony of the law-book *Glanvill* at the end of the 1180s: unlike other gifts, those made on the death-bed *required* the consent and confirmation of the heir.[42] This requirement contrasts with the relative freedom to alienate which tenants normally possessed.

(iv) The tenant's strengths

Why had the tenant in fee come to be in such a powerful position by 1135? The tenant's position in Normandy before 1066 had been in many ways a strong one. The process of settlement in England may have strengthened this position in some ways, for example in relation to the kin's claims to limit alienation, whilst weakening it in others, at least initially increasing the link between the tenant's hold on the land and his lord's gift of it to him. Simple continuity of tenure probably increased each

---

41. Note e.g. T. Madox, *Formulare Anglicanum* (London, 1702), no. ii; Hudson, 'Origins of property', p. 211.
42. *Glanvill,* vii 1, Hall, p. 70; Hudson, *Land, Law, and Lordship,* pp. 195–6.

successive tenant's hold on the family land, and reduced active lordly control. What was once land received by gift of the lord had become the family's inheritance. Charter language recording lords' regrants of lands to a tenant's heir suggest that they were seen as granting the heir what was due to him; they 'gave back' or 'rendered' (*reddere*) the inheritance to the heir, whereas they had 'given' (*dare*) the land to the first tenant.[43] Meanwhile, the very existence of charters could strengthen the tenant's position, especially if they promised that the lands be held by him and his heirs. In particular, obtaining a royal charter of confirmation constituted a promise of future royal help against any challenger, presumably including one's lord.

Moreover, the relative strength of the tenant's position could perpetuate itself in other ways. One should not assume that there was an endless supply of men clamouring to take grants on harsh terms. Rather, lords may have had to compete for good followers. In that case, if a lord desired to reward good service, to ensure loyalty, or to attract a new follower, he would have to make his gift conform to his follower's view of a proper transfer of land. The fullness of the transfer is sometimes emphasized by a phrase laying down that the tenant was to hold as freely as the lord ever had. The transfer was to be the fullest conceivable.[44]

Here we see the effect of the relative power of tenant and lord in the negotiation of a relationship. Such pressures varied between lordships. The position of the lord might be peculiarly strong in a compact honour, where almost all the tenants held of him alone. In general, however, lords' power over their men may have been declining in the Anglo-Norman period. It was becoming more common for men to hold of more than one lord; as one visitor commented, in England there were as many lords as neighbours. Moreover, even by 1087, some lords had powerful vassals, and the number of such men not easily controlled by their lords almost certainly had increased by 1135. Alienations could lead to a lasting drain on a lord's resources and on his capacity to enforce his will.

43. Hudson, *Land, Law, and Lordship*, pp. 72–7.
44. Hudson, 'Origins of property', p. 205.

All such developments worked to strengthen the tenant's position.[45]

Other developments may have strengthened and clarified land-holding customs. The Church reformers' working out of family, and in particular marriage, law must have been connected with the clarifying and hardening of inheritance practice. For example, increasingly clear positions on illegitimacy reduced the scope for dispute between offspring of different liaisons. The increasing classification of land-holding, and its effect upon disputes, may have had similar results. When an heir lost a case because the land was proved to be held explicitly only for life, the assumption that other lands were held heritably might be reinforced. Custom was re-affirmed as transactions occurred or disputes were settled within that customary framework. The tenant's peers in his lord's courts would help to enforce, perpetuate, and strengthen these customs. Let us, therefore, now turn to the procedures available in land disputes.

. . .

DISPUTES

(i) Modbert's case

On his death-bed, Grenta of North Stoke was surrounded by men not so much well-wishers as will-wishers, hoping to be favoured by his dying words. Most prominent were his son-in-law, Modbert, and the monks of the cathedral priory of Bath. The subject of their concern was land in North Stoke, Somerset. In the dispute which followed, the parties recalled versions of Grenta's wishes. According to the monks, when Grenta was making his last dispositions

> he was secretly asked by the members of his household to make a testament and publicly institute an heir. But he said 'This is the inheritance of the servants of the Lord, which I am

45. J. Laporte, ed., 'Epistolae Fiscannenses: lettres d'amitié, de gouvernement et d'affaires', *Revue Mabillon* 11 (1953), 30; see also e.g. P. Dalton, *Conquest, Anarchy and Lordship: Yorkshire, 1066–1154* (Cambridge, 1994), pp. 249–52, 285ff.; Hudson, *Land, Law, and Lordship*, p. 49; note e.g. Holt, 'Politics and property', 20–1 on toponymic family names.

"I'll take it all," she said sweetly, as the cashier, avoiding eye contact, quickly scanned her purchases.

Maggie picked up the small, brown plastic bag and went out to the bus stop in front of the strip mall. She took a seat on a concrete bench and waited for the 45 bus, which would take her home. She tore open the Snickers and took a small bite. With that first sweet taste of chocolate, she closed her eyes and remembered the magic of the campout—the gooey, chocolatey s'mores, toasted for dessert over the fire. They giggled as they licked each other's fingers clean under the light of the moon, eyes sparkling with promises of the night to come.

The squeak of tires announced the arrival of the 45 bus. Maggie tucked the rest of her candy bar into her purse along with her bag of purchases, freeing up her right hand to hold the rail as she climbed the stairs of the bus. She was grateful for the attentive driver who stood with a ready hand in case her legs didn't cooperate.

Tonight would have marked sixty years together. Maggie would place the new frame with Jimmy's picture in it atop the freshly dusted piano and she would play for both of them. Tonight would be theirs.

permitted to hold as long as I live by way of payment and not by law of inheritance, and now that I die, I leave myself with the land to the brethren to whom it belongs by right.' That is the testament he made and those are his last words, after which, having suffered for a few days, he died a monk.[46]

Modbert's claim, on the other hand, was 'that he most justly was the heir, since he was married to the daughter of the deceased (who during his lifetime had adopted him as his son) and that the father had held that land . . . freely and hereditarily'.

The dispute may have begun in the bishop of Bath's court shortly after Grenta's death, with Modbert making his claim to the land and having it rejected. However, our first evidence is a writ which Modbert obtained: 'William, the king's son, to John, bishop of Bath, greeting. I order you justly to seise Modbert of the land which Grenta of Stoke had held, to which he made him heir during his lifetime. Witness: the bishop of Salisbury.' The writ was brought 'in the month of June on the day after the feast of the apostles Peter and Paul, as Bishop John was sitting in his court at Bath with his friends and barons, who had gathered for the feast day'. The record of the case ends with the names of twenty-two men, including Bishop John. Amongst these are an Irish bishop and three archdeacons, as well as twelve laymen specified as witnesses. Very few of the laymen, perhaps only one, can be identified with reasonable certainty as tenants of the bishop. Possibly others were his men in a looser sense, tied by bonds other than land-holding. Yet the composition of the court reveals again that a lord's court need not be solely a meeting of his vassals.

The bishop's response to the writ shows the rationality, the awareness of the written word, and to an extent the informality of proceedings outlined in chapter 1. He agreed 'to do what has been ordered by the son of my lord through this letter, if it is just. However, my friends and lords . . . I beg you to discuss which is the more just cause in this matter.' The prior took counsel with the monks and

46. *Lawsuits*, no. 226. The narrative is from a Bath cartulary, and favours the church's case. Joseph Biancalana's unpublished paper, 'The administrative image of English society and the origins of the common law', has added much to my earlier analyses of this case.

then made his response to the attentive audience. He, too, latched on to the word 'justly' in the royal writ. He stated that the land was given to the brethren in the early days of the house in free possession, and had never been transformed into 'military right', by implication heritable. Grenta had left the land to the church on his death-bed. Thus Grenta neither could nor did make Modbert heir of the land. Lawful witnesses and a charter supposedly of the Saxon King Cynewulf, replete with fearsome curse, supported the prior's statement. Others, however, backed Modbert's claim. The court seems to have been unable to reach a decision as to whether Grenta had held the land heritably, whether he had made Modbert his heir, or whether he had bequeathed the lands to the church on his death-bed. The bishop therefore asked that those known 'to be neither advocates nor supporters of the parties' study the case and judge how it be settled. 'Those who were older and more learned in the law left the crowd, weighed subtly and wisely all the arguments they had heard, and settled the case.' They returned and one of them announced their opinion. Modbert was to prove his claim 'by at least two free and lawful witnesses from the familiars [close associates] of the church, who shall be named today and produced within a week, or by a signed and credible cirograph. If he fails in either, he shall not be heard again.' The court agreed that this was just, but Modbert remained silent. At least according to the account, this implied that he refused to accept the form of proof and thus surrendered his claim. He may well have felt harshly treated, for it was unlikely that either his agreement with, or the church's grant to, Grenta would have been recorded in writing, unless perhaps the latter were a life grant and hence less than helpful to Modbert. The demand was more appropriate for ecclesiastical written culture. Similarly, the requirement that witnesses be 'familiars' of the church seems to weight the process against Modbert. Concern that a discontented Modbert might revive the dispute helps to explain why the priory obtained a further confirmation from Henry I.[47]

47. *RRAN*, ii no. 1302.

The case is fascinating for many reasons. It shows an interesting combination of informality and precision in proceedings. It raises issues concerning heritability and life grants. It emphasizes that at least this honour was not a self-contained unit. Its court was of varied composition. Royal influence could be brought to bear upon it. Yet the royal writ was not simply an order permitting no discussion. Rather, it set under way proceedings in which the party who at first benefited from the written loan of royal support was in the end unsuccessful. One cannot discover how many men like Modbert obtained royal writs, but there is no indication that he was a man of peculiar status or with a link to the royal household. This writ must have been cheap enough to be worth obtaining in order to recover a fairly small plot of land. It may indicate that Henry I quite often provided royal backing in the internal disputes of at least ecclesiastical honours, prefiguring the general royal involvement in land litigation apparent by the end of the twelfth century.

(ii) Disputes: causes, conduct, courts

Disputes over land were likely to arise in a variety of circumstances. Political disruption bred disputes. This was true, as we shall see, of Stephen's reign, and also of the years immediately after the Conquest. William I's reign saw some notable hearings of land cases and one of the purposes of the Domesday enquiry was to settle conflicting claims.[48] Even in peaceful periods, some men may simply have invaded land to which they had no claim.[49] In most instances, however, there is evidence that strife arose from conflicting perceptions of claims. The succession of a new lord might be a particular occasion for disputes. If he was an outsider imposed upon the honour, he might seek to eject sitting tenants.[50] Any newly succeeding lord might seek an immediate assertion of his power, enquiring into any laxness which had slipped into his tenants' relationship with his predecessor. Alternatively, sitting tenants might

---

48. These are best recorded for church lands; see e.g. *Lawsuits*, no. 18.
49. See e.g. *Lawsuits*, no. 253.
50. See above, p. 95.

distance themselves from the new lord, for example by refusing homage and services.[51] Similarly, a tenant's death might lead to dispute, particularly if identification of the closest heir was difficult or the dead man had held only for life. Termination of any lease might cause strife. A large proportion of disputes concern the exaction of services due from the land, whilst others concern matters such as entry to and egress from lands, the destruction of hedges or the erection of sheepfolds.[52] Alienations, too, produced conflict. Donors sometimes nullified their own gifts, giving land successively to two different beneficiaries. On other occasions, heirs might seek to reverse their dead predecessor's gifts, or, more unusually, a previously unknown heir might appear and claim that his inheritance had been granted away in his absence.[53]

Much disputing took place outside court, as in the use of distraint for the exaction of services. Beyond the reigns of the Conqueror and Stephen, there is little evidence of outright violence, although later the royal plea rolls reveal interpersonal violence arising from land claims.[54] Aspiring tenants might use more subtle means of persuasion upon lords. When preaching, Anselm of Canterbury used the image of a prince's court containing men 'who labour with unbroken fortitude to obey his will for the sake of receiving back again an inheritance of which they bewail the loss'.[55] Such service might be linked to negotiation, where factors such as the prestige of the potential tenant, or the support which each party could raise, might have a crucial impact. Meanwhile, all such out-of-court activities could be combined with proceedings within court.

51. For instances involving ecclesiastical lords, see e.g. *Lawsuits*, nos 164, 257–9.
52. J. S. Loengard, 'The assize of nuisance: origins of an action at common law', *Cambridge Law Journal* 37 (1978), 147–52.
53. See *Lawsuits*, no. 380 for an example probably from the 1150s.
54. See Hudson, *Land, Law, and Lordship*, pp. 144–6; note also the Norman *Consuetudines et Iusiticie*, c. 6: 'Nulli licuit in Normannia pro calumnia terre domum vel molendinum ardere vel aliquam vastacionem facere vel predam capere' – C. H. Haskins, *Norman Institutions* (Cambridge, MA, 1918), p. 283. On the plea rolls, see below, pp. 210–12.
55. Eadmer, *The Life of St Anselm*, ed. and trans R. W. Southern (2nd edn, Oxford, 1972), p. 94.

If court proceedings were to move forward, there was a strong desire that both parties be present. Judgments because of default were not made lightly. The parties therefore might be given several chances to answer an initial summons and be permitted a variety of 'essoins' (excuses) for non-attendance. Practice with regard to essoins possibly varied between courts, and indeed between individual cases, and there may have been room for manipulation of custom by powerful parties.[56] Once in court, claims would be stated and rejected, and pleading, debate, and negotiation take place. Again, much information might be common knowledge. The facts of a case might be so clear that one party would be forced to withdraw its claim, hoping at best for some sweetener to compensate for the surrender. On other occasions, sworn testimony or – in particular in cases involving churches – documentary evidence could decide a case during pleading. In some instances, substantive argument about custom might be introduced. In Modbert's case no rules of law were explicitly stated, but throughout appeal was implicitly made to norms of land-holding; indeed, the norms seem accepted by both parties, leaving the dispute to turn on matters of fact. Thus, as we saw in the previous chapter, parties might accept a custom or norm, but plead that their case was exceptional. Sometimes such appeals to norms or such exceptions might bring the case to an abrupt conclusion. However, in other cases, much might depend on the eloquence and repute of the parties, and on their mobilization of supporters.

Such support was employed formally through warranty. Here the tenant 'vouched' his lord as warrantor. In effect, he was saying that he held the land from the lord, and that the latter, as a good lord worthy of honour, should take up his claim for him. Sometimes the great man's presence would suffice:

happy then was the tenant who could say to any adverse claimant: 'Sue me if you will, but remember that behind me you will find the earl or the abbot.' Such an answer would

56. See below, p. 132, for royal regulation of essoins in 1170, perhaps suggesting earlier variation or abuse.

often be final. ... He has a lord who may use carnal weapons or let loose the thunders of the church in defence of his tenant.

On other occasions, the lord was obliged to pursue the case, and, if he lost, to provide his tenant with an equivalent piece of land. Thus warranty provided a lordly guarantee that the tenant would be secure in his tenure of at least some holding against challenges by third parties.[57]

Judgment was generally made by the suitors, although clearly the president of the court would be influential. In Modbert's case the president selected those with no attachment to either party as the decision-making body. A wide range of factors could influence the suitors. Some might be fairly general such as desire to curry favour with, or to limit the discretion of, their lord, others particular to the case or the individual concerned. But in addition, suitors were influenced by their perceptions of correct land-holding practice. Usually, as in Modbert's case, their first decision following pleading was the 'mesne judgment': who should bear the burden of proof and what form that proof should take. Various forms were possible, for example documents, sworn testimony, oaths, or the decision of a body of neighbours.[58]

In hard cases, where evidence was lacking or unclear, or where the parties were quite irreconcilable, trial by battle might occur.[59] Compared with those over offences of violence or theft, such battles were likely to be between men of higher status, and altogether more dignified affairs. They were fought with swords rather than staffs or hammers. Moreover, they were not simply between the

---

57. Quotation Pollock and Maitland, i 306–7; see esp. P. R. Hyams, 'Warranty and good lordship in twelfth century England', *Law and History Review* 5 (1987), 437–503.
58. For a decision by a sworn body of twelve men, see e.g. below, p. 113 on Blackmarston. Domesday cases were often settled by the testimony of the hundred, or more rarely the shire. For the origins of the jury, see above, p. 10 n. 38. For oaths see *Lawsuits*, e.g. nos 166, 193, 280, and above, pp. 76–7. Evidence from witnesses of grant: e.g. *Lawsuits*, no. 248.
59. Other ordeals concerning land are only recorded as having taken place in England after 1066 in relation to the Domesday Inquest: Hyams, 'Ordeal', p. 114; Bartlett, *Trial*, p. 27.

principal parties. At least the demandant was represented by a man who swore that he witnessed the demandant's claim and would act as his champion. The tenant had the choice of himself fighting or finding a suitable champion.[60] Battle was offered more often than it was fought, and even when combat was undertaken, a compromise might still be struck. In the later years of Stephen's reign, a knight called Edward held a hide of land at Headington, for which he refused to do homage or any service to the prior and canons of St Frideswide. The prior obtained a writ and pursued his claim in the court of Robert earl of Leicester. The case

> was decided by judicial combat fought in the court of the said earl in a green meadow above the house of Godwin. Finally, after many blows between the champions and although the champion of Edward had lost his sight in the fight... they both sat down and as neither dared attack the other, peace was established as follows...[61]

If the case was decided entirely in favour of the tenant, he naturally remained in control of the land. If the demandant succeeded, the land was presumably transferred to him in some ceremony. Often, however, settlements were reached. These varied from genuine compromises, leaving no victor, to decisions which made the victor obvious, but allowed the defeated party some sweetener. Compromise might satisfy an ideological preference for 'love' over 'law', but also suit the circumstances of the dispute and render renewed trouble less likely.[62]

Procedure in land disputes probably did not differ greatly between different types of court. However, the relative importance of these courts is of great consequence. Were land cases the preserve of the courts of the honour concerned? If so, the possibility of peculiar honorial custom or of seignorial arbitrariness is increased. Alternatively, did the possibility of disappointed claimants resorting to the royal court to complain of injustice increase standard-

---

60. See above, ch. 3, also below, pp. 202–3; *Glanvill*, ii 3, Hall, pp. 23–5.
61. *Lawsuits*, no. 316; see also comments in Hudson, *Land, Law, and Lordship*, p. 47.
62. See e.g. *Lawsuits*, no. 242; and above, p. 16.

ization, decrease seignorial discretion? Henry I's 1108 writ concerning courts is again of central importance:

> if in the future there should arise a dispute concerning the allotment of land, or concerning its seizure, let this be tried in my own court if it be between my tenants in chief [*dominicos barones meos*]. But if the dispute be between the vassals of any baron of my honour, let it be held in the court of their common lord. But if the dispute be between the vassals of two different lords let the plea be held in the shire court.[63]

Clearly, Henry envisaged a considerable but not exclusive role for lords' courts. Because of the survival, and almost certainly the production, of evidence, we know most about the functioning of ecclesiastical lords' courts.

> In the year of the Incarnation of the Lord 1133 ... Bernard deraigned the land of Blackmarston in the chapter of St Mary and St Ethelbert by oath of twelve honest men and the judgment of the court, and was seised and invested thereof with the consent of the chapter, as well as his father Alward had had it and as the neighbours and those who knew the land had perambulated all around it, and he holds it for free service in fee farm.[64]

The identity of Bernard's opponent is uncertain; it may have been a third party, rather than his lord, Hereford Cathedral. However, seignorial courts did deal with complaints not simply between a lord's men but also against the lord, hard as it may have been in such cases for a claimant to succeed in the lord's own court.[65] Seignorial courts probably also dealt with cases between the lord's tenants and their own men. A disappointed sub-tenant might look to his overlord to right an injustice he felt he had suffered at the hands of his immediate lord.[66]

Henry I's writ stated that cases between tenants of different lords should go to county courts. Again, these may

63. *EHD*, ii no. 43.
64. *Lawsuits*, no. 281.
65. See above, pp. 41–2.
66. See Hudson, *Land, Law, and Lordship*, pp. 35–6, 38, 140–1, on overlords' courts; conceivably other great men of the area might become involved, ibid., p. 36.

have had an importance obscured by the paucity of sources. Probably in the 1120s, a certain 'Archembald the Fleming restored to Bernard [the King's Scribe] by judgment of the county of Devon land which was his grandfather's . . . as his inheritance'.[67] The shire court was in a sense a royal forum, and is one manifestation of royal involvement in land cases. This could also take various other forms. As in Modbert's case, one party might go – perhaps on a lengthy journey – to the royal writing office, obtain a writ, and bring it to the court hearing the case in the first instance. Writs could provide a temporary loan of royal support to those who might otherwise have lost the case, to those who desired a speedy success, or simply to those who enjoyed royal favour. Or, again probably at the request of one of the parties, royal justices might in person attend the court.[68] Such royal interventions could affect not only the men of the king's tenants in chief, but even those who held more distantly.[69] Cases concerning sub-tenants were also on occasion heard in the king's own court. The various forms of royal involvement were inter-linked. Some writs expressed the king's threatening will that he should hear no more about the issue for lack of justice having been done. And at least from Henry I's time, writs commanded that the king's instructions be obeyed, otherwise the case was to be heard before him or his justices. Procedures also existed for the transfer of cases should the disappointed party complain of 'default of justice'.[70]

In the Conqueror's reign, the process of sorting out disputes arising from the Norman settlement may have given an initial stimulus to the king's involvement in

67. *Lawsuits*, no. 267; note also e.g. no. 242.
68. See e.g. *Lawsuits*, no. 266.
69. Note e.g. *Lawsuits*, no. 175.
70. See M. Cheney, 'A decree of King Henry II on defect of justice', in D. E. Greenway *et al.*, eds, *Tradition and Change: Essays in Honour of Marjorie Chibnall* (Cambridge, 1985), p. 192; *Royal Writs*, pp. 147–8, 154–7. See generally on royal involvement, Hudson, *Land, Law, and Lordship*, pp. 36–44, 133–41. For suggestions that increased royal involvement in land cases began in the Conqueror's reign and was linked to the process of colonization and the Domesday Inquest, see R. Fleming, 'Oral testimony and the Domesday Inquest', *ANS* 17 (1995), 113–19.

settling land cases, particularly those between tenants in chief. Thereafter, it seems likely that demand for more general royal intervention increased up to *c.* 1135. One of the main sources was the Church, and the number of monasteries in England increased markedly during the reigns of the Anglo-Norman kings. Likewise royal servants looked to royal help, and their numbers also increased. Churches, royal servants, and increasing numbers of other laymen enjoyed written royal confirmations of their lands, or perhaps more personal protections. Either of these might constitute a royal promise of support should they become involved in a property dispute.[71] Moreover, the king also on occasion took a more active interest. He would be concerned to fulfil his royal rights, for example hearing cases of default of justice and unjust judgment. Most importantly, he would become concerned if the dispute threatened the peace.

Estimating the frequency of Henry I's involvement in land cases, and the regularity of the actions royal intervention set in motion, is almost impossible for lay honours, and very difficult for ecclesiastical ones. Modbert's case suggests that the king might become involved even in fairly minor cases at one party's request, but also indicates that the involvement did not extend to very close regulation, let alone observation, of procedure. Henry's regime was a very powerful one, but may have functioned in a significantly less routine fashion than would his grandson's later in the century. However, not merely actual royal intervention but also its potential had to be taken into consideration. In the 1120s or 1130s St Mary's, York, granted some land which Richard Tortus had held from it to a certain Ougrim of 'Frisemareis' and his heirs to hold in fee: 'if any heir of Richard Tortus can acquire that messuage of land from the king or deraign it against us or the said Ougrim and his heirs, we will not give exchange.' Claimants thus had some right in the land which they could enforce irrespective of the attitude of their predecessor's lord, and lords had to modify their actions accordingly.

71. See A. Harding, ed., *The Roll of the Shropshire Eyre of 1256* (Selden Soc., 96, 1981), p. lviii.

me now. He always had change in his pocket, surely he would have had fourteen cents. But he is gone, like everyone else, Gone. What's the point of living in a world where fourteen cents is going to make or break you?

Maggie looked up at the cashier, who nervously glanced at the growing line of impatient customers waiting to check out. Her eyes caught a flash of red as the clerk handed the declined credit card back to her. *Oh right! Damn it! My card expired and the bank sent me a new one.*

"I'm sorry, I used the wrong card. I knew there was money—" Maggie began, shaking her head. She stopped as she saw the look of disinterest on the girl's face. The cashier only wanted to get the line moving. Maggie turned and saw a young mother, frustrated as her toddler squirmed to get down. Behind them, a young man tapped his foot on the ground as he spun the wheels on his skateboard, impatient to get back to the streets.

"So, you want everything?" the young cashier said, unconsciously touching the penny dish by the cash register.

Maggie looked down at the three-dollar ceramic frame, etched with green ivy. It would be perfect for the picture she had found of Jimmy last night in an old box in the attic. It had been their first campout together and he was standing proudly on the riverbank, holding up a rainbow trout, broad smile on his face. The skin around his eyes crinkled with laugh lines behind round metal glasses. Next to the frame was a Snickers bar and bottle of water, a reward for getting out of the house. *I could probably do without those,* she thought, feeling the years of scarcity that had not allowed for extra treats.

Hearing movement behind her, Maggie glanced over her shoulder and saw a second cashier open up, relieving tension in the line. The young man, with his skateboard now propped against his leg, was making faces at the toddler in his mother's arms. The child giggled loudly, which echoed throughout the store, lightening everyone's mood, his earlier restlessness forgotten.

Maggie took a deep breath. *The world's not in that much of a hurry after all,* she thought. She adjusted her black felt hat, carefully held in place by two bobby pins, which barely contained the strands of gray hair trying to escape. Then, she opened her matching candy striped wallet, took the brand new card out and handed it to the cashier.

. . .

ANGLO-NORMAN LAND LAW AND COMMON LAW PROPERTY

We have thus seen that certainly by 1135 much of the language of common law land-holding had emerged, and also that the tenant 'in fee' enjoyed a strong position in relation to his lord as to control of his land. This position could be protected by a variety of courts, including the king's. If different perceptions of land-holding continued to coexist and sometimes conflict, the perception which was to predominate was already most prominent: in it, the tenant resembled in many ways the property-holder in thirteenth-century common law.[72]

Moreover, as far as the higher levels of society are concerned, there seems to have been little regional or honorial variation in the most important practices. Conceivably, there were procedural variations, for example concerning essoins, and perhaps more substantive ones, for instance concerning the allocation of dower.[73] However, there is no sign, for example, that settlers from areas which may have favoured partible inheritance, such as Brittany, imported these practices into areas they colonized, such as the honour of Richmond. In Kent, the partibility of inheritance which existed for gavelkind land did not lead to a partibility of land held in fee.[74] With such shared customs and the increasingly clear classification of land-holding, Henry II's advisers would be able to devise remedies which were routinely available and which applied throughout the realm.

. . .

CONCLUSIONS

During the period 1066–1135, Anglo-Saxon and Norman

---

72. *Early Yorkshire Charters*, i no. 310. For these conclusions generally, see also Hudson, 'Origins of property'. Note also Hudson, *Land, Law, and Lordship*, pp. 56–7 on warranty and tenant right, pp. 206–7 on royal power and alienability. However, for the cautious donor even royal involvement was not enough; see *Lawsuits*, no. 242 for Herbert fitzHelgot.
73. See below, p. 219 n. 121.
74. Hudson, *Land, Law, and Lordship*, p. 110.

practices, together with the impact of Conquest and colonization, had combined and inter-reacted to form important substantive and administrative bases for the common law. Continuity with England before 1066 was most notable in the hundred and shire courts, in land-holding in the lower levels of society, and in the treatment of offences against the person and moveable property. Norman innovation was clearer with regard to land-holding higher in society and seignorial courts. Flexibility and variation of custom and procedure no doubt existed. However, comparison, say, with France at the time suggests that the degree of standardization and uniformity in England was very significant. It had various causes: the pattern of land settlement, the continuing importance of shire and hundred as well as seignorial courts, and the relative smallness of the realm. In addition, there was the power of Norman kings, in the laudatory words of the *Leges Henrici Primi* 'the formidable authority of the royal majesty which we stress as worthy of attention for its continual and beneficial pre-eminence over the laws'.[75] After Henry I's death in 1135, the system of royal government, including judicial activity, was to break down. The renewal of royal power under the Angevins in the second half of the twelfth century would add further essential ingredients to the emerging common law.

75. *LHP*, 6.2a, *Downer*, p. 96.

Chapter 5

ANGEVIN REFORM

. . .

KINGSHIP, STEPHEN'S REIGN, AND ANGEVIN REFORM

Henry I's regime was one of very powerful kingship but of limited routine royal administration. The king's power was felt primarily through his exercise of a few great rights, through his use of *ad hoc* measures, and through his responses to requests from tenants in chief and their sub-tenants.[1] Such a powerful kingship collapsed during Stephen's reign. From the end of the 1130s until as late as 1153 many areas of the realm saw a breakdown of royal authority. Circumstances forced the king to decentralize elements of his power, for example through the creation of earldoms,[2] whilst lords also usurped royal rights and extended their own powers.

Such a breakdown naturally had an effect upon disputing and the administration of justice. There is evidence for continuing provision of royal justice, either by Stephen or by his Angevin opponents, the Empress Matilda and her son, the future Henry II. Some cases were held

---

1. It might be argued that had we, for example, a parallel to Howden's *Chronicle* from Henry I's reign, his administration of justice might seem far more similar to that of his grandson and great grandsons. Yet there is no sign that a royal justice and chronicler like Howden did exist or perhaps could have existed under Henry I.
2. See e.g. K. J. Stringer, *The Reign of Stephen* (London, 1993), p. 53; G. J. White, 'Continuity in government', in E. J. King, ed., *The Anarchy of King Stephen's Reign* (Oxford, 1994), pp. 126–9.

before royal courts, some judicial writs were issued.[3] There may, indeed, have been notable continuity from the end of Henry I's reign into the second half of the 1130s.[4] The worst disruption was in the middle of the reign and occurred particularly in the contested areas between the power bases of Stephen and his opponents. In certain other areas, such as the south-east, Stephen's control survived rather better.[5] Some revival of royal power occurred late in the reign, especially following the agreement between Stephen and the Angevins in 1153.[6]

Nevertheless, there was a marked diminution of royal control. We can find instances of royal orders being ignored, although of course this is not unique to Stephen's reign.[7] There is also considerably less evidence for Stephen than for Henry I intervening in inheritance disputes within honours.[8] Denied royal action, disputants substituted other means. The Church looked more to its own courts and to the papacy. For example, whereas a dispute between Ramsey Abbey and the Pecche family concerning land at Over, Cambridgeshire, had involved the king before 1135, under Stephen the abbey turned to papal help in its attempts to regain the land.[9] The influence of lay lords and their courts increased, through grants or usurpation of franchises, through simple exercise of strength, or through lack of better methods. Great men asserted their authority not only over their vassals, but throughout regions under

3. See e.g. *Lawsuits*, nos 299, 302, 303, 312, 315, 320, 321 (the case of William of Norwich), 331, 334, 335, 342; see also e.g. White, 'Continuity', pp. 131–3. For an optimistic assessment of royal judicial activity during the reign, see H. A. Cronne, *The Reign of Stephen* (London, 1970), ch. 9.

4. See e.g. White, 'Continuity', pp. 119–21.

5. See e.g. Stringer, *Stephen*, p. 58; see also E. Amt, *The Accession of Henry II in England* (Woodbridge, 1993), chs 2–4.

6. See e.g. *Lawsuits*, no. 363; note also *RRAN*, iii nos 129–31. On 1153 see also below, p. 127.

7. *RRAN*, iii no. 83 implies that no. 82 had been ignored; also nos 264 and 265. Such insistence that royal orders be enforced could, of course, be interpreted as a sign of energetic government, but for an interpretation like mine, see White, 'Continuity', p. 124.

8. Hudson, *Land, Law, and Lordship*, pp. 138–9; see also p. 39 on cases concerning services.

9. Hudson, *Land, Law, and Lordship*, p. 99; see also pp. 142–3, 243.

their power.[10] At the same time, however, some lords seem also to have been losing control over their own tenants.[11]

In such circumstances, claimants to lands turned increasingly to violent means. A letter in Henry II's reign records the following incident under Stephen:

> While Stephen [Dammartin] had the stewardship and mastery of all the land of Earl Gilbert [of Clare], he unjustly and against reason occupied the land of Pitley which belonged to William the reeve of Bardfield and his heirs, for he cruelly and unjustly caused one of William's sons to be killed, because he knew and perceived him to be nearer to his father's inheritance with regard to possessing that land.[12]

Or take the disputes between the abbot of Abingdon and Robert, son of a certain knight called Roger. Following Roger's death, Abbot Ingulf (1130–59) resumed a tithe Roger had held in Hanney. However, Ingulf was worn down by the prayers of Robert and his friends 'who were then powerful in war', and temporarily regranted the tithe to Robert. As for lands in Boarshill, with the help of his friends, Robert simply held on to them by force, although according to the abbey his father had just held them for life. Only with considerable difficulty and expense did Ingulf obtain a settlement with Robert whereby the latter gave up the lands.[13]

Furthermore, from Stephen's reign, unlike that of Henry I, we have evidence of magnates and other land-holders in England making treaties in order to regain their inheritances. Roger of Benniworth and Peter of Goxhill made an agreement in the earl of Lincoln's court concerning lands to which Roger was 'the rightful heir': 'this Roger and this Peter shall acquire them by their

10. See E. J. King, 'The anarchy of King Stephen's reign', *TRHS* 5th Ser. 34 (1984), 133–53; note also J. Biancalana, 'For want of justice: legal reforms of Henry II', *Columbia Law Review* 88 (1988), esp. 450–1.
11. Note Hudson, *Land, Law, and Lordship*, e.g. p. 49; also the suggestions of P. Dalton, *Conquest, Anarchy and Lordship: Yorkshire, 1066–1154* (Cambridge, 1994), pp. 242–7, on enfeoffments made under duress.
12. *Lawsuits*, no. 470; comment in Stenton, *First Century*, p. 82, and Hudson, *Land, Law, and Lordship*, p. 144.
13. *CMA*, ii 200–2, *Lawsuits*, no. 378.

common power and their common money'. It is conceivable that increased use of writing reveals such agreements which may have been made orally under Henry I, but it seems more likely that it was the conditions of Stephen's reign which created the need for partnerships to perpetrate violence.[14] Likewise, circumstances may have stimulated men to adopt new methods to secure those lands which they did possess. Thus within the charters of the earl of Chester, and perhaps those of other lords, written warranty clauses are more prominent in the 1140s and early 1150s than they would be early in Henry II's reign; special threats to the lands may have led men to resort to writing.[15]

There is also evidence of increased theft and rapine both at the lower levels of society and amongst knights. The following late, but plausible, story appears in an early thirteenth-century royal court record.

> In the war of King Stephen, it happened that a knight named Warin of Walcote was an honest itinerant knight and he fought in the war and at length he passed through the dwelling of Robert of Shuckburgh . . . . And Robert had a daughter named Isabel whom Warin loved and took, so that he asked Robert to give him his daughter, and he could not have her, both because of Robert and his son William who was then a knight. At length William went out to fight and was killed in the war. Hearing this, Warin came with a multitude of men and took Isabel away by force and without the assent and will of Robert her father and of Isabel herself, and he held her for a long time.

Warin descended still further from honesty as he entered upon a life of robbery, and his triumphs would only come to an end with the accession of Henry II.[16]

However, the breakdown of royal judicial power under Stephen did not mark a complete rupture in legal

---

14. Stenton, *First Century*, no. 6; Hudson, *Land, Law, and Lordship*, pp. 145–6.
15. Hudson, *Land, Law, and Lordship*, p. 55.
16. D. M. Stenton, ed., *Rolls of the Justices in Eyre, 1221–2* (Selden Soc., 59, 1940), pp. 167–9; see below, p. 139, for Warin's fate under Henry II; note also *Lawsuits*, no. 290.

development. Loss of control over hundred and shire courts did not last sufficiently long to prevent Stephen's successor re-employing them as key royal courts. Court procedures also survived, even if they were not under royal regulation. Groups of men on oath continued to settle cases at the request of the parties, and we also see Geoffrey de Mandeville as earl of Essex ordering a recognition to settle a land case, just as a king might have done.[17] The very fact that lords who usurped royal rights sought to imitate royal actions helped to preserve judicial procedures.[18]

Crucially, moreover, there is little suggestion of fundamental changes in substantive legal thinking, notably with regard to land-holding. Thus the principle of customary heritability of land was strong before Stephen's accession, and the pursuit of different claims based on this principle underlay many of the disputes of his reign.[19] Law had survived whereby Henry II might restore order to his newly acquired realm.

The Angevins renewed the power of the monarchy, but on a changed basis. It developed through considerable experimentation but came to be characterized by a new degree of routine royal contact with individual subjects. The need to re-establish peace after Stephen's reign and to settle disputes arising from it provided a very important impetus for such administrative action.[20] Those tenants who had been shuffling off seignorial control but were now denied the possibility of violent self-help might look to the king in pursuing their claims. And memories of the events of Stephen's reign provided a vivid image of bad lordship which might spur on the king and his servants in their assertion of royal power.

17. *Lawsuits*, nos 343, 309. For royal use of recognitions, see e.g. *Lawsuits*, no. 288, and also no. 298.
18. Note also e.g. the earls of Gloucester imposing a £10 forfeiture for disobedience of their orders; R. B. Patterson, ed., *Earldom of Gloucester Charters* (Oxford, 1973), nos 68, 89.
19. See e.g. Cronne, *Reign of Stephen*, pp. 157–62 on the Lacy inheritance; C. W. Hollister, 'The misfortunes of the Mandevilles', in his *Monarchy, Magnates and Institutions* (London, 1986), pp. 117–27; also Hudson, *Land, Law, and Lordship*, pp. 117–18.
20. See below, p. 127, 139.

. . .

THE EYRE

The new form of royal power was most obvious to the Angevins' subjects when the king's itinerant justices visited their locality. These visitations, known as eyres, were particularly frequent in the late twelfth century; sessions were held in Wiltshire in 1176, 1177, 1178, 1179, 1182, 1185, 1186, 1188, 1189, 1190, 1192, 1194, 1198 and 1202.[21] Loud criticism is testimony to the impact of the eyre. The itinerant justices, *justiciarii errantes*, supposedly wandered (*errauerunt*) from the path of equity. Roger of Howden reported of the 1198 eyre that 'by these and other vexations, whether just or unjust, the whole of England was reduced to poverty from sea to sea'.[22] Yet eyres were not all bad; their enforcement of royal financial rights may have induced much of the fear. Many disputants would have welcomed the advantages of royal justice being brought to them. Meanwhile, the assembly of large numbers ensured a lively social life and maybe a feast for the justices.[23]

The general eyre was responsible for all pleas. It heard cases between parties specifically summoned to appear before the eyre justices, and also those between litigants who had been suing at the central royal court. The justices brought with them a list of articles, of which the earliest surviving example comes from 1194.[24] Some articles concerned royal financial interests. Others dealt with recent political events, for example the troubles involving Prince John during Richard's absence on Crusade and in captivity. However, others were more directly legal.

---

21. C. A. F. Meekings, ed., *Crown Pleas of the Wiltshire Eyre, 1249* (Wiltshire Archaeological and Natural History Soc., Record Branch, 16, 1961), p. 4.
22. John of Salisbury, *Policraticus*, ed. C. J. Webb (2 vols, Oxford, 1909), i 345–6; Roger of Howden, *Chronica*, ed. W. Stubbs (4 vols, London, 1868–71), iv 62; also e.g. Pollock and Maitland, i 200–2.
23. Note also *Wiltshire*, p. 19 on proclamations to ensure supplies of reasonably priced victuals.
24. *EHD*, iii no. 15; on the Assize of Northampton's relations to the articles of the eyre, see below, p. 133; on changes in articles of eyre going into Henry III's reign, *Wiltshire*, pp. 27ff. On the procedure of eyres, see also *Surrey*, pp. 17ff.

[1] Of pleas of the crown new and old and all not yet concluded before the justices of the lord king.

[2] Also of all recognitions and pleas which have been summoned before the justices by writ of the king or of the chief justice, or which have been sent before them from the chief court of the king.

[7] Also of malefactors, and those who harbour them and those who abet them.

Further clauses concerned royal regulations such as the assizes of wine and measures, or mechanisms for the enforcement of justice in the localities.

Meanwhile, the sheriff and his bailiffs were busy preparing for the eyre's visit. They sought to ensure that when the eyre arrived numerous people involved in litigation were present, not just the parties themselves but also, for example, neighbours of people who had been killed.[25] Representatives of every hundred and village had to be summoned to answer the justices' enquiries. As the articles of 1194 specify

> In the first place, four knights are to be chosen from out of the whole county, who, upon their oaths, are to choose two lawful knights from each hundred or wapentake, and these two are to choose upon their oath ten knights from each hundred or wapentake, or free and lawful men if there are not enough knights, in order that these twelve together may answer to all the articles from every hundred or wapentake.

The formal empanelling of these men took place after the arrival of the justices, and after an opening ceremony. The representatives swore to answer the articles truthfully, with an oath such as the following:

> Hear this, ye justices, that I will speak the truth as to that on which you shall question me on the lord king's behalf, and I will faithfully do that which you shall command me on the lord king's behalf, and for nothing will I fail so to do to the utmost of my power, so help me God and these holy relics.[26]

25. *Surrey*, pp. 21–3.
26. *Bracton*, f. 116, Thorne, ii 329.

They were supplied with a copy of the articles, and were also instructed in private to arrest 'anyone in their hundred or wapentake [who] is suspected of some crime', or at least name them so that the sheriff could make arrests and bring the suspects before the justices. The representatives took the articles away, and then discussed their answers. They had to remember or uncover in any records all information relevant to the enquiries, for omissions laid them open to amercement. When ready, they presented their answers concerning royal rights and crown pleas, either out loud or in writing or perhaps both, and these were entered upon rolls.[27] The treatment and fate of those accused in these and other ways will be discussed in the next chapter.

The eyre thus was a major point of contact with royal government. It provided a review of local events. The activities of local officials were investigated. The Lincolnshire eyre roll of 1202 relates the fate of certain minor officials who had taken a stranger and placed him in the pillory because he could not find sureties.[28] He 'let his feet drop' and before help could arrive he died. The officials were asked by what warrant they placed him in the pillory and replied that it was by the command of certain men now dead. The reeves of Lincoln and the coroners denied any part in the matter, and the officials were taken into custody. In a similar way, the eyre watched over the actions of more senior officials, including the sheriff.[29] Any offences should result in amercement and the king's profit.

Although not all those gathered before the justices took an equally active part in events, royal business involved a large number of men. The gathering also provided a forum for the projection of royal authority. We have already heard the representatives' oath twice mention that the justices acted on the lord king's behalf. In addition, the proceedings opened with a reading of the writs which authorized and empowered the justices to proceed on eyre. One justice might then make a speech concerning the

---

27. *Bracton*, ff. 116, 143, Thorne, ii 329, 403–5; note also *Wiltshire*, pp. 92ff.
28. *Lincs.*, no. 1012.
29. *Lincs.*, p. xliii; however, see below, p. 182, for some limits to the eyre's supervision.

THE LOSS OF HOPE?

Sue Paterson

T HE OLD WOMAN LOOKED BLANKLY AT THE YOUNG GIRL BE-
hind the cash register as the words sunk in.

"Your card has been declined," the girl said in a loud whisper as she leaned over, pushing up smudged glasses that slid down her nose under curly red bangs. "Want me to try again?"

Maggie looked around, well aware that the people in line had heard the cashier. She felt her heart skip a beat and her face flush.

"No, dear, it's only $5.14. I should have that," she said. She took out her candy striped vinyl coin purse and carefully counted out the change. Three dollars in quarters and two one-dollar bills; short fourteen cents. She was suddenly aware that her hands were shaking as she scrambled in her black leather bag for the last fourteen cents. Tears threatened.

Isn't that the way of life? Always short fourteen cents. Almost to the finish line, then boom—out of nowhere something comes along and knocks you off your feet. If only Jimmy were still alive and here with

purpose of the eyre and the advantages of keeping the peace; the opportunities of sermonizing upon the majesty and the benefits of royal government are obvious. The eyre brought not just the practice but also the ideology of kingship to the localities.[30]

. . .

CHRONOLOGY

Such then is a picture of one manifestation of royal power and justice, based upon sources from late in our period and beyond. How did such power grow up? The first half of this book has argued for the existence by 1135 of a considerable degree of unity of custom within the realm and of royal involvement in important aspects of justice. Such were necessary preconditions for the reforms which occurred under Henry II and his sons. However, the Angevin period did produce a shift in the practices and the nature of royal administration. Reforms relating to law and justice consisted of a great variety of changes, some introduced by legislation, some by administrative innovation, others by decisions in the royal chancery or in the courts, others still by less conscious change. These reforms have often been discussed, but chronological accounts have generally concentrated on legislative innovations, producing a distorted picture. By drawing on the full range of sources, a sometimes inexact but nevertheless necessary sketch can be made.

(i) The early years

An initial problem is to set a starting point for the reforms. Often, relying on legislative texts, historians have looked to 1164 or 1166. Such a view receives some support from the Pipe Rolls, which for the first decade of Henry's reign display rather less judicial activity than in 1129–30, the date of Henry I's sole surviving Pipe Roll.[31] Yet there are

---

30. See *Bracton*, f. 115b, Thorne, ii 327. W. C. Bolland, *The General Eyre* (Cambridge, 1922), p. 36, estimates an attendance of 500 at a 1313 Canterbury session of the eyre.
31. Stenton, *English Justice*, pp. 62, 69, Amt, *Accession of Henry II*, pp. 179–81. For an important survey of, *inter alia*, matters covered in this chapter, see Biancalana, 'Legal reforms of Henry II', 433–536.

indications of significant developments before 1164, perhaps even before Henry's accession. In 1153 Henry and King Stephen, according to the chroniclers, promised to restore 'the disinherited', families who had held lands under Henry I but lost them under Stephen. This must have stimulated royal judicial activity; the royal declaration constituted a promise to help solve disputes. Further specific promises were made by the issue of royal confirmations, not just to great men but also to sub-tenants.[32] Cases arising from the Anarchy also encouraged the use of royal writs, and by 1158 appeared the phrase *breve de recto* ('writ concerning right/justice'). This need not refer to precisely the writ so named by *Glanvill,* but it already appears to be used as a classification.[33] Cases such as one involving two Lincolnshire peasants who obtained a royal writ (*breve recti*) show the wide availability of royal help.[34] Men were becoming re-accustomed to looking for royal justice, the king showing his willingness to intervene in disputes.

There are also signs of legislative activity. It is possible that by 1162 a *statutum* had been issued concerning the retrieval of lands lost under Stephen.[35] Other legislation concerned disseisin, with early mentions in cases involving advowsons. Then in 1162 Henry ordered the restoration of certain properties to St Benet's Holme, 'notwithstanding my assize'.[36] The meaning of these cases is unclear. Some legislation may have concerned only advowsons. Or the references only imply royal prohibition of disseisins whilst the king was abroad. Alternatively, part of the intention may have been more general: perhaps the king desired that

32. K. R. Potter, ed. and trans, *Gesta Stephani* (Oxford, 1976), p. 240, Robert of Torigny, in R. Howlett, ed., *Chronicles of the Reigns of Stephen, Henry II, and Richard I* (4 vols, London, 1884–9), iv 177; J. C. Holt, '1153: the Treaty of Winchester', in King, ed., *Anarchy,* pp. 291–316; Hyams, 'Warranty', 476–7. For an early edict concerning restoration of royal demesne, *Lawsuits,* no. 417.
33. *Royal Writs,* pp. 206–7.
34. F. M. Stenton, 'The Danes in England', *Proceedings of the British Academy* 13 (1927), 221–2.
35. See Hudson, *Land, Law, and Lordship,* pp. 256–7 for this and other early legislation.
36. D. W. Sutherland, *The Assize of Novel Disseisin* (Oxford, 1973), pp. 7–8.

the newly restored tenants in chief should not create problems by wholesale disseisin of existing sub-tenants.

Further legislation concerned distraint. In the early 1160s, the earl of Leicester promised that if he or his heirs failed to do or observe their homage to the bishop of Lincoln, the bishop would 'compel him by that land on the judgment of his court, according to the decree [*statutum*] of the realm'. Unfortunately, it cannot be told whether this *statutum* involved a new regulation that distraint by land required a court judgment, whether it reinforced a custom to that effect, or whether it was a more general prohibition of unreasonable distraints.[37] We know rather more about another decree of Henry II, concerning the transfer of cases from lords' courts to the king's, when the plaintiff accused his lord of default of justice. According to Guernes' *Life of St Thomas*, the enactment specified that:

> If anyone pleads about land in the court of his lord, he should come with his supporters on the first appointed day, and if there is any delay in the case, he should go to the justice and make his complaint. Then he shall return to the lord's court with two oath helpers, and swear three-handed that the court has delayed in doing him full justice. By that oath, whether false or true, he shall be able to go to the court of the next higher lord, until he comes to the court of the supreme lord [*seignur suverain* i.e. the king].[38]

This aroused the barons' suspicions: 'the king had made a constitution, which he thought would be very advantageous to himself.'

In addition to legislation and activities relating to land-holding, there were also significant measures relating to local administration. In the early 1160s notable changes in the personnel of sheriffs occurred, and resident local justices may have disappeared.[39] Thus the Constitutions of

---

37. *EHD*, ii no. 259.
38. A slightly modified version of M. Cheney's translation of Guernes de Pont-Sainte-Maxence, *La Vie de Saint Thomas Becket*, ed. E. Walberg (Paris, 1936), ll. 1401–10.
39. J. Boorman, 'The sheriffs of Henry II and the significance of 1170', in Garnett and Hudson, *Law and Government*, pp. 255–75; R. F. Hunnisett, 'The origins of the office of coroner', *TRHS* 5th ser. 8 (1958), 91.

Clarendon of 1164 cannot be taken as the starting point of reform, and the earlier dating reinforces the link between reform, the renewal of royal power, and the need to settle disputes and disorder arising from Stephen's reign.

(ii)   1164–89

The Constitutions of Clarendon, central to the dispute between Henry II and Thomas Becket, described themselves as 'a record and recognition of a certain part of the customs, liberties, and dignities of his ancestors, that is of King Henry his grandfather, and of other things which ought to be observed and maintained in the realm', Particularly significant because of the procedure adopted was a question of land-holding:

> If a dispute shall arise between a clerk and a layman, or between a layman and a clerk, in respect of any holding which the clerk desires to treat as alms, but the layman as lay fee, it shall be determined by a recognition of twelve lawful men under the direction of the king's chief justice, whether [*utrum*] the holding pertains to alms or to lay fee. And if it be recognised to pertain to alms, the plea shall be in the ecclesiastical court but if to lay fee, it shall be in the king's court, unless both of them shall vouch to hold [*advocaverint*] from the same bishop or baron. But if each of them vouches the same bishop or baron concerning this fief, the plea shall be in the court of the bishop or baron.[40]

This is the basis of the assize *utrum*, and the regular use of similar recognitions by twelve lawful men will be a central feature of the Angevin reforms.

In terms of its immediate effect on the conflict with the Church, however, an earlier clause was of much greater importance:

> Clerks cited and accused of any matter shall, when summoned by the king's justice, come before the king's court to answer there concerning that which shall seem to the king's court to be answerable there, and before the ecclesiastical court for

40. *EHD*, ii no. 126, c. 9. For precedents to *utrum*, *Royal Writs*, pp. 325–30.

what shall seem to be answerable there, in such a way that the king's justice shall send to the court of the holy Church to see how the case is there to be tried. And if the clerk shall be convicted or confess, the Church ought no longer to protect him.[41]

Moreover, Henry was concerned not only with clerical wrongdoing, and by late in 1165 or early in 1166 he was ordering local officials to implement a wide-ranging series of measures. The 1166 Assize of Clarendon, part of the process whereby Henry placed these measures in the hands of Geoffrey de Mandeville and Richard de Lucy as itinerant justices, states that:

[1] Inquiry shall be made throughout every county and every hundred, through twelve of the more lawful men of the hundred and through four of the more lawful men of each village upon oath, that they will speak the truth, whether there be in their hundred or village any man accused or notoriously suspect of being a robber or murderer or thief, or any who is a receiver of robbers or murderers or thieves, since the lord king has been king . . .

[2] And let anyone who shall be found on the oath of the aforesaid, accused or notoriously suspect of having been a robber or murderer or thief, or a receiver of them, since the lord king has been king, be taken and put to the ordeal of water, and let him swear that he has not been a robber or murderer or thief, or receiver of them, since the lord king has been king, to the value of five shillings so far as he know.

[5] And in the case of those who have been arrested through the aforesaid oath of this assize, let no man have court or justice or chattels save the lord king in his court in the presence of his justices; and the lord king shall have all their chattels.

Those failing the ordeal were to lose a foot. Even if they passed the ordeal, 'if they have been of ill repute and openly and disgracefully spoken of by the testimony of many and lawful men, they shall abjure the king's lands'. The king was seeking to rid the country of notorious

41. *EHD*, ii no. 126, c. 3.

wrongdoers. Further measures sought to ensure that the provisions be effective throughout the realm, and that standard peace-keeping measures, such as frankpledge, were properly enforced.[42]

Such measures emphasize Henry's desire to preserve his coronation promise to maintain the peace. A similar concern may also underlie another measure probably dating from the same period and perhaps the same council, which dealt with disseisins, and came to be called the assize of novel disseisin. Like the assize *utrum*, it used a recognition of twelve lawful men before the royal justices, and it provided a swift solution for accusations that another party had recently, unjustly, and without judgment, disseised a man of his land.

Although Henry was absent from England from March 1166 until 1170, and no legislation survives from this period, judicial and other administrative activity continued. There was an enquiry concerning knight service in 1166, an extensive forest eyre in 1167, and a very thorough visit of itinerant justices in 1168–70. The king's absence may have encouraged the regular employment of the exchequer court to decide cases even when the justiciar was not present.[43] The Pipe Rolls indicate men looking to royal help, for example in disputes concerning warranty of land. A highly significant change in the form of certain kinds of writs may also have occurred in the late 1160s. These started to be sealed 'closed', that is in such a way that the seal had to be broken in order to read the document. In addition, the writs were 'returnable' to specified courts, where the writs' details of the issue and form of the trial were to be read out.[44]

Measures taken upon Henry's return in 1170 display a similar emphasis upon royal control. Perhaps having learnt through the eyres many new details about local administration and its abuses, he ordered an enquiry, generally

---

42. Assize of Clarendon, *EHD*, no. 24, Assize of Northampton, c. 1, *EHD*, ii no. 25; Pollock and Maitland, i 151–3; on enforcement, see e.g. W. L. Warren, *The Governance of Norman and Angevin England, 1086–1272* (London, 1987), pp. 110–11.
43. Brand, *Making*, pp. 87–9.
44. See also below, p. 143; for further references, and the problem of dating, Hudson, *Land, Law, and Lordship*, p. 259.

known as the Inquest of Sheriffs, into royal and baronial administration. The direct result was the replacement of many sheriffs, and this may mark a significant point in the decline of any independent power that sheriffs had exercised. Moreover, one text of the Inquest articles contains a clause later referred to as an 'Assize of Essoiners', essoiners being those who brought excuses on behalf of those involved in law cases. This regulated essoiners' conduct in not only royal but also county and baronial courts. Whilst this may sound a minor procedural matter, the space devoted to essoins in both *Glanvill* and the early plea rolls indicates how important it was.[45]

Such active royal government may have contributed to baronial support for the revolt of Henry's son, the Young King, in 1173–74.[46] In turn, the restoration of control brought a new impetus to reform. A new eyre was the fullest yet conducted, and the itinerant justices received fresh instruction in 1176 with the Assize of Northampton.[47] These Assizes, the text uses the plural, were a revision of those made at Clarendon ten years before. Felons convicted by ordeal of water after communal accusation were now to lose not only a foot but also their right hand, and were to leave the kingdom within forty days. The rights of heirs were confirmed: 'if any freeholder has died, let his heirs remain in such seisin as their father had of his fief on the day of his death; and let them have his chattels from which they may execute the dead man's will. And afterwards let them seek out his lord and pay him a relief and the other things they ought to pay him from the fief.' A swift procedure, employing the recognition by twelve lawful men, was introduced for use by the heir whose lord refused his claim: the assize *mort d'ancestor*. Also at Northampton the justices were ordered to carry out inquisitions concerning novel disseisin, and to 'determine all suits

---

45. *EHD*, ii nos 48–9; *PKJ*, i 153–4. For words of caution, see Boorman, 'Sheriffs'. See also M. T. Clanchy, *From Memory to Written Record* (2nd edn, Oxford, 1993), pp. 64–5.
46. See Ralph of Diceto, *Opera Historica*, ed. W. Stubbs (2 vols, London, 1876), i 371.
47. *EHD*, ii no. 25; also below, chs 6 and 7; see below, p. 152, for *Dialogus*, p. 77; also Diceto, i 402 for enquiry concerning forest offences.

pertaining to the lord king and to his crown through the writ of the lord king, or of those who shall be acting for him, of half a knight's fee or under'. Further items for enquiry, like those concerning recent political events and 'escheats, churches, lands and women who are in the gift of the king', indicate that the Assizes of Northampton were the precursor of the articles of the eyre described early in this chapter. It may also be at this time that the justices began to keep extensive records, perhaps even plea rolls, although these do not survive until Richard I's reign.[48]

Other legislation comes from the latter years of Henry II, notably the Assize of the Forest of 1184.[49] Meanwhile, certainly on the Continent and perhaps in England, regulations were laid down concerning cases of debt. Also, from 1176 Henry's Pipe Rolls begin to mention amercements for sales of wine against the king's assize, the first of various measures regulating commercial affairs. In 1181 came another type of regulation with the Assize of Arms, laying down the arms freemen of different status were to possess, and prohibiting transfer or trading of arms. Since the arms to be possessed rested partly upon wealth qualifications, this involved enquiry into and the recording of the worth of the chattels and rents held by freemen. Henry's government was starting to reach the parts that other governments had not reached.[50]

Experiments with judicial organization continued. According to Roger of Howden, in 1178 Henry learnt that his use of 'a great multitude of judges', eighteen in number, had been burdensome to the realm. He replaced them with five members of his private household, two clerks and three lay, to hear all the complaints of the realm. However, this was not a lasting arrangement, and Ralph Diceto gives his impression of constant rearrangement:

48. Brand, *Making*, pp. 95–6; on fine rolls, see H. G. Richardson, ed., *Memoranda Roll 1 John* (PRS, ns 21, 1943), p. xxxii.
49. *EHD*, ii no. 28; see also D. J. Corner, 'The texts of Henry II's assizes', in A. Harding, ed., *Law-Making and Law-Makers in British History* (London, 1980), pp. 9–13.
50. *Surrey*, pp. 100–1, Bolland, *Eyre*, pp. 40–1 on eyre enforcement of regulatory assizes; Assize of Arms, *EHD*, ii no. 27. Note also the procedure for the 1188 Saladin tithe, *EHD*, ii no. 29.

the king made use now of abbots, now of earls, now of tenants in chief, now of members of his household, now of those closest to him to hear and judge cases. At length, after the king had appointed to office so many of his vassals of such diverse callings, who proved harmful to the public good, and yet he had not quashed the sentence of any official; when he could find no other aid beneficial to the interests of his private affairs, and while he was yet reflecting on the things of this world, he raised his eyes to heaven and borrowed help from the spiritual order. ... The king appointed the bishops of Winchester, Ely and Norwich chief justiciars of the realm.

Whilst Ralph suggests that Henry was hopeful of their godliness, the king no doubt remembered that the three bishops, Richard of Ilchester, John of Oxford, and Geoffrey Ridel had been his loyal supporters against Becket, his opponents then describing Ridel as an 'archdevil'.[51]

New procedures were also introduced. Probably at the Council of Windsor in 1179, the grand assize was established. This permitted cases concerning the right to land to be settled not by battle, but, in the presence of the king's justices, by twelve lawful knights of the area swearing as to which of the parties had the greater right in the land in question. *Glanvill* describes this as 'a royal benefit granted to the people by the goodness of the king on the advice of his magnates', and there are other signs that royal justice was proving popular, as in the rapid increase in the purchase of licences to agree recorded in the Pipe Rolls of the 1180s.[52]

(iii) Richard and John

Reforms continued under Richard I and John. Some were introduced by royal decree, although legislative measures

---

51. Benedict of Peterborough, *Gesta Regis Henrici Secundi*, ed. W. Stubbs (2 vols, London, 1867), i 207, Diceto, i 434–5.
52. Grand assize: *Glanvill*, ii 6–7, Hall, pp. 26–9. Final concords: Stenton, *English Justice*, p. 51. See also *Royal Writs*, pp. 330–5 on darrein presentment; Hyams, 'Warranty', 488 for reference to 'De Homagio Capiendo' in 1179; P. R. Hyams, *King, Lords, and Peasants in Medieval England* (Oxford, 1980), p. 223 on the action of naifty; Hudson, *Land, Law, and Lordship*, pp. 40–1 for jurisdiction concerning replevin passing from eyre justices to sheriffs; Brand, *Legal Profession*, p. 44 on attorneys.

were less significant than under Henry II. In part this was because of Richard's absences from the realm, although Howden did mention that whilst at Messina the king renounced his right of wreck.[53] Early in John's reign a decree was issued concerning baronial seneschals failing to answer properly on behalf of their lords at the exchequer.[54] Following the loss of the king's northern French lands, the threat of invasion from France became considerable, and a series of defence measures were issued, including a revised Assize of Arms.[55] New regulatory provisions were also introduced. In 1194 the king decreed that tournaments be allowed in England, and a system of licensing was introduced.[56] Then, in late 1196, came the Assize of Measures, another significant extension of government into commercial life: 'it is laid down that all measures throughout all England be of the same quantity.' A mechanism for local enforcement was specified, and thorough enforcement was obviously intended. The 1197 Pipe Roll records in its London and Middlesex account a payment of £11 16s 6d for 'a purchase to make measures and iron rods and beams and weights to send to all the counties of England'. The articles of the eyre of 1198 reveal the justices enquiring into the enforcement of the new legislation. It is notable, however, that enforcement was relaxed at least with regard to cloth; the emphasis was laid upon royal profit through licensing freedom from Richard's assize, not upon the regulation of commerce.[57] A decree issued at the start of his reign by King John concerning the sale of wine also

---

53 Howden, iii 68. For legislation concerning the crusading fleet and crusaders, Howden, iii 36, 45, 58–60. Note also *TAC*, lxxii, Tardif, pp. 68–9.

54. Howden, iv 152. The start of John's reign also saw a new scale of charges for royal documents.

55. *Rotuli Litterarum Patentium*, i 55; Gervase of Canterbury, *Historical Works*, ed. W. Stubbs (2 vols, London, 1879–80), ii 96–7, which is concerned also with internal disturbers of the peace; *Calendar of the Close Rolls, 1227–31*, pp. 395, 398.

56. Howden, iii 268; Diceto, ii pp. lxxx–i, 120; William of Newburgh, in *Chronicles Stephen, Henry II, Richard*, ii 422–3.

57. Howden, iv 33–4, 62, 172, *PR9RI*, pp. xxi–xxii, 160; *PR4J*, p. xx. See also William of Malmesbury, *Gesta Regum*, ed. W. Stubbs (2 vols, London, 1887–89), ii 487, for Henry I standardizing the length of the yard at the length of his own arm.

dissociation. I play these visions in my head, over and over again, and try to reach some sort of conclusion. It is true that my mom and dad were always pretty bad parents, who screamed at and threatened me, and who responded to my various mental illnesses with denial and disgust. It is true that I clung to them simply because I did not trust anyone else. It is also true that my parents took me out for ice cream, bought me absurd quantities of video games, and made me feel secure. But all of that is gone, now, because I don't have a home anymore. As I write this on the night before Christmas Eve, the illusion of a happy family, so convincing for so long, lies in tatters. Since that declaration of support a little over a year ago, my parents have insulted me and mocked me and threatened me with misgendering, and I have cried and trembled and screamed and fled and tried to kill myself many times.

I always knew it would come to this, though that does not make it easier. Or maybe I didn't really know, only suspected it. I had been mistreated my whole life, and thought the worst of everyone for it. Maybe there is no knowledge, in the end, no memory, and no continuity of reality. Sometimes, I start to think that maybe there is nothing except my mind. But even in my mind, there is this: I was happy, to a point. I had a family who made me happy, sometimes. And that's all gone now.

I like to think that I am past the point where all of this is still raw, but the truth is, I am still in it. I still live in my childhood home, because remarkably few people want to hire a trans woman. I have not told my parents that they are lost to me, even though they have been lost to me for some time now. I have felt my family slipping through my fingers all my life, and I have desperately tried to stop it. I now realize that this is simply how it has to be. There is still that final choice to be made, and I will make it. I will go down to the shore, and try not to look back too often, so as not to lose my nerve. And maybe some day I will come back and visit. For now, I cannot abide the air upon my skin.

proved unenforceable in its original form; the price of wine was reduced, 'and thus the land was filled with drink and drinkers'.[58]

Judicial activity continued. General eyres were less frequent than under Henry II but still quite regular, visiting in 1194/95, 1198/99, 1201/3 and 1208/9. Forest eyres toured in 1198, 1207, and 1212, and there were also commissions with more limited competence.[59] The supply of royal remedies was increased and refined. Some writs started to be issued *de cursu*, cheaply and readily available from the chancery. The forms of writs and procedures were modified and multiplied. Particularly important were to be writs of entry, which brought cases before the royal justices. These writs focused a recognition's attention on one alleged flaw in the tenant's title, for example, that he had inherited the land from his father who had disseised the tenant. Such was one form of the 'writ of entry *sur disseisin*', and in 1204 an apparently chance note in the royal records declared it henceforth a writ *de cursu*.[60] Existing remedies were improved or extended. Thus it was decided that damages should be awarded to every successful plaintiff at novel disseisin, and novel disseisin also began to be used for the retrieval of rents.[61]

Behind at least the last of these measures may lie Richard and John's great minister, Hubert Walter, justiciar 1193–98, chancellor 1199–1205. He certainly was an extremely influential figure, who, according to Gervase of Canterbury, 'knew all the laws [*iura*] of the kingdom'. His contributions were manifold, but those in the field of record-keeping are particularly notable, especially for the

---

58. Howden, iv 99–100. Note also the 1205 Assize of Money, *PR7J*, pp. xxvjff., *Rotuli Litterarum Patentium*, i 54. See below, p. 239, on the introduction of English law to Ireland.

59. See e.g. *Lincs.*, pp. xli–ii.

60. *Rotuli Litterarum Clausarum*, i 32. For caution on the impact of writs of entry in John's reign, Holt, *Magna Carta*, p. 139; note also *Lincs.*, pp. lxxi–ii, Milsom, *Legal Framework*, pp. 101–2.

61. Sutherland, *Novel Disseisin*, pp. 50–2. See also R. C. Palmer, *The County Courts of Medieval England* (Princeton, NJ, 1982), pp. 184–7 on the emergence of viscontiel *justicies* writ of debt; Holt, *Magna Carta*, p. 181 on the writ of attaint.

historian reliant on documents.[62] Thus, in the first three years of John's reign start our run of charter rolls, close rolls, and patent rolls.

Agreements had long been recorded in bipartite documents called cirographs. The agreement was written out twice, between the two texts was written the word CIROGRAPHUM, and then the parchment was cut through, dividing this word generally with a wavy line. One half went to each party. Should a dispute arise, the auth- enticity of each side's document could be tested by seeing if the two halves fitted together again. Then in 1195, an agreement between Hubert Walter's brother Theobald and William Hervey had the following note written upon its back:

> This is the first cirograph which was made in the court of the lord king in the form of three cirographs [under the instructions of] the lord of Canterbury [Hubert Walter] and the other barons of the lord king, so that by this form a record could be handed over to the treasurer to place in the treasury.

This third copy was referred to as the 'foot of the fine'. Here we see an emphasis upon the keeping of a regular series of royal records, and the increasing use of multiple copying. Both are essential characteristics of bureau-cratization.[63]

Hubert also had a notable effect on the judiciary and their activities. During this time, the Common Bench, the most important royal tribunal for civil cases for the remainder of the middle ages and beyond, emerged as a court independent of the exchequer, reflecting the increasing pressure of business and the growth of specialization.[64] Hubert as justiciar presided over these royal courts. His impact upon the composition of the eyre

---

62. Gervase, ii 406; C. R. Cheney, *Hubert Walter* (London, 1967), pp. 107–9. However, see above, n. 48, for evidence of records starting earlier than our surviving series. Hubert's role may have been one of significant regularization.
63. *Feet of Fines, Henry II and Richard* (PRS, 17, 1894), p. 21; see also Clanchy, *Memory*, pp. 68–9.
64. B. R. Kemp, 'Exchequer and Bench in the later twelfth century – separate or identical tribunals?', *EHR* 88 (1973), 571–2.

is apparent within a year of his becoming chief justiciar.[65] From 1194 and 1198 come our first surviving texts of articles of the eyre. Amongst their concerns was local administration, and in 1194 it was specified that 'in each shire are to be elected three knights and one cleric as keepers of the pleas of the crown'. This marks the appearance of coroners, whose inquests remain a part of legal procedure today. The early plea rolls reveal much of their activities, notably the holding of an inquest whenever a corpse was found. The inquest was recorded in the coroner's roll, for presentation at the time of the eyre.[66]

Further evidence of concern for order in the localities comes in 1195, when Hubert Walter sent a 'form of oath' throughout England. This re-affirmed traditional methods such as the hue and cry, and instructed that specially assigned knights make all those within their jurisdiction aged fifteen or older swear that they would keep the king's peace. The knights were also to receive criminals who were taken, and deliver them to the sheriff. As so often, we see the leading men of the localities becoming further involved in royal judicial activity. The decree clearly had a major impact on the populace, for Howden records that, forewarned and of bad conscience, many fled, leaving behind their houses and possessions. Further torment was added in 1198 with a general eyre and a forest eyre enforcing a renewed version of the Assize of the Forest.[67]

Such complaints arose from the regular imposition of justice. Under John, further grievances were added as, following the loss of the Continental possessions and particularly from 1209, justice was more concentrated on the king and the court which travelled with him, notably with its visits to the north of the country. Such developments seem to have been disruptive and unpopular, and will be considered in the final chapter in the context

65. C. R. Young, *Hubert Walter, Lord of Canterbury and Lord of England* (Durham, NC, 1968), p. 51.
66. See R. F. Hunnisett, *The Medieval Coroner* (Cambridge, 1961), esp. ch. 2; also below, p. 178.
67. Howden, iii 299–300, iv 61–6; Cheney, *Hubert Walter*, p. 93; *PR7RI*, p. xxvi, *PR9RI*, p. xvii, *PR10RI*, p. xxx. There were also enquiries into the conduct of royal officials; see Howden, iv 5 (1196) and the articles of the 1198 eyre.

of the background to Magna Carta. The impetus for reform had temporarily shifted from the king and his men to his opponents.[68]

. . .

THE STAGES AND NATURE OF REFORM

Having sketched a chronology, some suggestions can be made about the stages of reform. Henry II began his reign with two major problems. He had to govern his far-flung dominions. And more specifically in England he had to restore peace and royal authority. The doing of justice had, therefore, to be central to Henry's activities. To a large extent, in the early years of the reign Henry and his advisers sought only to restore the traditional devices of local authority, to make the old system work according to its own terms. Respect, or at least lip-service, was paid to the limits of royal jurisdiction: complaints of default of justice were to go initially to overlords' courts, the Constitutions of Clarendon allowed certain *utrum* cases to baronial courts.[69] Further action relied on complaints being brought to the king. This was most clearly true of land cases, but is also evident with theft or violence. We earlier left Warin of Walcote enjoying his life with Isabel of Shuckburgh, whom he had abducted, and entering upon a life of robbery. Under Henry II, he found that 'he fell into poverty because he could not rob as he used to do, but he could not refrain from robbery and he went everywhere and robbed as he used. And King Henry, having heard complaints about him, ordered that he should be taken.' Eventually he was captured, brought before the king, and Henry 'that he might set an example to others to keep his peace, by the counsel of his barons, ordered Warin to be put in the pillory, and there he was put and there he died'.[70] Here royal justice was hardly being taken to the localities as it would be from the mid-1160s. Yet the king was far from passive, and in his declarations of peace and his promises

---

68. Stenton, *English Justice*, ch. 4; see below, p. 222. R. V. Turner, *The English Judiciary in the Age of Glanvill and Bracton, c. 1176–1239* (Cambridge, 1985), pp. 133–4; *PR12J*, pp. xiv–xxiij.
69. See above, p. 129.
70. Stenton, *Rolls of the Justices in Eyre*, pp. 167–9, and see above, p. 121.

to restore the disinherited, he was inviting claimants to come to him. This initial shifting of the focus of cases back to the king and his court was vital to later developments.

The period from *c.* 1164–84 saw more obviously dramatic change. New procedures were announced at major councils, such as those at Clarendon, Northampton, and Windsor. Importantly, there came into routine use the few, easily reproducible, administrative reforms which were to dominate key aspects of legal procedure. Writs originating hearings and recognitions to settle those disputes were obtained by one party looking to the king, but at the same time royal justice began to be taken to the localities on a much more regular basis through eyres. These were primarily concerned with royal rights and the maintenance of the peace, but they also made much more readily available the new actions affecting land. This fresh assertiveness is reflected in the phraseology of reforms such as the Assize of Clarendon which emphasize that existing interests are not to block royal administration of justice.[71]

Thereafter reform was more gradual, in part because the necessary machinery had been brought into existence. New procedures were introduced, but these tended to be modified versions of existing ones. Sub-sets of writs appeared, such as the writs of entry. Standardization continued, and in this respect a most notable development is that of regulation, such as that affecting wine and measures. Again the standardizing impulse of royal government was taken to the localities through legislation and through the enforcing agency of the eyre.

The nature of the reforms can be linked to the above stages. Whilst new writs could be created, major measures were not invented from scratch. The reformers drew on a variety of sources for their thinking and practices.[72] Experiments were made with existing materials; some failed, others succeeded and ended in many cases by transforming the original form. Many of the measures which characterize the Angevin reforms, such as the use of sworn bodies of men either to present criminals or to give

71. See below, pp. 157, 180.
72. E.g. for ecclesiastical influence see below, p. 150, and also Pollock and Maitland, i 151–3 on presenting juries.

verdicts on specific questions of land-holding, had previously been used on an *ad hoc* basis, sometimes involving royal justices, sometimes at the choice of the disputants, sometimes through a decision of a local community.[73] The reforms took such measures, regularized them, and enforced them from above. The result was a few easily reproducible, easily adaptable forms which were central to common law procedure. The eyre, the returnable writ, and the jury and recognition, would remain at the heart of law and of the royal administration of justice.[74] Crucially, they allowed both active assertion of royal rule and responsive capacity to satisfy requests for justice. The king's government came to his subjects, the king's subjects came to his government.

Such a conclusion warns against categorizing the reforms simply as centralization. Certainly, far more than ever before, royal courts, particularly the eyre, became courts of first resort for the whole realm. Certainly, Henry's attacks upon crime must have curtailed at least the customary exercise of baronial franchises, franchises which had expanded under Stephen. Yet the local contribution continued to be vital to royal government. Central to the reforms was the jury or recognition, 'a body of neighbours . . . summoned by some public officer to give upon oath a true answer to some question'.[75] Judicial activity and law continued to be characterized by a considerable degree of local self-government, but in important aspects it was self-government at the king's command.

The Angevin reforms have sometimes been lauded as a triumph of rational justice over older irrational methods, encapsulated in the replacement of ordeal by jury trial. Certainly, the reformers regarded reason as laudable.[76] Yet as we have seen, the existing methods of trial only

---

73. For recognitions in Normandy before 1154, see e.g. C. H. Haskins, *Norman Institutions* (Cambridge, MA, 1918), ch. 6. On not the creation but the preservation of the various forms of 'jury' as a characteristic of English law, see S. M. G. Reynolds, *Kingdoms and Communities in Western Europe, 900–1300* (Oxford, 1984), pp. 33–4.
74. Note though the limits to regularity, e.g. *Wiltshire*, p. 10, on eyre arrangements.
75. Pollock and Maitland, i 138.
76. See e.g. *Glanvill*, Prologue, Hall, p. 2.

occasionally resorted to the supernatural, and it is hard to see the reformers as pursuing rationality throughout all their activities.[77] Indeed, their dominant figure in the later years of Henry II's reign was a man, Ranulf de Glanville, who may well have believed that his rise to prominence was sealed by the miraculous intervention of Thomas Becket in allowing him to capture the king of Scots in 1174. Not surprisingly, therefore, the reformers did not reject the supernatural. At least for those they saw as undesirable members of the lower orders they extended use of trial by ordeal. Even with the grand assize, primarily intended for more respectable people, justification was not based on rationalist principles. Their preference for new methods in land cases may have had more to do with the capacity of royal justices to control proceedings and perhaps outcomes. It certainly had to do with speed, and the text of *Glanvill* reveals noteworthy debate over procedure regarding the non-appearance of parties in court. Efficiency, not rationality, was the reformers' conscious aim.[78]

Rather than seeing the Angevin reforms as based upon principles of centralization or rationality, therefore, it is better to describe them in terms of routinization, bureaucratization, and regulation.[79] Nowhere is this more obvious than in the royal plea rolls. One might expect these to be filled by decisions of cases. In fact they reveal that a great mass of the work of the king's court was procedural: hearing essoins, checking those essoins, arranging for attorneys, granting licences to come to an agreement. This is a neglected historical development of the utmost importance: the birth of red tape. Men's actions were increasingly being brought under administrative scrutiny. Actions which might perhaps have been satisfactorily left to individuals, such as out-of-court compromise, were being directed through the 'proper channels' by royal servants. Everything must be made official.

77. See above, p. 72.
78. *Glanvill*, i 32, vi 10, xi 3, Hall, pp. 20–1, 63–4, 134; these constitute three of the total of six debated points where names were attributed to opinions – see below, p. 154.
79. On bureaucratization, see Clanchy, *Memory*, pp. 62ff., and below, p. 192, on the writ rule.

Closely connected with these developments is the increased use of writing, in administration and in courts.[80] Bureaucracy is based on the bureau, the writing desk. On such desks were written the ever-expanding financial and judicial records of Angevin administration. Significantly, in terms of bureaucratization, increasing numbers of these records were produced in multiple copies.[81] Also coming from the writing desks of Angevin chanceries were increasingly standardized writs. The writer of *Glanvill* may have had some sort of register of writs,[82] and certainly his own work reveals the development of a core of writs to be reproduced in set forms for set situations. Thereafter further writs, notably those of entry, were created to fill holes left by those currently available. Most of the writs created in the Angevin period were sealed closed and therefore could be used just once. This expendibility contrasts with older, reusable writs which were sealed open, and it suggests a more routine use of writing. Moreover, these new writs were returnable; they were sent to the sheriff who set proceedings in motion, for example organizing a recognition. He then wrote the names of the recognitors upon the writ, and was obliged to produce it before the royal justices on the day of judgment. Anglo-Norman writs had been growing more specific in detailing that their orders be carried out justly or by some particular method, and they may have been accompanied by oral messages with further details. However, they lacked the standardization and precision which the Angevin returnable writ gave to royal control over judicial proceedings.[83]

The details required by the returnable writ also fit another feature of Angevin administration, the gathering of information. This was manifested on a national scale not only by the general eyre but also by the 1166 enquiry into

---

80. Note an isolated plea roll instance from Richard I's reign, *CRR*, vii 346, of a case disrupted because the writ was taken to a man who later protested that he had had no cleric with him to read the writ, and when he had sent for a cleric, the other parties left.
81. See above, p. 137, below, pp. 148, 185.
82. See esp. *Glanvill*, xii 10–22, Hall, pp. 141–7; contrast the earlier part of the Norman *Très Ancien Coutumier*.
83. See also above, p. 114; note *Royal Writs*, index *sub* 'writs, judicialisation'.

knight service, the 1185 enquiry into the king's feudal rights, and most ambitiously the 1170 Inquest of Sheriffs. Information gathered in these ways and illustrating, for example, the problems of seignorial justice, must have influenced later royal administrative activities.

Overall, therefore, the Angevin reforms constituted a considerable extension of royal control of justice, and a change in the nature of that control. They were not, however, intended as a head-on attack upon baronial power and justice, or other local jurisdictions. Rather, the localities participated in the application of the reforms and, crucially, provided much of the demand which stimulated them. Given, then, that consumer demand was one of the forces behind legal and judicial change, let us look more closely at the other causes which set reform in motion.

· · ·

HENRY II AND REFORM

Many have referred to the changes of the period 1154–89 as 'Henry II's legal reforms', but how far was the king personally responsible for them? Explanations based on Henry's own genius, his lawyerly characteristics, are enticing in their simplicity but encounter serious difficulties. Kings certainly were interested in judging cases, and in the considerable profits raised by legal and judicial business, but there is far less evidence that they were concerned in any but the broadest sense with the details of judicial administration, let alone the content of substantive law. Moreover, whatever intentions Henry did have in these respects surely had only a limited effect upon the end results of the changes. Yet royal intentions must not be ignored, for Henry and his sons did have motive conducive to the reform of justice and law.

It is surely best to begin by taking Henry at his word: he wished to return the realm to its state in his grandfather's time. He saw Henry I's reign as a time of peace, justice, and law, in contrast to the time of war under Stephen. Moreover, he associated such peace with the strength of royal power, the activities of his grandfather as the Lion of Justice. Retrospect may have exaggerated the degree to which earlier kings had controlled justice, but it is Henry's perception of the past which is the essential point here.

Such ideas reinforced his coronation oath, with its promises to protect the Church and his subjects, to forbid all kinds of rapine and unlawfulness, do justice, and, in an apparently new clause, to protect the rights of the Crown. To achieve these ends he had to ensure that disputants did not seek violent solutions to their difficulties, for example simply seizing back lands which they believed to be their own or turning to force when they believed themselves to have been denied justice. Such would have been a recipe for a multitude of private wars. Desire to prevent disorder helps to explain the concern with disseisins and the provision of remedies for default of justice. The king had to ensure the availability of peaceful solutions, be it through the proper functioning of seignorial and local justice, or through royal remedies.

Was there a deliberate attempt to extend royal power? The answer must be yes, at the very least in so far as royal power had declined under Stephen. In comparison with the situation under Henry I, or with Henry II's perception of that situation, an answer is more difficult. Certainly, in the early stages of reform Henry made specific promises to allow cases to go to lords' courts, the Assize of Clarendon allowed the chattels of those convicted other than by presentment to go to the traditional beneficiaries, and even *Glanvill* does not show royal justices as entirely hostile to baronial jurisdiction.[84] Moreover, many of the new writs, one of the best indications of the thinking of reform, reveal that they were only to apply in cases where lords had first failed to do justice. It has been suggested that this represented a working compromise between king and lords. However, this may be to underestimate the assertiveness of the king and his counsellors. In the early 1160s the barons feared that the king had instituted the decree concerning default of justice because he thought it 'would be very advantageous to himself'. After such a dispute all must have been aware that the king could use the notion of default of justice to justify the extension of his own jurisdiction.[85]

84. See above, p. 129, for the assize *utrum*; *EHD*, ii no. 24, c. 5; *Glanvill*, viii 11, Hall, pp. 102–3.
85. See above, p. 128; cf. Biancalana, 'Legal reforms of Henry II'.

That summer, after I quit my job and had more time for obsessive late-night research, I finally accepted that I was a woman. I felt a kind of ecstasy that I hesitate to describe, because description might sully it, and bring it down to Earth. I told my parents, and they seemed hesitant at first, but basically accepting. My dad told me he had always wanted a daughter. I was tremendously relieved, and berated myself for having been so nervous. Everything was going to be fine. But a few months later, when I decided to start hormone replacement therapy, my parents informed me that they would not allow me to use their insurance. I was going terribly fast, they said; could I really be sure this was what I wanted?

I spent long nights thinking very carefully about all the evidence I might muster to prove that I was really trans, and how badly I needed this. When the time came to talk to my parents again, I followed my dad around the house, unloading all that I knew. At one point, he came close to tears, and I thought he had listened to reason. After the conversation, however, I asked my parents again if I could use their insurance—the answer was still no.

I thought long and hard on the knives in the kitchen, the good sharp ones, but in the end, after sulking in the bathroom for a while, I went back downstairs and told my parents that I would finance the hormones myself, if need be. They threatened to forbid me from using their car, so I couldn't get to my job. I told them I would walk if I had to. At that point, they switched back to trying to talk me out of it, but I was not to be persuaded. Eventually, they went to sleep and we didn't talk about it the next day. The following day, they told me they had changed their minds, and would support me fully. I was relieved.

That spring, my family went on vacation to Sanibel, an island off the coast of Florida. We had been there often in the past, and always stayed in the same hotel. I remember telling my girlfriend that everywhere I went, I felt the ghosts of the happy family that had been there before. But, of course, I felt that everywhere. And we had never really been a happy family. I doubt that my mother was ever truly happy. I certainly was not. The nostalgic visions of my beatific childhood are no true ghosts, because they were never alive, and so could not have died.

But it is not enough to say this, because in the end, you need ghosts. You need a past, a substance to fill the void of twenty-odd years of

So the king was assertive, without having either an overall plan for legal and judicial reform, or any precise perception as to where his general intentions and his piecemeal actions might lead. The provision of royal justice took off in a way which no one at first could have expected. Reforms intended initially to be of limited scope, perhaps associated with particular political circumstance, became general and lasting remedies.[86] This snow-balling of reform occurred in part because of consumer demand, particularly in the area of land-holding, in part because of the nature of administration and administrators under the Angevin kings. I shall concentrate on legal and judicial aspects of administration, but the practices, ideas, and ideals of the king's men were driven by many forces, not least royal financial needs arising from war.[87]

. . .

THE ADMINISTRATOR'S MENTALITY

(i) Richard of Ilchester

Rather than simply listing royal servants and their activities, let us begin by looking in detail at one official. Richard of Ilchester was born in the diocese of Bath, quite possibly in Sock Dennis, Somerset, close to Ilchester.[88] His background may well be a minor knightly family, with connections to the bishop of Bath and to royal administration. In addition, he was a kinsman of Gilbert Foliot, the learned abbot of Gloucester, bishop of Hereford and of London. During Stephen's reign, Richard probably advanced through the household of the earls of Gloucester. This led him into the administration of Henry II, and already in the second year of Henry's reign he was referred to as the king's scribe. He is prominent in the lists of those who witnessed the king's

---

86. See above, p. 127, on decrees concerning disseisin possibly associated with royal absences; also M. Cheney, 'The litigation between John Marshal and Thomas Becket in 1164: a pointer to the origin of novel disseisin?', in J. A. Guy and H. G. Beale, eds, *Law and Social Change in British History* (London, 1984), pp. 9–26.
87. See Holt, *Magna Carta*, ch. 2.
88. On Richard, see K. Norgate in *Dictionary of National Biography*; C. Duggan, 'Richard of Ilchester, royal servant and bishop', *TRHS* 5th Ser. 16 (1966), 1–21.

charters. In 1162–63 he became archdeacon of Poitiers, later being appointed treasurer of the same church. Although from the point of view of the church of Poitiers he was notable by his absence, Richard was clearly active in the king's service on the Continent. In England he was generally with the king at the key royal centres of Westminster, Winchester and Woodstock. He undertook a wide range of duties, for example being 'keeper' of the vacant bishopric of Lincoln from 1166–67. Not surprisingly for a well-rewarded royal servant and a kinsman of Gilbert Foliot, he was prominent on the king's side in the Becket dispute, even though he had probably served as a clerk in the chancery under Thomas. Although he seems not to have incurred the personal animosity of the Becket party, Richard was twice excommunicated for his various services to the king during the dispute.

In the early 1160s Richard was increasingly influential in judicial affairs, and following the Assize of Clarendon, according to one account, 'by the king's order he exercised the greatest power throughout England'.[89] He served as an itinerant justice in several shires in the south, the west, and the midlands. Amongst the records of his activities are some brief mentions of rolls belonging to him, perhaps an early form of eyre roll, perhaps simply records of amercements. His appointment as bishop of Winchester in 1173 may well have curtailed his royal judicial activities, although Ralph of Diceto recorded him as one of three bishops amongst the five justices the king appointed in 1179.[90]

Typically of Henry II's great administrators, Richard was also prominent in financial affairs. He may have taken a leading role in the restoration or reform of the Norman exchequer in 1176. Meanwhile in England, the *Dialogue of the Exchequer* stated that Richard 'is a great man and should not be busied except in important affairs', and provided a curious insight into the 'important affairs' of Angevin administration by stating that one of Richard's duties was to stop the treasurer from falling asleep; the somnolent treasurer was, of course, the author of the *Dialogue*, Richard

89. *Lawsuits*, no. 446; see also e.g. no. 417.
90. See above, p. 134.

fitzNigel. Richard of Ilchester's other main concern at the exchequer was record-keeping. He had a true bureaucrat's love of ever-mounting piles of parchment, and fitzNigel described how Ilchester introduced a system whereby a copy was kept of every summons sent to sheriffs concerning their debts: 'but as time went on, and the number of debtors enormously increased so that a whole skin of parchment was scarcely enough for a single summons, the number of names and the labour involved became over-powering, and the barons were satisfied, as of old, with the original summons'.[91]

Richard's election to the see of Winchester was one of six to vacant bishoprics in 1173, elections which revealed Henry's intention of obtaining loyal bishops following the Becket dispute. Richard contributed to the adjustments and reconciliation between king and Church which followed the Compromise of Avranches. He also became involved in matters of canonical interest, although there is no indication that he had any academic training in canon law. He acted as a papal judge delegate, and papal instructions to him entered into canonical collections.

From the mid-1170s, Richard was very prominent amongst the counsellors of Henry II. In mid-1174, the justiciars were desperate to obtain Henry's personal help in putting down the rebellion in England, whereas he had so far concentrated his energy on his Continental problems. Hence they unanimously agreed to send their message by Richard, 'knowing that he would speak to the king much more familiarly, warmly and urgently than anyone else'. Well before his death in 1188, therefore, Richard was at the very heart of the group of men who produced and administered the Angevin reforms. He was one of those who could influence entry into the group, ensuring its continuing close-knit quality. In *c.* 1181 he appeared with Richard fitzNigel and Ranulf de Glanville in the charter witness list which contains the first known reference to Hubert Walter. Richard's illegitimate son Herbert le Poer enjoyed a successful career in the Church, becoming a canon of Lincoln in 1167–68, archdeacon of Canterbury in

91. *Dialogus*, pp. 27, 74.

1175, and bishop of Salisbury in 1194. But he, like his father, also had a royal administrative career, probably working at the exchequer under Henry II, and acting as a royal justice under Richard I. Like the Angevin reforms, the Angevin reformers were reproducible.

(ii) Henry's servants

We can get some indication of the numbers of this crucial central group of Henry's servants. Whilst at least seventy men sat as justices in the exchequer between Michaelmas 1165 and Henry II's death, an inner core of fifteen provide about two-thirds of the recorded appearances of named justices. These included the justiciars, Robert earl of Leicester, Richard de Lucy and Ranulf de Glanville, and other key royal servants such as fitzNigel, Ilchester, and Hubert Walter. Similarly, whilst we know of eighty-four men who served Henry as itinerant justices, only eighteen travelled on three or more eyres. Seven of these were also amongst the inner core of fifteen in the exchequer court.[92]

Some members of the inner group of Henry's administrators had grown up together, many had close personal connections, notably to the chief justiciar.[93] To such connections they might owe their entry to the group, and thus bound together, they were separated to only a limited degree by any specializations within administration. Ranulf de Glanville was a sheriff, a military leader, and a justiciar. They saw themselves above all as the king's servants, and they brought similar methods to various areas of administration, most notably finance and justice, for both of which the exchequer provided a focus. Increasingly, their social origins were below the top ranks of society, notably in knightly families.[94] Yet such close ties and such origins did not mean that the circle lacked

92. Brand, *Making*, pp. 91–3.
93. See e.g. Cheney, *Hubert Walter*, pp. 19ff. for Hubert and Glanville; Richard de Lucy may have been another central individual, and he, like Richard of Ilchester, had a son who was prominent amongst royal administrators. Many had East Anglian connections, see e.g. Turner, *Judiciary*, p. 105; note also p. 143 on leading figures emerging from lesser administrative families.
94. Turner, *Judiciary*, p. 63.

broader perspectives, geographic and intellectual. These men combined learning and practical experience, and united the two in their work and their discussions. They produced ever-increasing written records and the first administrative manuals.

The formation, intellectual and communal, of the circle may have been associated with the Becket dispute. Henry now had with him men who could respond to the intellectual challenge posed by the archbishop and his supporters. About half of the leading judicial figures were clerics, and they expressed their own justifications for serving the king.[95] Some, like their erstwhile opponents in Becket's camp, were educated in the learned laws, Roman and canon. Although only three of Henry's justices, Jocelin of Chichester, Geoffrey Ridel, and Godfrey de Lucy, bore the title 'master' which links them to lengthy study at the schools, others may have studied the learned laws more rudimentarily, whilst judicial activities brought still more, like Richard of Ilchester, into contact with such law. The influence of the learned laws upon reform was not through academic study and then through careful application of learned remedies. Rather, elements of legal learning helped to stimulate and shape thinking and writing about law and the administration of justice. For example, in *Glanvill*, it is not the majority of the procedure and substantive law covered but the structure of arguments, and some of the vocabulary and rhetoric, which shows the influence of Roman law.[96] Likewise, whilst people could already separate notions of being seised of land and having a right to it, from *c.* 1140 such notions were refined by churchmen bringing into more frequent use the learned law distinction between 'possession' and 'property'. Such ideas penetrated the circles which constructed the new measures concerning land-holding, and helped to produce a clearer conceptual distinction between seisin and right.[97]

95. See e.g. *Dialogus*, p. 1; however, Howden criticized Henry II in the context of the Becket dispute; i 241.
96. *Glanvill*, pp. xxxvi–xl.
97. See above, p. 88, below, pp. 186, 198; M. Cheney, '*Possessio/proprietas* in ecclesiastical courts in mid-twelfth-century England', in Garnett and Hudson, *Law and Government*, pp. 245–54; *Lawsuits*, no. 641; Hudson, *Land, Law, and Lordship*, pp. 267–8.

Within the circle of royal servants, discussion and debate concerning matters of law, justice, and administration furthered regularization and standardization. They may lie behind the development of certain principles which characterize the reforms, for example the desire to create swifter actions which avoided the continual use of essoins, and also perhaps a desire for alternatives to trial by battle. More generally, debate and experience may have produced an increasingly aggressive attitude to powers and privileges which interfered in regular royal administration. Angevin royal servants seem to have had an unprecedented desire for uniformity in the administration of the country. The king was responsible for all his people – or at least all his free men – under whomsoever's lordship they lived. According to Richard fitzNigel, 'God has committed [to the king] the care of all his subjects alike'.[98] Eyres for the first time covered the whole country. Royal courts sat for prolonged sessions, whereas the older courts had in general met only for one day. This further increased the likelihood that regular participants in the royal courts would develop a more specialized expertise and greater routine in their activities.[99] Moreover, the role of the royal justices themselves within court was probably changing. Whereas cases traditionally had been decided by the suitors of a court, with the justices simply presiding over that court, from 1176 royal justices on eyre seem to have taken a more active role either in actually making the judgments or in guiding recognitions and juries to their verdicts. As king's men, knowledgeable in the practices of the king's court, they would ensure that royal custom was applied in the localities.[100] Such practices and attitudes helped to ensure that the law became common to the kingdom.

(iii) Literature and ideals

Our clearest indications of the views of this circle of king's men come from the two administrative manuals it produced.

98. *Dialogus*, p. 101, preceding the passage on natural enemies cited below, p. 152.
99. See *Lincs.*, no. 764 for an early mention to 'justices learned in law'.
100. Brand, *Making*, pp. 77–102, and the comments of Hudson, *Land, Law, and Lordship*, pp. 266–7; see below, pp. 179, 207.

Richard fitzNigel composed the *Dialogue of the Exchequer* in the late 1170s. A decade later an anonymous writer, possibly a clerk attached to the justiciar Ranulf de Glanville or to Ranulf's protégé Hubert Walter, produced a *Treatise on the Laws and Customs of the Kingdom of England*, commonly referred to as *Glanvill*.[101] The *Dialogue* makes most obvious their devotion to the king. The noble king's 'great deeds win the highest praise'. In particular he is committed to peace: 'from the very beginning of his rule he applied his whole mind to crushing rebels and malcontents by all possible means, and sealing up in men's hearts the treasure of peace and good faith.' Following the rebellion of 1173–74, 'when the kingdom was saved from ship-wreck and peace restored, the king again strove to renew the times of his grandfather'. To do so, he chose six circuits of itinerant justices, to 'restore the rights which had elapsed. They, giving audience in each county, and doing full justice to those who considered themselves wronged, saved the poor both money and labour.' According to Richard, Henry's servants were 'alike in their zeal for the king's advantage, when justice permits it'. And no wonder, for Henry and his servants' promotion of each other was also self-promotion: 'the greatest of earthly princes, the renowned king of the English, Henry II, is always striving to augment the dignities of those who serve him, knowing full well that the benefits conferred on his servants purchase glory for his own name, by titles of undying fame.' Indeed, as men who owed their great position almost solely to royal favour and their connections within the circle of the king's servants, they may well have exceeded even the king himself in their insistence on royal rights, and perhaps in antagonism to the nobility; fitzNigel, at least, referred to lords as the 'natural enemies' of their men, who in turn were to be protected by the king.[102]

101. *Glanvill*, pp. xxx–xxxiii.
102. Quotations: *Dialogus*, pp. 9–10; 75; 77, 8; 61; 101. See also pp. 14, 26 on the royal seal; 27–8; 117 on the noble inspiration of legislation; 113 for a rather apologetic tone; 120 on royal kindness. On the protection of the weak against the powerful, see also *Glanvill*, Prologue, cited below, and viii 9, p. 82 concerning heirs facing violence from their lords. Hyams, *King, Lords, and Peasants*, p. 261; *TAC*, esp. vii 1, Tardif, p. 7; such principles are more prominent in the *Très Ancien Coutumier* than in *Glanvill*.

Such ideological stances are generally less clear in the other great manual, *Glanvill*, except in its Prologue. This opens with the words 'Royal Power', and, echoing Justinian's *Institutes*, states that 'royal power not only must be furnished with arms against rebels and peoples rising up against the king and kingdom, but it is also fitting that it should be adorned with laws for ruling subject and peaceful peoples'. After praising Henry's victories, it goes on to proclaim that

> nor is there any dispute how justly and how mercifully, how prudently he, who is the author and lover of peace, has behaved towards his subjects in time of peace, for his Highness's court is so impartial that no judge there is so shameless or audacious as to presume to turn aside at all from the path of justice or digress in any respect from the way of truth. For there, indeed, a poor man is not oppressed by the power of his adversary, nor does favour or partiality drive any man away from the threshold of judgment.[103]

Later in the Prologue, the writer cites the Roman maxim that 'what pleases the prince has the force of law'. The rest of the text is not taken up with such grandiloquence, although mention is made of the lord king's crown and dignity, the lord king's mercy, the benefits of the lord king's legislation, the absence of any equal, let alone superior, of the lord king, and the superiority of fidelity to the lord king even over the homage bond.[104]

However, what the *Treatise* best reveals are the attitudes and atmosphere which increased royal control of justice and law.[105] Whilst compared with the *Dialogue* the author's tone is not didactic, and his first person pedagogical comment very limited, he was correct in judging that his *Treatise*'s contents could most usefully be preserved in writing. No fewer than nine manuscripts of the text survive which probably date from before 1215.[106] At least one

---

103. *Glanvill*, Prologue, Hall, pp. 1–2.
104. *Glanvill*, i 1, ii 7, ii 19, vii 10, ix 1, x 1, xii 21, xii 22, Hall, pp. 2, 28, 36, 84, 104, 116, 146, 147; cf. vii 17, p. 91 on the king not wishing to infringe the rights of others.
105. See also below, ch. 8.
106. Hall, pp. viii–ix, lxv–lxx; in contrast, no twelfth-century manuscripts of the *Dialogus* survive.

other must have existed, for none of our manuscripts seems to be the original, and it is most likely that others too have been lost. We have then a text which rapidly spread amongst the court circle, even the possibility that most of the regular royal justices had a copy. The quality of the texts varies. The existence of some manuscripts of high quality, even decorated, suggests the prestige which was attached to the text. Others are sloppy, such as that copied by the royal justice and chronicler Roger of Howden, which may indicate rapid production and considerable desire for working texts. The content and form of the texts also shows some variation, again suggesting practical use. Probably within a decade of the work's completion, a slightly revised version had been made and was being copied. Many of the revisions are purely stylistic, although some are intended for legal clarification and others detract from the work. Most significant, though, are the attempts to improve the clarity of the work by dividing it into books and chapters. These eased cross-referencing and made the text more readily accessible, thereby producing a more user-friendly manual. Clearly the text was being used and commented upon, and this process is reflected in the early 'glossing' of the manuscripts, the writing of comments in the margin, be they simple cross references or, more rarely, critical comments.[107]

The possession and study of a legal manual by numerous justices even by 1200, and certainly by 1210 would have further standardized the administration of justice.[108] This view is reinforced by another feature of the *Tractatus*. At various points diverse opinions are mentioned, and some of the early manuscripts at these places give names either in the margin, or inter-lineated in the text, or within the text itself. The number of names given varies markedly between manuscripts, but the names themselves are generally consistent,[109] and it seems quite plausible that the author himself included such names in the margin of his text.

107. On glosses and divisions of the text, Hall, pp. xlvii–liv.
108. If some manuscripts of *Glanvill*, extant or now lost, were owned or read by people outside the royal circle, such a reception of royal ideas on law and justice could also have been a force for standardization.
109. Hall, p. xliii n. 4 suggests that the one exception (vii 3) is an error, presumably caused by scribal confusion.

They give us our best indication of the circle of justices for whom the text was produced. All except Henry II's justiciar Richard de Lucy were still alive. Of the remaining six, one appears in four places, Hubert Walter, one in two places, Osbert fitzHervey. The rest appear only once. They include Henry II's justiciar Ranulf de Glanville, and all the others were both itinerant and central justices. The names are those of the authorities holding those opinions. Whilst when more than one authority is cited, the point is left unresolved, it is nevertheless clear that certain figures were seen as lending weight to an opinion, and were worth naming in a manuscript.[110] The same men must have been those whose opinions lay behind increasing standardization of procedure.

The texts of *Glanvill* and the *Dialogue* confirm that the inner circle of king's men debated certain points of law and procedure. One manuscript of *Glanvill* even includes in its margin at appropriate places in red the word *Distinctio*, and abbreviations for *quaestio* and *solutio* (that is, question and answer). These are terms familiar from the academic Schools, and re-affirm Peter of Blois' statement that in Henry II's court it was school every day.[111] In its assimilation and comparison of materials, its emphasis upon classification, its production of new genres of writing, and its encouragement of personal advancement through specialized knowledge, Angevin reform was a practical manifestation of the 'Twelfth-century Renaissance'.

. . .

CONCLUSIONS

Royal officials according to Peter of Blois were like locusts: as soon as some left, others arrived.[112] But how did Henry II

---

110. Hall, pp. xliii–xlvii. The *Dialogue* similarly gives evidence of debate in the exchequer, but Richard is much readier to reject one opinion, to back another; e.g. *Dialogus*, p. 121. Such contrasting of opinions, not always with resolution, was of course a feature of academic study in the twelfth century, e.g. in Abelard's *Sic et Non* and Gratian's *Decretum*.
111. Balliol College, Oxford, ms. 350, e.g. ff. 51v, 52, 54v; J. C. Robertson, ed., *Materials for the History of Thomas Becket* (7 vols, London, 1875–85), vii 573.
112. Turner, *Judiciary*, p. 5.

to choose between what I knew and the infinite, seductive unknown. In the end, the unknown won. I was terribly sad, but this was what was supposed to happen, and I could not deny it. My friends and family were sad, too, but they understood, and they threw me a huge going-away party. In the midst of this party, as I looked around me and saw everyone I cared for, I hesitated, and changed my mind. I could not abandon these people; they were my whole world. I would stay on land, and live my life, and forget who I was.

Puberty was hell. The changes it caused in my body were more wrong than it's really possible to describe. They are a curse, one I will never entirely shake. I came so, so close to killing myself, but for reasons that still escape me, I did not. I carried on, and slowly acclimated to the hell of my body, and tried not to think about what might have been.

Every day, I would come home from school and feel my muscles relax. Only then would I realize that they had been tense all day. I stopped going over to friends' houses, and scrupulously avoided the various school dances and other events. When I went to college—the same college my mother taught at—and had to live in a dormitory, I broke. I contracted a terrible illness, which pretty well cemented my horror of my new school, and I abandoned any notion of making friends there. I spent every possible moment at home, with my family, where things were okay. I dreaded being at school with an almost religious intensity. My mother and I frequently got into arguments about how much I would stay at home, until I broke down crying at the dinner table one night, and she relented. That was the last year I lived in a dorm.

I hoped that my malaise would be alleviated when I left college and got a teaching job, but I was more miserable than ever. I made the terrible decision to take on five classes in three different grades, teaching two different subjects at two different schools. During the week, I stayed in a large, empty house near one of the schools where I taught. My dad drove me home on the weekends. I would talk politics with him on the drive home, snacking on the cookies he always brought me. When I got home, I was finally able to exist again. I collapsed, and let my dog jump on me, and did not move for some time, as though all the emotional weight of the week had caught up with me all at once.

get away with inflicting such a plague? Major measures were introduced, or so at least their texts tell us, with the counsel and consent of the great men of the realm. Many of the reforms discussed above, for example in record-keeping, would anyway have been uncontroversial. Others were popular, designedly so in some cases such as the grand assize. In certain instances, like novel disseisin, a measure which may have constricted a man in his position as lord would help him in his position as tenant. Yet there was resistance to at least some of the reforms, resistance which did not stop the process. Part of the explanation must simply lie in the amount of authority and force upon which the king could draw. Opposition which had arisen for various reasons in 1173–74 was effectively crushed. Royal power is not, however, the only answer. Kings pulled back from particularly unpopular measures, or adapted them to their own profit. Privileges were granted to individuals, or, notably in the case of economic regulation, reforms were no longer enforced but used to raise money through the sale of licences to avoid the regulations.

There is also another, more fundamental reason which may be lost in hindsight. Men at the time can only have noticed the reforms in very piecemeal fashion. Even from the point of view of royal administrators, the reforms snow-balled in a not entirely intended fashion and certainly produced unintended results. Others can have had still less of an idea of what was going on. Soon procedures which had been new seem to have been accepted as part of custom. When protest did arise, most notably in 1215, the protests concerning royal jurisdiction focused not on the routinized measures which were the products of Angevin reform but the continuing personal impact of the king and his officials upon justice.

Chapter 6

CRIME AND THE ANGEVIN REFORMS

Pleas are either criminal or civil. Some criminal pleas belong to the crown of the lord king, and some to the sheriffs of counties.

Glanvill, i 1.

And concerning those who are taken by the oath of this Assize, none are to have court or justice or chattels except the lord king in his court in the presence of his justices, and the lord king will have all their chattels. Concerning those who are taken other than by this oath, let it be as is accustomed and proper.

Assize of Clarendon, c. 5

In 1166 Henry II set the country to work for the maintenance of the peace: 'And in the several counties where there are no gaols, let such be made in a borough or some castle of the king at the king's expense.'[1] Words were backed by money, royal money. Acting primarily through the eyre, the regime sought to eradicate those whom the usual methods had failed to touch, most explicitly the notorious offender.[2] Developments epitomize the assertion of royal authority, the modification of procedure, and the processes of classification which, as we have just seen, characterize Angevin reform.

1. Assize of Clarendon, c. 7, *EHD*, ii no. 24. Gaols were used to hold prisoners awaiting trial, not for custody as a punishment; see above, p. 56.
2. For developments in proof in canon law relating to notoriety, see e.g. J. A. Brundage, *Medieval Canon Law* (London, 1995), pp. 94–5, 144–51.

However, whilst the late twelfth century was a period of important change, there were also very notable continuities. It was not just that there were precedents for the new royal procedures. Rather, various old methods remained of crucial importance, as indeed is suggested by clause five of the Assize of Clarendon quoted above. Frankpledge, the sheriff's tourn, hue and cry, and appeal all remained central to the prevention and prosecution of crime. Local arrangements and actions remained the most effective way of dealing with wrongdoing.[3] The rapid capture of the wrongdoer remained essential if there was to be much chance of a successful prosecution; otherwise the system remained, at least in our eyes, notably inefficient at catching and punishing offenders.[4] The options open to a criminal – capture and the answering of accusations, taking sanctuary, or simple flight – remained the same. Meanwhile, victims still sought physical and monetary recompense for injury and dishonour. Types of wrongdoing and the motives of wrongdoers – vengeance, drunkenness, and so on – underwent no revolution.[5] Almost all killings were by men, often acting with accomplices, and most victims too were male.[6] Although there was some gentry violence, most killers and other criminals were poor, as were their victims.[7] Much trouble could be caused by difficult individuals or families.[8] Border areas were

3. See *PKJ*, iii no. 703 for an instance where the criminal takes the horn which was being used to sound the pursuit. J. B. Given, *Society and Homicide in Thirteenth-Century England* (Stanford, CA, 1977), esp. pp. 172–3, suggests that in the thirteenth century homicide rates tended to be lower in areas of strong lordship and nucleated settlement.
4. E.g. *PKJ*, ii nos 620, 751; for more qualified comment, see below, p. 184.
5. See e.g. H. E. Butler, ed. and trans, *The Chronicle of Jocelin of Brakelond* (Edinburgh, 1949), pp. 92–3 for a gathering degenerating into a brawl with wounding; *Lincs.*, no. 773 has a barbarity which suggests a feud; and the judgment may suggest some sympathy on the part of the court. More generally, see Given, *Homicide*.
6. Given, *Homicide*, pp. 41, 48. Groups accused of crimes: e.g. *PKJ*, iii no. 761; iv nos 3444–8.
7. See e.g. H. Thomas, *Vassals, Heiresses, Crusaders, and Thugs* (Philadelphia, PA, 1993), pp. 61, 65; Given, *Homicide*, p. 69.
8. For possible examples see *CRR*, i 63 (Giffards), *PKJ*, iii no. 698.

especially dangerous, and night remained a time when crime was particularly feared: according to *Bracton*, journeys to market should be made 'by day and not at night, because of ambushes and the attacks of robbers'.[9]

.   .   .

AILWARD'S CASE

In all these aspects, the picture provided by the new and much more extensive evidence of the royal court records is generally consistent with that of earlier and contemporary narrative sources. An account derived from the not entirely reliable evidence of Becket miracle stories illustrates such continuity, as well as other themes of this chapter.[10] Ailward was a peasant in the royal manor of Westoning. His involvement in wrongdoing was made unusual not only by St Thomas's belated protection of him, but also by the fact that he was baptized on Whitsun eve. According to popular opinion, this made him immune from sinking in water or being burnt by fire; ordeal by water, therefore, would always prove him guilty, ordeal by hot iron prove him innocent. Early in the 1170s Ailward was owed a penny by his neighbour, but the neighbour refused his demands for payment, pretending that he could not afford to pay. One feast day, Ailward showed appropriate goodwill; he asked for half of the debt so that he could go to drink some beer, but would allow the neighbour to keep the other half. The debtor refused, Ailward grew angry, drunk, and vengeful. He left the tavern and broke into the neighbour's house. As security for his debt, he took away the padlock which secured the house, a whetstone, a gimlet, and some gloves. However, the debtor's children saw the break-in and informed their father. He pursued Ailward, tore the whetstone from him and

> launched it against his head, thus breaking the whetstone on his head and his head with the whetstone. Drawing also the sharp knife that he was carrying, he pierced his arm, got the better of him and took the miserable man in fetters as a thief, robber, and burglar to the house into which he had broken. . . .

9. *Bracton*, f. 235b, Thorne, iii 199; for nocturnal offences, see *PKJ*, ii nos 734, 735, 739. For borders, e.g. *PKJ*, i pp. 132–3.
10. *Lawsuits*, no. 471; I have conflated the two versions of the story.

> A crowd gathered together with Fulk the reeve who, since
> the theft of goods worth one penny does not justify mutilation,
> suggested augmenting the importance of the theft by
> pretending that more goods had been stolen. This was done
> and beside the fettered man was placed a package containing
> hides, wool, linen cloth, a garment, and a . . . pruning knife.[11]

Ailward and the goods were brought before the sheriff and
the county. However, judgment was suspended for a
month, and he was kept in public custody in Bedford until
finally he was taken to a meeting of judges at Leighton
Buzzard. He denied theft, saying that he had taken only the
whetstone and gloves, and these as security for a debt.
Ailward asked either to fight a judicial combat with his
accuser or to undergo the ordeal of fire. However, at the
wish of Fulk the reeve, who had received an ox for that
purpose, it was adjudged that Ailward should undergo the
ordeal of water and thus – on account of his baptism on
Whitsun eve – have no way of escape. After another month
in prison in Bedford, he failed the ordeal of water, and
'was led away to the place of execution' where 'a not
inconsiderable crowd of people had gathered to see the
spectacle, whether compelled by public authority or moved
by curiosity'. Ailward was mutilated, his accuser and the
royal reeve putting out his eyes and cutting off his testicles.
Fortunately for Ailward, his devotion to St Thomas at
length restored him to wholeness, although his new
testicles were small and one of his eyes no longer
multicoloured but black.

·   ·   ·

CLASSIFICATION

(i) Crimes, pleas of the crown, and felonies

In chapter 3, we noted the absence of a category called
crime in Anglo-Norman England, but in chapter 5 we saw
that the Angevin reforms involved a tendency to
classification.[12] As the quotation at the start of this chapter
indicates, *Glanvill* employed the categories criminal and
civil, which he adopted from Roman law and which are

11. Cf. *LHP*, 22.1, Downer, p. 124 on accusers inflating charges.
12. See above, pp. 56, 142–56.

comfortingly familiar to us. So too are some of the characteristics he attributed to criminal pleas: they are against the king and his peace, and are punished. However, his emphasis in fact differs from ours, in particular with regard to the bringing of private appeals, as opposed to crown prosecutions, for crimes. Nor do plea rolls use the term crime in order to categorize cases. In *Glanvill* and elsewhere, two other terms are preferred, pleas of the crown and felony.

According to *Glanvill*,

> The following [criminal pleas] belong to the crown of the lord king: ... the crime which in the [Roman] laws is called *lèse-majesté*, namely the killing or betrayal of the lord king or of the kingdom or army; fraudulent hiding of treasure trove; the plea of breach of the peace of the lord king; homicide; arson; robbery; rape; the crime of forgery and anything similar; all these are punished by death or cutting off of limbs. The crime of theft which pertains to sheriffs and is pleaded and decided in counties is not included.

As the exclusion of thefts suggests, for *Glanvill* not all crimes – in his terms or ours – were crown pleas. Moreover, he defined certain non-criminal cases as 'pleas pertaining to [the king's] crown and dignity', for example land cases coming to royal courts in the context of the assize *utrum*, pleas concerning advowsons, and harm to royal tenements, ways, or cities.[13] Similarly pleas of the crown were a category used in plea rolls,[14] but whilst all cases of violence and robbery appear as pleas of the crown, far from all pleas of the crown were concerned with violence and robbery. Rather, they were – as their title suggests – matters which touched the royal interests particularly closely.

Felony had been a term used to denote disloyalty – the name of the traitor in the *Song of Roland*, Ganelon, rhymed nicely with felon. However, probably in the time of Henry II, the word begins to appear with an additional meaning.

13. *Glanvill*, i 2, xii 22, iv 13–14, ix 11, Hall, pp. 3–4, 146–7, 52–3, 114. The Norman *Très Ancien Coutumier* does not separate criminal pleas in the way *Glanvill* did; *TAC*, liii, lxx, Tardif, pp. 43, 64–5. Note also A. Harding, ed., *The Roll of the Shropshire Eyre of 1256* (Selden Soc., 96, 1981), p. xlii.

14. Note *Lincs.*, no. 765.

It is not used in the Assize of Clarendon, but was employed in 1176 in the Assize of Northampton, meaning a particularly serious wrong. The association of the word with this category of offences probably stemmed from the view that serious offenders were breaching their oath of loyalty to the king, and any promise they had made not to commit or to aid in the commission of such wrongs. Such an oath, as noted earlier, was probably sworn in the Anglo-Norman period and almost certainly dates back to the Anglo-Saxon. Quite why the word felony came into use in its new sense specifically in Henry II's reign remains uncertain, but it is notable that the Assize of Northampton also ordered the taking of oaths of fealty from all who wished to remain within the realm.[15]

By the early thirteenth century, the criteria of a felony were fairly clear:

(i) A felony is a crime which can be prosecuted by an appeal . . . (ii) The felon's lands go to his lord or to the king and his chattels are confiscated. (iii) The felon forfeits life or member. (iv) If a man accused of felony flies, he can be outlawed.[16]

At the time of *Glanvill* too, these criteria seem to have applied. Writing of treason, he stated that 'if the ordeal convicts him of this kind of crime, then judgment both as to his life and as to his limbs depends on royal clemency, as in other pleas of felony'.[17] Less clear is whether by *Glanvill*'s time there was a set list of felonies. In the thirteenth century the following were so categorized: homicide, be it secretive murder or simple killing, arson, robbery, rape, maiming, wounding, burglary, larceny.[18] Not all of these were explicitly mentioned as felonies by *Glanvill,* and only the first three appear by name in the

15. *EHD*, ii 25, c. 6. Understanding of the link between serious offences and the oath to the king has been transformed by Patrick Wormald, see above, p. 30. Cf. S. F. C. Milsom, *Historical Foundations of the Common Law* (2nd edn, London, 1981), p. 406; also Pollock and Maitland, ii 465. The connection may also be related to the fact that the lands of either type of felon returned to his lord.
16. Pollock and Maitland, ii 466.
17. *Glanvill,* xiv 1, Hall, p. 171.
18. Pollock and Maitland, ii 470.

Assize of Northampton, together with forgery and theft.[19]

Theft indeed exemplifies the problems of categorization. The Assizes of Clarendon and Northampton included theft as one of the serious offences to be presented by juries, and Northampton by implication included it amongst felonies, but *Glanvill* seems less certain of its place as a crown plea. He insisted that thefts which belong to the sheriff were to be distinguished from his other criminal pleas which belong to the Crown. Meanwhile, distinctions between theft and robbery may have remained unclear in many eyes.[20]

Overall, the impression is of various attempts at categorization based on various criteria. The one constant emphasis is upon the seriousness of the offence. Whilst a wound constituted a felony, a scratch did not, and the amount stolen might make theft a plea of the crown.[21] However, other criteria complicate the situation. Some were procedural: rape was not included in the Assizes perhaps because it was not considered suitable for presentment.[22] Others were jurisdictional: thefts to be heard before the sheriff were not pleas of the crown. Others still were a matter of royal interest: hence the wide variety of crown pleas heard by the eyre. The intellectual elegance of *Glanvill*'s initial categorization is a sign of the climate of

19. *EHD*, ii no. 25. On forgery, see Pollock and Maitland, ii 504, 540. On presentments made in the period 1166–76 for offences other than those specified in the surviving texts from Clarendon and Northampton, see N. D. Hurnard, 'The jury of presentment and the Assize of Clarendon', *EHR* 56 (1941), 401.

20. *EHD*, ii nos 24, 25; see above, p. 159 for Ailward's case. Milsom, *Historical Foundations*, p. 286 suggests that if *Glanvill* had conceived of writing a list of felonies, he would have included theft, at least above a certain amount. Note also *Dialogus*, pp. 102–3. Cf. *TAC*, lix, Tardif, p. 50 attributes thefts to lords in Normandy. In Henry III's reign, thefts are very prominent in the rolls of commissions of gaol delivery. It is conceivable that such commissions took over jurisdiction previously exercised by sheriffs. (I owe this point to Dan Klerman.)

21. See *Bracton*, f. 144, 151b, Thorne, ii 407, 427–8; also Pollock and Maitland, ii 468–9; above, p. 160 for Ailward's case; Assize of Clarendon, c. 2, *EHD*, ii no. 24; F. W. Maitland, ed., *Pleas of the Crown for the County of Gloucester* (London, 1884), no. 20.

22. R. D. Groot, 'The crime of rape *temp.* Richard I and John', *Journal of Legal History* 9 (1988), 323–34.

reform, not of its substantive achievement, but nevertheless late in the twelfth century we are seeing the beginning of common law classification.

(ii) Wrongs and trespasses

After mentioning the crime of theft, *Glanvill* then listed certain other offences over which lords or sheriffs had jurisdiction: 'brawling, beatings, and even wounding unless the accuser states in his claim that there has been a breach of the peace of the lord king.'[23] Such offences would later have been termed trespasses. Trespass is familiar to us as a rather archaic-sounding word for sin or wrong, 'Forgive us our trespasses', and this general usage also existed throughout the middle ages. However, it is also one of the first legal words that most modern English children encounter, on signs stating that 'Trespassers will be prosecuted' or shortened to 'Trespassers will' outside Wol's house in *Winnie the Pooh*. The separation of the legal category from the general word began late in our period, and trespass is not a term used in any technical sense by *Glanvill* or the early royal court rolls. Rather it meant wrongs in general: every felony was a trespass, though not every trespass a felony.[24] In the later middle ages, too, legal usage was somewhat vague: even in its technical sense, trespass denoted the residue of an undifferentiated category of wrongs. This residuary nature helps to explain why it is so hard to treat the 'emergence' of the legal category. Rather than *emerging*, trespass *remained*, with the divergence of other clearer categories, such as felony, providing whatever bounds it had.

There was no clear jurisdictional distinction characterizing trespasses in our period or beyond. However, beginning with the Angevin reforms, there emerged an action of trespass heard in the royal courts. A long tradition existed of kings hearing their people's complaints of wrongs, and then either promoting a settlement or ordering that the wrong be corrected. The instruction to this effect might be oral or by writ. Most notable in this

23. *Glanvill*, i 2, Hall, p. 4.
24. See *Bracton*, f. 119b, Thorne, ii 337.

context are a considerable variety of writs which we see being issued by the end of the twelfth century, asking the addressee to show why (*ostensurus quare*) they had taken a certain action. After 1215 a limited number of these would develop into 'writs of trespass'. Again, we see not so much the emergence of a category but the reduction of a previously less differentiated grouping. But how did the reduction, and the routinization of the procedure, occur? How did there come to be a so-called action of trespass in the king's court? Rather as *ad hoc* decisions had always been made about whether to hear individual complaints, so now the royal court must have selected certain types of wrong which it would handle on a regular basis.[25] The two key elements seem to have been the threat to peace and the contempt of the king's special orders and protections.[26] The allegation of breach of the peace, or of the use of force and arms, could develop into a formal means whereby many wrongs were brought before the king's court. This broadened use of trespass was to be very significant, particularly as the thirteenth century progressed. Extending royal jurisdiction beyond the few serious crimes addressed by the Assizes and *Glanvill*, it led to the routine treatment in the king's court of a wide range of minor injuries, a development which has been described as 'comparable in significance to Henry II's introduction of new actions protecting land'.[27]

Yet within our period and beyond, it remained lords and sheriffs who had jurisdiction over a wide variety of the wrongs which in later common law would be categorized as trespasses. In addition to *Glanvill* mentioning brawling, beatings and woundings which did not lead to claims of breach of the king's peace, other records similarly show lords dealing with a wide variety of wrongs, for example insults and minor scuffles.[28] If we had sufficient evidence to

25. S. F. C. Milsom, 'Trespass from Henry III to Edward III' in his *Studies in the History of the Common Law* (London, 1985), p. 1; see also above, p. 28.
26. *Shropshire*, pp. xlviii–xlix, lviii.
27. *Shropshire*, p. liv.
28. *Glanvill*, i 2, Hall, p. 4; see also *Bracton*, f. 154b–155, Thorne, ii 436–7; Pollock and Maitland, ii 519–20 on the thirteenth century; Milsom, *Historical Foundations*, pp. 286–7.

all the out-spread oddities of my life. This place was my everything, and I never spent long away from it.

Only my dad could make other places safe. I went to the zoo with him during weekdays, when it was empty. We walked amidst the various animals, serenely confident that he and I were the only humans for some distance. I went with him to the school where he taught, and played games on the computer in his office, the ones that the computer at home could not run. Sometimes he even brought me into his classes, and allowed me to opine on certain texts. I did not fear the college kids; they were subordinate to my father, and thus I was in a *de facto* position of power. It felt good.

I never did anything with my mom, not without my dad present. She was friendly in a distant sort of way. She would sometimes hug me, but I would feel no warmth in her embrace. In spite of this, I knew she tried, and loved her for it.

I liked to think that my parents could protect me from the monsters, but there were things that they had no desire to protect me from. As the years crawled by and I learned more about what it meant to be a teenage boy, I grew increasingly frantic. Up until then, there had been a certain amount of ambiguity. One could shy away from traditional modes of masculinity, even decide to not really be a boy at all. But it seemed to me that the changes brought on by puberty had a certain terrible finality to them. I tried to find a way out, but could not, at least not one that I would consciously entertain.

One day, while I was riding home in the car with my dad, I asked him what he thought of transgender people. He told me that, in general, his attitude was "whatever floats your boat" (his exact words), but that trans people in particular struck him as just plain weird. This discomfited me, but he was my dad, and I did not wish to think ill of him. So I told myself that, of course, he was right—trans people, while not worthy of death, necessarily, were certainly to-be-shunned.

It was around this time that I had a dream. I do not always remember my dreams, but I remember this one. In it, I discovered that it was my destiny to become a mermaid. The problem, of course, was that if I transformed, and took to the sea, I would never be able to return. I would never see my friends and family again. And so, in the dream, I had

analyse these types of cases and still lesser ones, the pattern of continuity through the Angevin reforms would be re-emphasized. Whilst reform led to changes in jurisdiction and procedure for the most serious cases, it had much less of an impact on the most numerous. Moreover, trespass – even when dealt with in the royal court – provided continuity in settlement method. It gave the plaintiff a means whereby to exact punishment upon the offender and to extract compensation from him, both for material loss and for the shame or dishonour suffered. It thus clearly resembles the settlements discussed in chapter 3, and the continuing desire for compensation will remain a theme of this chapter.

. . .

THE CONTINUATION OF TRADITIONAL METHODS

Continuity is also apparent throughout our period and beyond in the traditional methods of peace-keeping and of catching and prosecuting wrongdoers. Indeed, these were sometimes re-emphasized by kings. The Assize of Clarendon sought to ensure that wanderers be brought under surety whenever they entered a borough and that frankpledge function properly, whilst the decree of 1195 emphasized the obligation to raise the hue and cry.[29] Offenders caught red-handed continued to be summarily tried and executed, although such acts should be reported to the eyre, and were then open to investigation. Actions relating to theft continued to rely on a tracing of the possession of the goods. Thus a 1201 eyre roll records that

> Roger Corbin, asked how he acquired a certain cloak and napkin which William le Burguinin says were stolen from him together with other things when his house was broken into and burgled, comes and says that he bought the cloak and napkin from Robert Triz . . . . And he vouches Robert Triz to warranty, and if he does not wish to be his warrantor therein, he offers to prove against him as the court shall adjudge. Robert Triz comes and denies altogether that he ever sold that cloak or napkin to him. And he says that on another occasion in the full shire Roger had appealed him thereof and

29. *EHD*, ii no. 24, cc. 9, 15–16; *SSC*, p. 258.

afterwards took this back and vouched another, William son of Richard, and the whole shire bears witness to this. And because Roger was found seised of the stolen goods and varied in his statement and in vouching his warrantor, it is adjudged that he be hanged. Let Robert Triz be quit therein. William son of Richard outlawed for this.[30]

As for prosecution of other serious crimes, *Glanvill* distinguished two types of procedure.[31] Historians of the Angevin reforms have tended to concentrate on presentment, where no specific accuser appeared and the accusation was based on public notoriety. However, the other type, in which a specific accuser appeared and the case was prosecuted by appeal, continued to be much the more common.[32] Ailward's case provides one instance, but more can be revealed by assembling the various stages of an appeal from the plea rolls. Much remained similar to the procedure sketched in chapter 3, and I therefore emphasize the new elements, in particular the coroner's role.

Let us imagine a case of wounding in breach of the king's peace, which along with robbery, rape, homicide and assault was the most common subject of appeal.[33] It was the victim's duty to raise the hue and cry,[34] aiming to obtain help from his or her own and neighbouring townships in

30. *PKJ*, ii no. 741; see also no. 347; Pollock and Maitland, ii 157–66; *Dialogus*, pp. 102–3; *Glanvill*, x 15–17, Hall, pp. 130–2; *Bracton*, ff. 150b–2, Thorne, ii 425–9.

31. *Glanvill*, xiv 1, Hall p. 171.

32. See e.g. *Lincs.* On appeals by approvers, see above, p. 75, C. A. F. Meekings, ed., *Crown Pleas of the Wiltshire Eyre*, 1249 (Wilts. Archaeological and Natural History Soc., Record Branch, 16, 1961), pp. 91–2; note, however, H. Summerson, 'Maitland and the criminal law in the age of *Bracton*', in Hudson, *Centenary Essays*, p. 119, on the situation early in Henry III's reign. See above, p. 162 on the availability of appeal as one criterion for felony in the thirteenth century.

33. See e.g. the 1202 Lincolnshire eyre roll (*Lincs.*); also *Surrey*, pp. 117ff. On appeals by women, see below, pp. 235–6.

34. See *Lincs.*, p. lviii. Obviously in homicide cases, appeal had to be made not by the victim but his kin or those bound to him by homage or lordship who 'can speak about the death from what he has seen himself'; *Glanvill*, xiv 3, Hall, p. 174. This latter phrase seems to mean that either he saw the killing or found the body; see also *Lincs.*, no. 931.

order to capture the felon, and also bring the accusation before the bailiff or sergeant of the hundred and the coroner preliminary to bringing an appeal in the county court.[35] The victim showed his wounds to the strong-stomached coroner, who was responsible for measuring them. Failure to show wounds could lead to the appeal being quashed.[36] In other cases the hundred sergeant might go with some knights to the wounded man and make a view of him. In the improbable event of the accused being present, the coroners and sergeants were responsible for 'attaching' him, that is ensuring he had sureties to appear in court, or, particularly if it looked likely that the wounds would be fatal, for arresting him until it could be decided whether he was to be treated as a homicide.[37] In practice, most felons fled immediately. The coroners recorded their names, and also those of their tithings so that these might be amerced by the eyre if the felon could not be found. Either then, or in the next county court, appellors had to give sureties, generally two, that they would pursue their appeals. Finally, the appeal was made before the county court, where the coroner enrolled the appeals verbatim.[38]

Cases then awaited the arrival of the king's itinerant justices – a situation which may have grown less satisfactory as the period between eyres became longer.[39] However, very few were actually pursued to a decision there in the presence of both parties. Often the eyre records state that an appellor did not prosecute or, less frequently, that he withdrew himself.[40] Although the difference between

---

35. R. F. Hunnissett, *The Medieval Coroner* (Cambridge, 1961), pp. 55–7; *Bracton*, ff. 139b–140, Thorne, ii 394.
36. *Lincs.*, no. 899. Note also the coroner's responsibilities in rape cases; e.g. *Lincs.*, no. 590.
37. *Lincs.*, pp. xlv–vi; *Bracton*, f. 122b, Thorne, ii 345. *Wiltshire*, pp. 46–51 suggests that the system of attachment was 'reasonably efficient'.
38. *Glanvill*, xiv 1, Hall, pp. 171–2, see also i 32, p. 21; *Lincs.*, p. lii, *Wiltshire*, p. 71. See e.g. F. W. Maitland, ed., *Select Pleas of the Crown* (Selden Soc., 1, 1888), no. 4 for display of wounds to county court; see also above, p. 160, for the stages in Ailward's case.
39. See above, p. 123.
40. Together these form the largest group of cases in e.g. the Lincolnshire eyre roll of 1202, *Lincs.*, p. lix.

non-prosecution and withdrawal is now somewhat unclear, the court rolls seem firm in their distinction, which may reflect the timing and formality of the abandonment of the appeal: withdrawal might be more formal and take place before the eyre justices.[41] Why was non-prosecution so frequent, despite measures such as the requirement for sureties? Perhaps some were wild appeals, made in the highly emotional aftermath of a crime. Perhaps others were dismissed because of some unrecorded failure in a technicality; in the heat of the moment and through misunderstandings of law, errors might be made in the initial accusation, for example. Perhaps appellors grew scared of confronting, and in particular of fighting, their opponents in court.[42] Probably most, however, were cases settled outside court by negotiation. Victims had not lost their desire for compensation. Out-of-court settlements might allow sensitivity to particular circumstances; an accidental wound might merit no punishment, but the victim and/or their relatives might still feel some moral right to compensation.[43] Settling outside court was not very expensive. The appellor's amercement for failure to prosecute an appeal was generally only half a mark, which the accused might reimburse as part of any compensation payment.

Some, however, waited until they appeared before the eyre justices in order to confirm their settlement: 'William [de la Dune] appeals William de la Bruere that... [he] came up and struck him on the head with a staff, so that he made wounds on him. They are brought into agreement by the licence of the justices.'[44] Such agreements cost more than the amercement for an appeal not prosecuted,[45] but did have certain advantages. They provided the parties, and

---

41. Note e.g. *Lincs.*, no. 1010; however, note also no. 671 'et non est prosecutus quia retraxit se'.
42. See below, p. 173, for a widow Bela failing to prosecute someone with the threatening sobriquet of 'the champion'.
43. See also below, p. 182; generally for cases of homicide, Hurnard, *Pardon.* Payments of compensation for wounds survived explicitly in some urban customs; see e.g. *Borough Customs*, i 30–1.
44. *PKJ*, ii no. 385; see also no. 591 for an amercement of 100s for a license to agree connected to this case.
45. See *Lincs.*, e.g. no. 1033.

in particular the accused, with a written warrant approved by the justices. They thus reduced the possibility of future denial of the agreement, and may have protected the accused against future presentment for the offence.[46] It is significant, though, that the justices did not grant such licences in cases of homicide.[47]

What of the occasions when the appeal was taken further? Let us make the rash assumption that both parties came to the court. The appellor made a statement such as:

A. appeals B. that [on a specified day in a specified place] the said B. came with his force and attacked him in breach of the king's peace, feloniously, and in a premeditated assault, and dealt him such a wound in such a part [of his body] with such a kind of weapon. And that he did this wickedly and feloniously he offers to prove against him by his body or as the court may award.[48]

The appellee might simply deny this word for word, or he might bring an exception, give a specific reason why the appeal was incorrect. He might claim that the appeal had not been properly pursued, for example that wounds had not been displayed. Such arguments might be checked against the records or testimony of the coroners and sheriff. Alternatively, the appellee might claim that he was not a thief removing goods but a lord rightfully retrieving his dead villein's chattels.[49] Particularly notable is the

46. See also pp. 189, 207–8, on royal attitudes to *privatae conventiones*. For the value of a powerful warrantor for a concord, see *Lincs.*, no. 846. Amercements for withdrawing were similar to payments for concord, perhaps reflecting the greater finality of withdrawal as opposed to non-prosecution: see R. D. Groot, 'The jury in private criminal prosecutions before 1215', *American Journal of Legal History* 27 (1983), 134, also e.g. *Lincs.*, no. 1044. Following withdrawal, appellees were generally said to go 'quit' rather than *sine die*, although see the alterations in *Lincs.*, e.g. nos 615, 620–1, 624 for one scribe's confusion; also e.g. nos 563, 584, 1009 using 'quit'.

47. See Hurnard, *Pardon*, p. 22, where she suggests that the issuing of such licenses in homicide cases was a personal monopoly of the king. None of the licenses to agree following appeals in the 1202 Lincolnshire eyre roll relates to homicide.

48. *Bracton*, f. 144, Thorne, ii 406.

49. See *Lincs.*, no. 561; Ailward pleaded that he was distraining, not stealing, see above, p. 160.

exception that the appeal was not brought in good faith. The bringing of an appeal still contained elements of vengeance: it gave the appellor a chance to fight the accused, and if victorious to punish him. However, appeals were not to be brought merely through hatred. The appellee could purchase an inquest from the king as to the appeal having been brought through 'spite and hatred' (*odio et atia*), and the issue was decided by a jury of local men. Thus a certain John appealed his cousin Andrew of going to the house of Thorold, John's father, and ejecting Thorold and his people, and so treating him that he was ill until the day he died. Andrew also robbed Thorold of four swords, four hatchets, two bows, fifteen arrows, two sheets, five yards of linen, and certain charters concerning his inheritance. Andrew came and denied all the charges, but stated that Thorold was his uncle and the son of a priest, so that the land should descend to him after Thorold's death; and that when Thorold began to die, Andrew, without any force, entered Thorold's house which should descend to him. Andrew gave the king ten marks to have justice hastened and to have an inquisition as to whether the appeal was made by just cause or by spite and hatred, and to have a licence to make an agreement concerning another appeal. The case is very interesting, not only in revealing the minor arsenal a man might keep in his house. It demonstrates the way in which violence and inheritance cases might become entwined, and suggests that the death of Thorold saw the culmination of ill-feeling between his near kinsmen.[50]

Inquests concerning hatred were to become common. Generally they would decide whether the appellee's claim concerning spite was true, and if so he would go free; if they dismissed the claim, he would go to proof by battle, or when appropriate to ordeal. The issue of 'spite and hatred' may have been taken very broadly, to cover the truth as much as the motivation of the appeal.[51] Perhaps it was assumed that all false appeals were in some sense motivated by 'spite and hatred', perhaps the phrase came sometimes to be a matter of form, the real issue being the guilt or

50. *Lincs.*, no. 594.
51. See Groot, 'Private criminal prosecutions'.

innocence of the appellee. At the same time, some inquests were purchased simply into issues such as whether a man was guilty of a death or not.[52] The Lincolnshire roll of 1202 contains three examples concerning 'spite and hatred' and four without mention of 'spite and hatred'. This may seem very few in terms of the total number of appeals, but is a larger proportion of those where both parties appeared in court, and very significant compared with the four ordeals and two duels adjudged.[53] It may be that by the early 1190s, and certainly by 1215, appellees had a strong chance of insisting that such an inquest should precede physical proof.

If no exception were successfully brought, the appeal proceeded towards trial by battle. The parties produced sureties and swore oaths to back up their position, and then the battle would take place on the day fixed by the court. The fight no doubt was fierce, and *Bracton* noted the value of incisors – as opposed to molars or grinders – for success in such a trial.[54] The court was then notified of the result, and judgment pronounced. However, in some cases the appellee might, according to *Glanvill*,

> refuse trial by battle . . . on account of age or serious injury. The age must be sixty years or over. Serious injury means a broken bone, or injury to the skull by cut or bruise. In such a case the accused must purge himself by ordeal, that is by hot iron or water according to his status: by hot iron if he is a free man, by water if he is a villein.

This option was also open to appellors, and it was of course particularly likely in cases of wounding that the victim should have to plead as a maimed man.[55]

Such an account would suggest that the royal justices took a relatively passive role in cases brought by appeal, but

---

52. See e.g. *Lincs.*, no. 555.
53. *Lincs.*, pp. lvii–lx, nos 555, 561, 594, 607, 841, 909, 938.
54. *Bracton*, f. 145, Thorne, ii 410. For further details on battle, see *Bracton*, ff. 141b–142, Thorne, ii 399–401; see also above, pp. 75–6.
55. *Glanvill*, xiv 1, Hall, p. 173; see e.g. *Lincs.*, no. 851, where the appellee is given a choice as to which of them will carry the hot iron; he chooses that the appellor should do so, but in the end withdraws his appeal.

other evidence reveals their more active participation. They sometimes insisted that the appealed appear before them even though the appellor had not followed up his case, sometimes allowed cases to be heard which might have been dismissed on technicalities, sometimes rejected appeals on seemingly tenuous technicalities.[56] Their enquiries concerning an appeal might involve the jurors present before the eyre. The jurors' role could take various forms, and is perhaps peculiarly common in appeals by women.[57] They might act as witnesses, concerning evidence of the deed and the general character of one party; one's honour, one's standing in the community remained important.[58] Or, if the appellor had not pursued his case or had had it dismissed because of a technicality, the justices might then ask the jurors whether or not they suspected the appellee:

> Ernald the champion, William his brother, Peter his brother, and William son of Ernald were appealed by Bela widow of Roger of beating and wounding her and Bela has withdrawn herself. . . . The jurors, asked, say that Bela was so beaten by them and therefore let them be taken into custody.[59]

Alternatively, after the appellee had denied the accusation, the jurors might state that the appeal was brought through hatred or give their opinion of the facts.[60] On other occasions the whole shire bore witness after an appeal had been withdrawn, or responded to a question as to the character of an offender:

56. *PKJ*, ii no. 744, *Lincs.*, nos 855, 773; see also *Bracton*, ff. 137, 138b, Thorne, ii 386, 390.
57. See the instances cited in the text below, and also *PKJ*, ii nos 265, 734, 735.
58. See e.g. *PKJ*, ii no. 285; cf. ii no. 399 where the failure of a woman's appeal of robbery is related to the jurors' assessment of her as a harlot.
59. *PKJ*, ii no. 310. Jurors not suspect after appeal withdrawn: e.g. *Lincs.*, no. 540 (wounding), *PKJ*, ii no. 329 (burglary). Technicality, jurors suspect appellee: *PKJ*, ii no. 265 (homicide); jurors not suspect appellee, ii no. 383 (theft). See also *PKJ*, ii no. 351 and *Lincs.*, no. 1004 for cases where the potential appellor has died. See also below, p. 178.
60. E.g. *PKJ*, ii nos 323, 345.

Eva of Babington appeals Richard Frend of the death of Ralph her son and that he wounded her in the breast, and this she offers to prove etc. The knights of the shire, asked of what repute he is, say that before this deed he was accused of sheep stealing and of other evil deeds so that on one occasion he fled for suspicion into the church and stayed in it and afterwards fled secretly. They also say that he fled for the aforesaid death and hid himself away and therefore they suspect him. Richard comes and denies the whole.

In this case, as in others, the opinion of the jurors or the shire did not lead to the immediate punishment of the accused; rather he faced proof – 'Judgment, Let him purge himself by water'.[61]

If defeated in battle or proved guilty in some other way, the accused faced punishment. For the criminal pleas of the king, according to *Glanvill* the punishment was death or the cutting off of limbs, whilst the *Dialogue of the Exchequer* specifies that

> Whoever is convicted of an offence against the royal majesty is condemned in one of three ways according to the degree of his offence to the king. For minor wrongs he is condemned in all his moveable goods; for major wrongs he is condemned in all his moveable property, his lands and rents, so he is disinherited of them; and for the greatest and most heinous offences he is condemned in life and limb.[62]

However, the prospect of painful or deadly punishment helps to explain why few of the accused actually appeared to answer appeals pursued before the justices, leaving their sureties to suffer amercement. Fear of the processes of law, perhaps combined with differing conceptions of liability and doubts that royal administration would render justice, also persuaded to flee those who had committed acts for which they would probably have escaped punishment, for example accidental killing. In so doing, they might even harm themselves. Flight might be taken as an admission of

---

61. *PKJ*, ii no. 742; see also e.g. nos 729, 739. Note below, p. 179, on the effect of the abolition of ordeal.
62. *Glanvill*, i 2, Hall, p. 3, *Dialogus*, p. 113: see also above, pp. 78–9, for mutilation, below p. 179 on Ralph Diceto.

guilt, thus leading to outlawry.[63] And, as in the Anglo-Norman period, it was with the flight and outlawry of the accused that many prosecutions by implacable appellors ended.[64]

This analysis of appeal demonstrates notable continuity from the earlier period. Most cases still began by appeal, although few concluded with battle and the punishment of one party. Individual action, the pursuit of vengeance or satisfaction through the courts, remained vital. The procedure underwent some modifications, notably with the appearance of coroners, but even some of their duties may previously have been treated by royal sergeants. The major change was the predominance of the eyre in the hearing of appeals of felonies. The extension of royal authority with regard to serious offences thus once again becomes a major theme.

. . .

PRESENTMENT AND THE EXTENSION OF ROYAL AUTHORITY

Pipe Rolls of the 1150s and 1160s and the articles of the Inquest of Sheriffs suggest that it had been quite normal for sheriffs or local justices to deal with crown pleas in the county court.[65] By the end of our period, this was no longer the case. The sheriff in his tourn still heard accusations, including presentments made by representatives of each village or tithing. He would amerce those whom a jury of freeholders found guilty of minor offences. However, those suspected of grave crimes were merely taken by the sheriff and held or temporarily released in return for sureties guaranteeing appearance in court. Their

---

63. See e.g. *PKJ*, iii no. 736. *PKJ*, ii no. 267 records a whole village fleeing and being outlawed. Also Hurnard, *Pardon*, pp. 131, 135–6; *Bracton*, f. 132, Thorne, ii 371–2.

64. See above, pp. 68–9; cf. *Dialogus*, p. 102; *Bracton*, ff. 125–9b, Thorne, ii 352–64 (note the suggestion of special conditions in the border counties of Gloucester and Hereford, p. 362). The length of treatment in *Bracton* shows the importance of outlawry. Even when an appeal were quashed, if some of the accused did not appear their sureties were still held to be in mercy; e.g. *PKJ*, ii no. 399, cited above, p. 173 n. 58.

65. See above, p. 37.

From the beginning, I relied on books—especially fiction, films, shows, and video games. They allowed me to live briefly in other worlds, which was crucial, because I certainly couldn't stand living in this one. Some of my fondest memories are of reading books. I think that I would have died long ago without them. Many of them provided a common narrative structure that I so dearly loved: a sad, purposeless child lives a normal life and seems condemned to a normal future, but then a great destiny abducts them and plunges them into various dangerous situations.

Perhaps the first of these was given to me when I was six months old. It's about a selkie—a seal-boy taken from the sea by his adoptive human parents. They prevent him from ever swimming in the ocean for fear that he will never come back. But, of course, one day he does go out into the water, and becomes a seal, fully, and is gone. His parents are sad, but accept that this is what is best for him. Their loss is lessened somewhat by his periodic returns for brief, presumably awkward visits. Yet I still couldn't accept this as a happy ending. All the same, I kept coming back to this book. It haunted me. I would stare at the pictures of the child staring out to sea, and feel so terribly sad.

I was always afraid of the world, or almost always. Its vast, dark reaches could contain anything, and one had to be cautious. As I grew older, my fear was focused on people, but as a kid, I was afraid of monsters. This can be traced back to any number of scary stories, most notably those told to me by a particular woman. She was a friend of my aunt's, or perhaps my grandmother's, I cannot recall for certain. Nor can I remember much from the stories she told me, except a bit of one, the end, I believe. A vampire is chasing a woman, and she tries to flee by running across a bridge, but the vampire catches her. Then he rips open her chest, tears out her heart, drains it dry, and tosses it into the river below.

My home was the only safe place, the only respite from the terrible darkness all over. Even the yard and the driveway sometimes terrified me. When I first learned that mosquitoes suck blood, I assumed that they did so in the same way that vampires did. I tried to never leave the house, and ran to and from the car at top speed, until someone told me that mosquito bites weren't actually dangerous, and I felt foolish. My house was a place unto itself in my mind, a series of shrines containing

fate must await the coming of the royal justices.[66] Again, methods familiar at least from Henry I's reign were being reinforced and integrated with the eyre.

Overall, the royal courts, particularly the general eyre or lesser commissions, were hearing an ever-increasing number of cases.[67] Certainly in criminal matters, the extension was a matter of royal policy, exercised through itinerant justices, and most clearly described in the Assize of Clarendon in 1166. Powerful barons and indeed franchises were not to stand in the way of the prosecution of crime.[68] Co-ordination of action between different administrative areas was to be improved, with the sheriff as the crucial co-ordinator of local activities:

> And if any sheriff shall send word to another sheriff that men have fled from his county into another county, on account of robbery or murder or theft or the harbouring of them, or on account of outlawry or of a charge concerning the king's forest let him [the second sheriff] arrest them. And even if he knows of himself or through others that such men have fled into his county, let him arrest them and guard them until he has taken safe sureties for them.[69]

The Assizes of Clarendon and Northampton extended and regulated presentment. Through presentment juries, the Assizes targeted those accused or notorious of being murderers, robbers, or thieves, or receivers thereof, and from 1176 also those accused of forgery or unjust burning.[70] All were to be put to ordeal. Other proofs, such as compurgation, were not available. Previously reserved

---

66. See above, pp. 124–5; Pollock and Maitland, i 559.
67. On lesser commissions, see e.g. Stenton, *English Justice*, pp. 83, 97; in Henry III's reign and after, commissions of gaol delivery would become extremely important.
68. See below, p. 180, on c. 11 of the Assize of Clarendon.
69. Assize of Clarendon, c. 17, *EHD*, ii no. 24; see also Hurnard, 'Presentment', 398. In practice, co-ordination of different local administrative areas and officials remained a problem.
70. See above, pp. 130, 132. For the method of choosing jurors, see articles of eyre for 1194, *EHD*, iii no. 15; cf. *Bracton*, f. 116, Thorne, ii 328; both display a preference for knights; see also Pollock and Maitland, ii 642–3. Even in 1198 cases could still be referred to as carried out 'according to the assize', e.g. *PKJ*, i p. 133.

primarily for hard cases, the use of ordeal was thus being extended – hence the need for the digging of ordeal pits. Ordeal by water, unlike hot iron, gave an immediate result, and so was preferable for the planned mass processing of suspects. Those who failed the ordeal were, according to the Assize of Northampton, to lose a foot and their right hand, the latter an addition to the punishment specified at Clarendon. The use of mutilation rather than the death penalty seems peculiar in measures aimed at ridding the country of felons. Conceivably, there existed a sense that the death penalty was not as appropriate in the new procedures as in an appeal, where the accuser had risked his own life in combat. Nevertheless, following present-ment, even success in ordeal was not final. Men of particular ill-repute, or presented for 'murder or some other base felony' had to 'abjure' the realm, that is leave England under oath never to return.[71] The penalization of the notorious even if they passed the ordeal was not unique to the Angevin Assizes, but its use does emphasize royal single-mindedness.

Late twelfth- and early thirteenth-century records allow us to see these and related procedures in action, with modifications such as the appearance of coroners. As with appeal, the difficulty was actually laying hands on the offenders. Swift action was necessary before they fled.[72] Those men of ill-repute who were taken in possession of stolen goods, and were unable to produce a 'warrantor' who had given the goods to them, were not even allowed the benefit of ordeal.[73] Those found guilty at a coroner's inquest into a death, if present, were arrested and given to the sheriff to be kept in the county gaol. In cases other than homicide, those notorious were attached by sureties 'to the first session of the king's justices when they come to these parts', the sureties being amerced if the accused failed to appear.

71. Assize of Clarendon, c. 14, Northampton, c. 1, *EHD*, ii nos 24–5. On procedure, Hyams, 'Ordeal', 121–4, esp. p. 123 n. 184 on ordeal by water, which may also have been selected because of its association with lowly status; Bartlett, *Trial*, pp. 62–9, esp. pp. 67–9 on exile for those who passed ordeal.
72. For flight, see e.g. *PKJ*, ii no. 51, iii no. 715.
73. Assize of Clarendon, c. 12, *EHD*, ii no. 24.

At the arrival of the eyre, the coroners' rolls were produced and it was the sheriff and the coroners' responsibility to ensure the presence of those who had been attached.[74] Those whose names were presented and who were actually in court or could be arrested might be sent to ordeal immediately or have their cases further investigated. According to *Glanvill,* in cases based on public notoriety,

> the truth of the matter shall be investigated by many and varied inquests and interrogations before the justices, and arrived at by considering the probable facts and possible conjectures both for and against the accused, who must as a result be either absolved entirely or made to purge himself by the ordeal.[75]

The justices' main helpers in their enquiries were men of the locality, again showing the characteristic reliance of Angevin reform upon the harnessing of local power and personnel. In particular there were the juries of the hundreds and villages who had made the original presentments. The rolls often make a distinction between the communal accusation and the further opinion given by the jurors as their own: they stated whether they suspected the accused, and if so the accused was to go to ordeal.[76] The jurors thus sifted the accusations brought by communal opinion. Their judgment might be based on a fact which they believed to show the accused's guilt, or – and generally only in cases where no such fact was available – by obtaining an additional opinion from the jurors of the four neighbouring villages.[77] Thus presenting juries had a

74. See *Wiltshire*, pp. 46–51.
75. *Glanvill,* xiv 1, Hall, p. 171.
76. See R. D. Groot, 'The jury of presentment before 1215', *American Journal of Legal History* 26 (1982), 1–24, who notes that the pattern is not true of all rolls. See also e.g. *Lincs.*, nos 1488, 1496. They were not amerced if their own opinion contradicted the communal one which they had presented.
77. E.g. *Lincs.*, no. 588d (translated p. li, and note also the other cases cited at p. lii). Occasionally we see the presenting jury being overruled, for example by the knights of the shire; e.g. F. W. Maitland, ed., *The Rolls of the King's Court in the Reign of Richard I* (PRS, 14, 1891), p. 86; see also e.g. *PKJ*, ii no. 621.

certain adjudicatory function even before ordeal was abolished in England early in Henry III's minority in accordance with a decree of the 1215 Fourth Lateran Council. With the removal of ordeal, the jurors' decision as to whether they trusted or suspected the accused grew very close to a 'not guilty' or 'guilty' verdict. The criminal trial jury, now one of the most widely recognized characteristics of common law, was emerging.[78]

As for punishment, perhaps as the initial sweeps of the countryside proved to be of limited success, or as presentment was fully accepted, there came to be a greater emphasis upon the death penalty. Although he does not specify whether his concern is appeals, presentments, or both, it is notable that Ralph Diceto in his account of 1179 recorded that homicides were to be hanged, those guilty of lesser crimes mutilated. *Glanvill* confirms the general applicability of such penalties, writing that 'if the ordeal convicts [the felon] . . . then judgment both as to his life and as to his limbs depends on royal clemency'.[79] Mere mutilation could thus be presented as merciful.

Within these procedures, as in appeals, royal justices provided pressure for a common law. Some made general statements of law in court.[80] They could also insist that a court follow what the justices regarded as the custom of the king's court. And cases heard in the localities might be referred to royal courts after claims of default of justice.[81] The exceptional nature of border regions and the rare highly privileged areas became ever clearer as royal procedures brought greater standardization to law and the administration of justice.[82]

Comparison with royal action elsewhere in twelfth-century Europe is also revealing. First, take an admittedly

78. See also above, pp. 170–2 on inquests and the pleading of exceptions. On the abolition of ordeal, see Bartlett, *Trial*, pp. 137–9; note also *Wiltshire*, pp. 51–3.

79. Ralph of Diceto, *Opera Historica*, ed. W. Stubbs (2 vols, London, 1876), i 434, *Glanvill*, xiv 1, Hall p. 171.

80. See e.g. *Lincs.*, p. xxiii.

81. See also above, p. 51.

82. See e.g. *Borough Customs*, i 30, emphasizing compensation for homicide in Archenfield (Herefordshire), an area of Welsh law; also Holt, *Magna Carta*, p. 332 n. 167 on a limitation of amercement in Westmoreland.

rather exceptional but still highly revealing statement in Frederick Barbarossa's 1186 edict against fire-raisers:

> c. 1.16 If an arsonist in his flight comes to a castle and the lord of the castle happens to be his lord or vassal or relative, then he need not hand him over to his pursuers, but will help him to leave the castle for the forest or some other place that he deems safe. But if he is neither his lord, vassal nor relative, he should hand him over to the pursuers or he will be guilty of the same crime.

Now compare particularly the first part of the above statement with clause 11 of the Assize of Clarendon:

> And let there be no one in a city or a borough or a castle or without it, not even in the honour of Wallingford, who shall forbid the sheriffs to enter into his land or his soke to arrest those who have been accused or are notoriously suspect of being robbers or murderers or thieves or receivers of them, or outlaws, or persons charged concerning the forest; but the king commands that they shall aid the sheriffs to capture them.[83]

Such a contrast again brings home the degree of control to which the Angevin reformers were aspiring.

. . .

THE LIMITS OF ROYAL AUTHORITY

Clearly then, there was considerable aspiration and considerable pressure towards greater royal control, greater standardization, greater efficiency. But how effective were such royal measures, and, indeed, the whole system of dealing with offences? We know that hundreds of people either fled or went to ordeal after the Assizes of Clarendon and Northampton. However, the surviving records, which are financial and interested only in the accused's forfeited chattels, do not differentiate between those who were tried and those who fled. The success of the Assizes in ridding the country of criminals – as opposed to filling it with outlaws – cannot be assessed.

---

83. *Monumenta Germaniae Historica: Legum*, sectio iv, *Constitutiones*, t. 1, 451; *EHD*, ii no. 24. See also M. T. Clanchy, *England and its Rulers, 1066–1272* (Oxford, 1983), pp. 144–5.

Nevertheless, in our discussion, the limitations of royal capacity to deal with crime have been very clear. This applies not only to the many lesser offences which were left to local or seignorial courts but also to the select serious offences which were the royal target.[84] There may have been a mass of corruption amongst powerful local officials, such as Edward I's hundred roll enquiries would reveal a century later; it might take the form of bribes received from offenders seeking to escape the consequences of their deeds or, as in the case of Ailward, from accusers wishing to inflate their charges.[85] The other major problems were ensuring that appellors pursued their appeals and getting the accused, be he appealed or presented, into court. Only very rarely was a suspect taken and persuaded to confess:

> Richard Francus, the sergeant of the hundred, with the hundred, bears witness that in the hundred court, called together about this, and before him and the hundred, Peter acknowledged that they made the wound whence Reginald died, and he said that in three days he was willing to be hanged himself should Reginald die of that wound. By the assize, let Peter be hanged for his admission and let Walter and Maud purge themselves by the judgment of iron.[86]

Even once captured, criminals sometimes escaped the clutches of local officials.[87] Very few cases reached court. Of those that did, many were then compromised or quashed by the justices, perhaps because only those accused who were confident of a reasonable settlement actually appeared. Ordeals, duels and executions were few; if Ralph Basset really did hang forty-four thieves at 'Hundehoge' in 1124, his was a success of which his Angevin and later medieval successors would be jealous.[88]

Besides its limited efficiency, there are further reasons for rejecting any view of the extension of royal justice as an

---

84. On sheriffs and theft, see above, p. 163; on the 'sheriff's peace', see *Lincs.*, p. l.
85. See above, p. 160; for the later thirteenth century, see H. M. Cam, *The Hundred and the Hundred Rolls* (London, 1930).
86. *PKJ*, ii no. 732.
87. E.g. *Lincs.*, nos 986, 1011.
88. See above, p. 78; also *Lincs.*, pp. li–lii, lx; for mid-thirteenth century figures, see e.g. *Wiltshire*, pp. 79, 98ff., *Surrey*, p. 128.

utterly overwhelming tide. There are signs of resistance, leading sometimes to compromise, sometimes to defeat for the royal efforts. Henry II clearly wished serious crime to be prosecuted as vigorously as possible. However, in the case of homicide, there are hints that he faced some obstruction from the families who dropped their appeals when they settled out of court. They sought to protect themselves against any possible limitation of their freedom for self-help, whether aimed at revenge or at settlement. If the eyre brought a more impersonal element to the doing of justice, it may not have been at the desire of the parties in disputes; hence the prevalence of uncompleted appeals.[89]

Moreover, the reforms set under way at Clarendon had only a limited impact upon baronial franchises and regional variations. Border areas were not brought under frankpledge and preserved their own methods of peace-keeping. Nor is there any indication, for example, as to whether Henry or his advisers ever expected the Assizes of Clarendon and Northampton to apply in Cheshire. Henry promised the bishop of Durham that the enforcement of the new procedures in his lands was from necessity and would not form a custom. At the end of the century, Jocelin of Brakelond's chronicle provides much evidence for the jealousy with which privileged lords sought to protect their rights.[90]

The continuing exercise in particular of minor franchisal jurisdiction, most notably the right to execute thieves caught red-handed, no doubt reflects royal acceptance of the fact that this remained by far the most effective way of dealing with crime.[91] Lords remained an essential part of the Angevin regime, alongside the king and his officials. However, ambiguity in attitude to lords' continuing role

89. See Hurnard, *Pardon.*
90. G. V. Scammell, *Hugh du Puiset, Bishop of Durham* (Cambridge, 1956), ch. 5, esp. pp. 190–1; Jocelin, pp. 50–3, noting the combination of royal involvement and forceful self-help, 100, 102, 134–5; see also p. 45 for the abbot arranging a compromise settlement following a complaint of rape. See in general N. D. Hurnard, 'The Anglo-Norman franchises', *EHR* 64 (1949), 289–323, 433–60.
91. For infangentheof in Henry III's reign, see e.g. the Tewkesbury annals in H. R. Luard, ed., *Annales Monastici* (5 vols, London, 1864–9), i 130, 140, 144–5.

may also reflect some divergence in the views of the king and certain of his administrators. The latter sought to promote standardization, at the expense, if necessary, of seignorial power. The king, on the other hand, does not seem to have personally opposed franchises in general, and indeed granted them himself. The administrators therefore lacked the personal backing of the king which they would have needed if they were to take on seignorial interests.

Yet the most emphatic reverse to royal efforts came in an area where advisers and king were united in their desire for greater uniformity of procedure, that is in their attempt to bring clerical crime under royal control. We can be certain that Henry did not intend the clergy to be excluded from his clamp-down on crime. Yet his efforts to deal with clerical wrongdoing through the royal courts quickly became central to his dispute with Thomas Becket.[92] Canon law did not provide a definitive answer to the question, but the martyrdom of Becket, together with a hardening of papal attitude, did. Following the negotiations of the early 1170s, a settlement is recorded in a memorandum sent by the king to the pope, and recorded by the chronicler Ralph Diceto: 'a clerk shall not be brought in person before a secular judge for any crime, nor for any wrong, except wrongs of my forest, and except about a lay fee from which lay service is owed to me or another secular lord.'[93] Certainly, clerics still had to prove their ecclesiastical status before they enjoyed the benefit of being handed over to church courts; certainly, if a cleric fled before making his proof of status, he could be outlawed like any other fugitive; and certainly, early in the thirteenth century there are cases of criminous clerks having to abjure the realm. Yet still Henry's efforts had failed. The court rolls reveal clerics committing serious crimes and being handed over to the church courts.[94] Particularly notable are certain cases where clerics joined with laymen in committing crimes. As was so often the case, the laymen fled; however, the clerics stayed to face justice.[95] Royal punishment could not strike into them the fear that drove away their lay accomplices.

92. See above, p. 129–30.
93. Diceto, i 410.
94. E.g. *PKJ*, ii no. 311.
95. E.g. *PKJ*, ii nos 321, 322.

. . .

CONCLUSIONS

The limits of royal power, and more generally of methods of dealing with crime, are therefore very clear. However, our awareness of such inefficiencies, and of disparities between royal aspirations and achievements, is undoubtedly greater than that of people at the time. The system could satisfy the interests of the various parties.[96] From the royal point of view, the eyre maintained a check on the local workings of justice, ensuring that there was no politically significant breakdown of order. Later visitations sustained the efforts begun at Clarendon and Northampton.[97] The eyre also collected useful revenue for the king, for example the forfeited chattels of felons and a wide range of amercements. Furthermore, the king and his advisers may have been aware that the very possibility of royally enforced justice and punishment encouraged parties to come to settlements, whether within or outside court. The same possibility of settlements must have been desirable both to appellor and to appellee. One can imagine instances, indeed, where an appeal might be brought collusively, and then withdrawn or concorded, in order to clear the appellee's name following local rumour. Alternatively, parties could fight their feuds in part at least through the royal courts.[98] Finally, from the point of view of the local community, the system generally succeeded in ridding them of disruptive criminals, usually because they fled, occasionally because they were punished.

Moreover, contemporary perceptions were probably determined not so much by continuing inefficiencies but by the impact of innovations and the displays of justice when it was applied. The realm's rulers – kings, administrators, and lords – strove hard to maintain respect and, indeed, awe for criminal justice. The royal right of

96. Summerson, 'Maitland', independently comes to similar conclusions for a slightly later period.
97. Pipe Rolls figures might suggest that 1166 and 1176 marked not so much the beginning of a royal clamp-down but its peak; however, this stems from changes in the form of Pipe Roll entries, as can be shown by comparison with eyre rolls.
98. See e.g. *Lincs.*, no. 931, *PKJ*, ii no. 736.

pardoning could both ensure royal popularity and reinforce the impression that the king was the fount of all justice.[99] Other measures encouraged fear. The fate of those who were caught might be advertised. Following their inquests into the deaths of the small proportion of outlaws who had been pursued and beheaded, the coroners might send the outlaws' heads to the county gaol where, presumably, they were displayed.[100] Mutilation left a shameful mark upon a criminal, and one that announced the ferocity of royal justice.[101] We have also seen the publicly humiliating and potentially fatal use of the pillory. Likewise, although we must not underestimate the spectator appeal of an execution, one of the many interesting features of Ailward's case was that a crowd might be *compelled* to attend a punishment session, an act reminiscent of many an authoritarian regime.[102]

Let us end, then, with another story drawn from a collection of miracles, which well illustrates the fear, indeed the paranoia, caused by the intrusions of Angevin justice into the localities:

> By royal command, men who had committed homicide, theft, and the like were traced in the various provinces, arrested and brought before judges and royal officers at St Edmunds and put in jail, where, to avoid their liberation by some ruse, their names were entered on three lists by command of the judges. Amongst them was one Robert, nicknamed the putrid, a shoemaker from Banham, who was certain that he saw and heard himself put on the list. In the midst of his prayers, afflictions, tears and devotions he made a vow to God and St Edmund that if he saved him from this peril he would give him the best of his four oxen. At daybreak, when they were taken out and their names checked against the written list, for them to be purged by the ordeal of water, the name of Robert was found in none. Pleased and full of joy he returned home and, not forgetting his vow, took the ox and offered it to God and St Edmund with great devotion. . . .[103]

99. Hurnard, *Pardon*, ch. 9.
100. Hunnisett, *Coroner*, p. 34; *PR7RI*, p. 9.
101. See Summerson, 'Maitland', p. 138.
102. See above, pp. 125, 139, 160.
103. *Lawsuits*, no. 501.

ALWAYS

Evelyn Tanner

AS A CHILD, I WAS ALWAYS RELUCTANT TO GO TO BED, SO MY father would tell me stories. When he got tired of coming up with new stories every night, he began to record the stories on tape, so I could listen to them in the future. And I did listen to them, endlessly, until it was not so much about the words as the sound, which filled the awful, infinite silence of my bedroom. The tape that touched me the most was filled not with stories, but with songs—all sung by my dad. I did not play it often, for it was very old, and somehow, not as comforting as the others.

There were several songs that I was obsessed with, especially as I got older. One of these songs was "Show Me the Way to Go Home." Whether through a fault in my memory or my dad's—or an embellishment on his part—I recall the song including a line that does not appear in the standard version: "You can always go home." Even as a child, I thought there was something vaguely forced about that line, but I believed it, with the desperation of one who cannot afford to believe otherwise.

Chapter 7

LAW AND LAND-HOLDING IN ANGEVIN ENGLAND

Whilst Henry II's own primary concern was the maintenance of peace and the punishment of crime, new procedures concerning land cases also featured prominently in the Angevin reforms. These developments had an impact not just upon the conduct of cases in court but also the enabling and preventative functions of law, and upon security of tenure, heritability, and alienability. However, it is vital to remember that the changes in land law in the Angevin period were not merely caused by the reforms. Some influences, such as the learned law notions of *possessio* and *proprietas*, worked both through and independently of the reforms. Moreover, the various longer-term causes which had been securing the position of the tenant and his heirs by 1135 continued to work throughout our period.[1]

As with crime, the circumstances in which many cases arose remained similar to the earlier twelfth century. Matters of honour and vengeance still lie hidden beneath some lawsuits.[2] Family disputes were frequent, as were ones over particularly valuable economic resources, such as meadows and mills.[3] From *c.* 1180, inflation – as far as it was perceptible – may have made lords expend still greater efforts in ensuring that grants for life or shorter periods returned to them as due. Control of officials was vital to a

1. See above, pp. 103–5, 150, and below, pp. 212–13. See above p. 90 for my concentration upon land-holding in the higher levels of society.
2. Note e.g. C. T. Flower, *Introduction to the Curia Regis Rolls* (Selden Soc., 62, 1944), pp. 298–9.
3. E.g. *CRR*, vi 81–2, *Lincs.*, no. 394, and see below, pp. 194, 198.

lord's success, and issues arising therefrom also resulted in court cases.[4] Political disruption, such as that during Stephen's reign or John's attempted usurpation of power in the early 1190s, also produced rashes of disputes.[5] To obtain a more concrete impression, let us look in detail at the activities and concerns of one lord, passed down to us by the chronicler, Jocelin of Brakelond.

. . .

ABBOT SAMSON OF BURY ST EDMUNDS

Jocelin saw the quality of the lord as vital to the control of the abbey's estates. The ageing Abbot Hugh

> was pious and kindly, a strict monk and good, but in the business of this world neither good nor wise. . . . The villages of the abbot and all the hundreds were given out to farm; the woods were destroyed, the houses of the manors threatened with ruin, and from day to day all went from bad to worse.[6]

In contrast is his description of Samson's acts on becoming abbot. Samson took the homage of his men. He asserted his control over the officials who would serve him. Meeting resistance to his demand for an aid, he made his displeasure known:

> he was angry and said to his friends that, if he lived, he would render them like for like, and trouble for trouble. After this the abbot caused an enquiry to be made as to the annual rents due from the free men in each manor and as to the names of the peasants and their holdings and the services due from each; and he had them all set down in writing.

He also repaired, restocked, and extended the abbey's estates, appointed new officials, and produced a mass of new records of his abbey's rights. Samson's lordship was

4. E.g. *CRR*, i 109, H. Thomas, *Vassals, Heiresses, Crusaders, and Thugs* (Philadelphia, PA, 1993), p. 63.
5. See e.g. *Rotuli Curiae Regis*, i 39–41, 47. For a case arising partly from the division of England from Normandy, *CRR*, vi 81–2.
6. H. E. Butler, ed. and trans., *The Chronicle of Jocelin of Brakelond* (Edinburgh, 1949), p. 1; note also p. 38 on the number of seals having got out of hand.

active and very personal. When necessary he resorted to vigorous self-help, but he could also act with a good lord's generosity when compromise was desirable.[7]

As a lord, Samson heard cases in his honorial court, in this instance a court reinforced by the liberties of St Edmund. On one occasion, the justiciar Ranulf de Glanville allowed a recognition, which had been summoned to be made by twelve knights in the king's court, to be held in the abbot's court at Harlow.[8] Jocelin commented upon the rigour of Samson's judgments, but these could still be swayed by personal considerations, for example the abbot's memory of hospitality he had received.[9]

In dealing with worldly business, Samson was regarded as rather unwilling to take counsel. However, from the start he had at least one special adviser. Having rejected the requests of his kinsmen to be taken into his service, he made one exception: 'one knight he kept with him, an eloquent man and skilled in the law.' Similarly, when he became a papal judge delegate, he both began to study canon law and took counsel from two clerks experienced in law. In 1194 Samson was sufficiently trusted in legal matters for him to act as an itinerant justice.[10]

So much for the nature of Samson's lordship; what more can be said of his major concerns? He strove to control his rights in his liberty, his markets and their tolls, and advowsons.[11] Most obviously he strove to control his estates and tenants. Again, a particular concern was that estates leased out for limited periods might become hereditary. This is epitomized in the Cockfield case. The Cockfield family had gradually assembled various lands and rights, held from the abbey.

> On the death of Robert of Cockfield [in *c.* 1191], his son Adam came and with him his kinsfolk, Earl Roger Bigod and many other great men, soliciting the abbot concerning the

7. E.g. ibid., pp. 27–9, 31–2, 50–3, 59–60. See also pp. 63, 120 for further record-making.
8. Ibid., p. 62.
9. See e.g. ibid., pp. 44–5.
10. Ibid., pp. 26–7, 24; *PKJ*, iii p. xcviii.
11. Jocelin, pp. 50–3, 59ff., 75, 95, 132–4; also p. 5 for concern about the papal legate.

holdings of the said Adam and more especially concerning the holding of the half-hundred of Cosford, on the grounds that it was his by hereditary right; for they said that his father and grandfather had held it for eighty years past and more. But the abbot, when he got a chance to speak, put two fingers against his two eyes and said 'May I lose these eyes on that day and in that hour, when I grant any hundred to be held by hereditary right, unless the king, who has power to take away my abbey and my life, should force me to do so.'

He explained that such a grant might imperil the abbey's liberty, and that anyway Robert had never claimed the hundred hereditarily. As a result of Samson's stout resistance, according to Jocelin, Adam renounced his right in the hundred, and received estates at Semer and Groton for life. This settlement made no mention of Cockfield.

Both Jocelin and the royal pleas rolls record the next dispute, in 1201.[12] When Adam died, he left a three-month-old daughter as his heiress. After a struggle, the wardship passed through the hands of Hubert Walter to Thomas Burgh, brother of the king's chamberlain. Thomas then sought seisin of Cockfield, Semer, and Groton, but the abbot refused, on the grounds that Robert of Cockfield on his death-bed had publicly declared that he had no hereditary right in Semer or Groton, and that Adam in full court had reconsigned those two manors to the abbey, confirming this with a charter. According to Jocelin,

Thomas therefore demanded a writ of recognition in this matter and caused knights to be summoned to come to Tewkesbury and to swear before the king. Our charter was read in public, but in vain, since the whole court was against us. The knights having been sworn said that they knew nothing about our charter or our private agreements, but that they believed that Adam, his father, and his grandfather had for a hundred years back held the manors in fee farm, one after the other, on the days on which they were alive and dead; and thus by the judgment of the court after much labour and much expense we were disseised, save for the payment of the annual rents as of old.

12. Ibid., pp. 58–9, 97–8, 123–4, 138–9; *CRR*, i 430; J. C. Holt, 'Feudal society and the family in early medieval England. (ii) Notions of patrimony', *TRHS* 5th Ser. 33 (1983), 193–8.

The plea roll records that an assize of *mort d'ancestor* came to recognize whether on the day he died Adam had been seised in demesne as of fee farm of the manors of Cockfield, Semer, and Groton, and whether Margaret was his closest heir. The abbot argued that the assize should not proceed about Semer and Groton as Adam's father Robert had held them only for life and had admitted so at the time of the Saladin Tithe (1188) and on his death-bed. Samson also produced a cirograph stating that the subsequent grant to Adam had only been for life. Samson admitted that Robert had said Cockfield was his right and his inheritance. The roll goes on to state that

> It is decided that the assize proceed about the aforesaid two manors and that Margaret have her seisin of Cockfield. The jurors say that Adam father of the said Robert held the said two manors for a long time, well, and in peace, and died thus, and that after him Robert his son held for all his life, and Adam his son, father of Margaret, held them in the same way until his death and he died holding them. But they know well and because of the long tenure of the aforesaid they believe that Adam died seised thereof as of fee farm. And they say that Margaret is his closest heir. Judgment. It is decided that Margaret have her seisin thence; and the abbot is in mercy.

Various points are notable here. There are the differences between the two records. The plea roll omits an initial stage, where Thomas asked the abbot for seisin. It makes the proceedings sound as if they progressed very formally, in set stages; the chronicler is more concerned with the court's bias against the abbot and his church. Despite such differences, significant points of procedure and substance emerge. The abbot pleads an exception, a reason why the assize should not proceed: the land is not hereditary. It is rejected, and indeed Samson's acceptance that Cockfield might have been held by hereditary right led to Margaret being placed in seisin without more ado. Documentary proof was not decisive, and according to Jocelin was rather contemptuously dismissed.[13] The jurors had their own ideas

13. There may have been a technical reason for the rejection of documentary evidence; that Margaret was a minor, and a rule perhaps already existed against minors having to answer deeds produced against them in court. (I owe this point to Paul Brand.)

of proper proof, and so in the case of Semer and Groton, long tenure was taken to constitute hereditary right.

Control of services was also of great concern to Samson, and he risked entering a dispute with his whole body of knights.

> He put to them that they ought to do him full service of fifty knights in respect of scutages, aids, and the like, since, as he said, they held that many knights' fees; why should ten of those fifty knights do no service, or for what reason and by whose authority should those forty receive the service of ten knights. They all replied with one voice that it had always been the custom for ten of them to help the forty, and they neither would nor ought to answer nor enter into a plea on this matter.

The case came to the king's court, whereupon the knights employed delaying tactics. Eventually, the support of the justiciar broke the deadlock in the abbot's favour, for the justiciar stated 'in full council that every knight ought to speak for himself and for his own holding'. Gradually, the knights admitted the service they owed, with the exception of castle-guard at Norwich.

> And because their acknowledgement of this in the court of St Edmund was not sufficient, the abbot took them all to London at his own expense and their wives and those women who were heiresses of lands, to make their acknowledgement in the king's court. And each of them received separate cirographs. ... Aubrey de Ver was the last who resisted the abbot, but the abbot seized and sold his beasts, so that he was forced to come to court and answer like his peers. After taking counsel, he finally acknowledged the right of St Edmund and the abbot.[14]

Despite Samson's emphasis upon the preservation of Bury's liberties, the king was not entirely excluded from its affairs.[15] The abbot looked to royal help in disputes over rights to tolls and markets and in trying to prevent a hereditary claim to the stewardship of the abbey. The abbot

14. Jocelin, pp. 65–7.
15. See ibid., p. 3 for the king becoming involved because of rumours of Abbot Hugh's ill-management; also pp. 46, 105.

also obtained a royal writ in his attempt to obtain the knight service which the king was insisting that the abbey provide for his campaigns overseas, although it is notable that Samson ended up by reaching a compromise with his knights.[16]

Not just the king personally but also the Angevin reforms more generally affected Bury and its affairs. This is most striking in a dispute where the convent of Bury asked Abbot Samson to disseise the townsmen of some holdings. Samson replied that he desired to do the convent justice in so far as he could,

> but that he was bound to proceed in accordance with the law [*ordine justiciario*], and that without a judgment of the court he could not disseise his free men of their lands or revenues which, justly or unjustly, they had held for a number of years; if he did so disseise them, he would fall under the king's mercy by the assize of the realm.

As in the Cockfield case, we see a combination of the old and the new. Long tenure greatly strengthened the tenant's position, whilst the impact of new royal measures, notably novel disseisin, is clear both in settling disputes and in shaping men's thinking.[17]

. . .

NEW PROCEDURES

Chapter 5 identified as key characteristics of the Angevin reforms their regularity and their use of replicable forms, most notably the eyre, the assize and the jury, and the returnable writ. The connection between writs and royal control was close. By *Glanvill*'s time, it was a maxim that, according to the custom of the realm, no one need answer in their lord's court concerning their free tenement without a royal writ. This rule was most likely of customary origin, although its development may have been affected, for example, by royal rulings that disseisins during the king's absence abroad were only permissible by royal writ.[18]

16. Ibid., pp. 27, 75, 85–7, 132–4.
17. Ibid., p. 78; see also below, p. 213.
18. *Glanvill*, xii 2, 25, Hall, pp. 137, 148 the former specifying the lord's

I shall concentrate upon three key procedures begun by royal writs, those of novel disseisin, of *mort d'ancestor*, and of right. The eyre was the main forum for such cases, and eyre records give an indication of their relative frequency.

	Novel disseisin	*Mort d'ancestor*	Actions of right for lands
1198 Herts., Essex, Middlesex	19	35	13
1202 Bedfordshire	11	37	8
1227 Buckinghamshire	89	87	62 [19]

(i) Novel disseisin

Novel disseisin became the predominant land action in the thirteenth century and its popularity is attested in the earliest plea rolls by its use concerning small plots of land.[20] It is also the assize most closely related to Henry and his advisers' desire to maintain peace in the realm. According to *Glanvill*, 'the defeated party, whether he be the appellor or the appellee, is always in the lord king's mercy on account of violent disseisin'.[21] Novel disseisin focused on the actions and antagonism of the two parties. It could be brought only against the disseisor, not his heir. The disseisee was said to be complaining of the disseisin, rather than seeking his land as in *mort d'ancestor*.[22] Some

---

court. See J. Biancalana, 'For want of justice: legal reforms of Henry II', *Columbia Law Review* 88 (1988), 448–9 n. 56; Milsom, *Legal Framework*, pp. 57–64; Hudson, *Land, Law, and Lordship*, pp. 255–6 n. 6 includes further refs.

19. D. W. Sutherland, *The Assize of Novel Disseisin* (Oxford, 1973), p. 43. On other actions, see e.g. Pollock and Maitland; W. L. Warren, *Henry II* (London, 1973), ch. 9; *Lincs.*, pp. lxxv–vi.

20. Sutherland, *Novel Disseisin*, p. 48; note that whereas initially the assize dealt only with recent disseisins, particularly in the later years of John's reign the time limit was extended, allowing ever-older disputes to be heard; ibid., pp. 55–6. The following account rests initially on ibid., esp. pp. 64ff., which in turn draws largely upon *Bracton*.

21. *Glanvill*, xiii 38, Hall, p. 170; on which see Sutherland, *Novel Disseisin*, p. 27 n. 2.

22. But see e.g. *Rotuli Curiae Regis*, i 48 for use of the word 'seeking'.

amercements for disseisin were very heavy.[23] However, novel disseisin was not merely a police measure, but was important within the whole range of land actions. It ensured that a claimant could not simply seize the disputed land and then enjoy it throughout the lengthy process of establishing the greater right, or even argue that being in seisin backed up his claim.[24]

Few recorded cases explain their underlying origins. Some complaints were against lords, oppressing their vassals or simply enforcing their rights – the difference may often have been in the eye of the beholder. Alternatively, a lord, having received new estates, was over-enthusiastic in dispossessing sitting tenants if they did not submit immediately.[25] Another significant set of cases concerned nuisances, for example the raising of mill-ponds to the detriment of another's mill. A series of such disputes might occur, amounting to a minor feud.[26]

Feeling that a disseisin had occurred, the plaintiff generally went to the chancery and purchased a writ:

The king to the sheriff, greeting. N. has complained to me that R. unjustly and without a judgment disseised him of his free tenement in such-and-such a place since my last voyage to Normandy. Therefore I command you that, if N. gives you security for prosecuting his claim, you are to see that the chattels which were taken from the tenement are restored to it, and that the tenement and the chattels remain in peace until the Sunday after Easter. And meanwhile you are to see that the tenement is viewed by twelve free and lawful men of the neighbourhood, and their names endorsed on this writ. And summon them by good summoners to be before me or my justices on the Sunday after Easter, ready to make the recognition. And summon R., or his bailiff if he himself cannot be found, on the security of gage and reliable sureties to be there then to hear the recognition. And have there the

23. Sutherland, *Novel Disseisin*, p. 27.
24. On awareness of the practical advantage of being in seisin, see Jocelin, pp. 50–1.
25. See e.g. *Rotuli Curiae Regis*, i 62–3; note also e.g. *Lincs.*, no. 477.
26. See e.g. *Lincs.*, nos 121, 140, 324, 341, 371, 413; J. S. Loengard, 'The Assize of Nuisance: origins of an action at Common Law', *Cambridge Law Journal* 37 (1978), 144–66; also Sutherland, *Novel Disseisin*, pp. 11–12; Flower, *Introduction*, pt. II ch. 18.

summoners, and this writ, and the names of the sureties. Witness, etc.[27]

Next, usually in the presence of the sheriff, the plaintiff had to nominate two sureties as security that he would prosecute his case; otherwise plaintiff and sureties would be amerced. Likewise, the sheriff, generally through one of his bailiffs, 'attached' the defendant or, failing him, his bailiff; that is, he had to provide two sureties that he would appear in court on the specified day. Failure to appear would lead to the sureties and the defendant being amerced. Meanwhile, the sheriff formally instructed his bailiff to empanel the necessary recognitors. The plaintiff and defendant were invited to this empanelling, and might challenge nominations. More than twelve recognitors might, therefore, be empanelled, to prepare for challenges or later essoins. The recognitors were assigned a day in court and then sent to view the land. In the presence, if he so wished, of the defendant or his bailiff, the plaintiff indicated to the recognitors the disputed land or the nuisance he claimed to have suffered.

Now came the day for appearance in court. According to *Glanvill*, 'No essoin is allowed in this recognition. Whether or not the disseisor comes on the first day, the assize shall proceed.' Default led to immediate loss of his plea. Similarly, the defendant was allowed no delay. If neither he nor his bailiff appeared, the assize gave its verdict in his absence. Only if too many recognitors essoined themselves was the case postponed, although even then the court would proceed as far as it could, short of a verdict.[28]

Even if both parties appeared, the assize might still not have to proceed. Of just over sixty cases decided before the 1202 Lincolnshire eyre, in four the parties were granted licence to agree and in another four the defendant admitted his wrongful deed. Plaintiffs too might not

27. *Glanvill*, xiii 33, see also e.g. 36 (nuisance), Hall, pp. 167–9. Sutherland, *Novel Disseisin*, pp. 64–5 notes that 'if the disseisin had been committed during a general eyre in the county, the justices in eyre could issue the original writ themselves'.
28. *Glanvill*, xiii 38, Hall, p. 169; *Lincs.*, no. 460; *Rotuli Curiae Regis*, ii 19–20. *PKJ*, iv 4051 shows the assize proceeding in the defendant's absence; the recognition found against him, and he was in mercy.

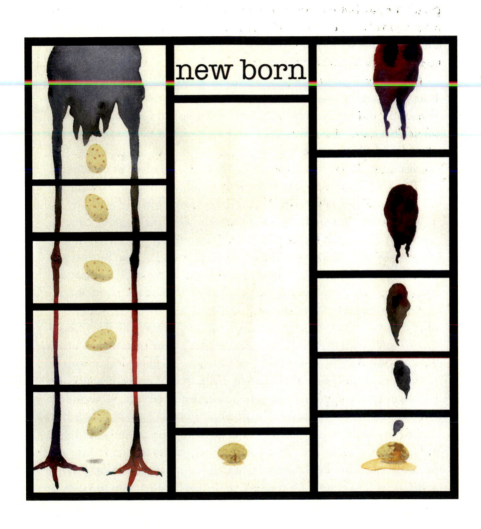

Newborn
Illustration by Ligang Luo

proceed; in six instances the case was not prosecuted, in another five the plaintiff retracted, in one more he is simply recorded as having placed himself in the king's mercy.[29] The majority of cases, however, did proceed with the assize. The writ makes it sound as if the assize was taken immediately the parties were in court. However, the plea rolls reveal that the alleged disseisor or his bailiff was asked whether he wished to say anything in his defence, and *Bracton* advised that justices should not rush the assize but should enquire into the case by a series of questions. The defendant might at this stage bring forward a technical objection to the complaint against him, for instance that the plaintiff was a married woman suing without her husband.[30] Alternatively, he might produce further evidence and arguments, for example that the plaintiff had given him the tenement, or that the disseisin was in fact by judgment, or that the plaintiff was a villein or the tenement not free.[31] As in the latter instances, such exceptions often admitted that the disseisin had taken place, but that the disseisor was acting within his rights. These pleadings might require further action, the proffer of a charter, the appearance of the suitors of the court which had adjudged the disseisin, or the production of the plaintiff's relatives to prove that he was a villein.[32] If such a pleading depended on a point of law, it could be decided by a ruling of the court. Much more often pleading turned on specific points of fact which led to a trial by jury. Sometimes a jury was then summoned, but on other occasions it was constituted by the existing recognitors being re-employed to try the special issue.[33]

---

29. *Lincs.*, nos 37, 84, 183, 423 license to agree; nos 51, 172, 410, 413 defendant admits wrong; nos 52, 252, 376, 403, 419, 420; 24, 34, 93, 311, 371; 368, plaintiffs not proceeding. Failing to proceed could again mean that an out-of-court settlement had been reached.
30. E.g. *CRR*, iii 345.
31. See e.g. *Lincs.*, nos 36, 251, 423. See also *PR16HII*, p. 149; Sutherland, *Novel Disseisin*, pp. 12, 19–20; Milsom, *Legal Framework*, p. 21.
32. E.g. D. M. Stenton, ed., *The Earliest Northamptonshire Assize Rolls, A.D. 1202 and 1203* (Northants. Record Soc., 5, 1930), no. 638; *CRR*, iii 126.
33. Such instances clarify the often confusing distinction in land cases between an *assize* and a trial *jury* in its stricter sense at this time. An assize (other than the Grand Assize) was summoned by the original

If the assize went ahead, the parties were given a final chance to challenge the recognitors. Next, the recognitors took their oath: 'Hear this, O justices, that I will speak the truth as to this assize and as to the tenements of which I have made the view by order of the king.' They then deliberated in a private place, before returning to give their verdict. Again the justices might give guidance, through a series of questions concerning the facts of the case and the recognitors' reasoning.[34]

According to *Glanvill*, 'In this recognition the party who has proved the recent disseisin can require that the sheriff be ordered to see that the chattels and produce, which have in the meantime been seized by the command of the lord king or his justices, are restored to him'.[35] From 1198 the procedure changed and instead of a restoration of produce and chattels, the assize was called upon to assess damages, the Lincolnshire eyre of 1202 recording amounts varying from four pence to twenty marks.[36] Finally, the judgment was carried out. If the complaint had been successful, the sheriff restored the plaintiff to seisin, with the recognitors pointing out where the relevant land was. The disseisor was amerced and from him the sheriff was entitled to an ox or the monetary equivalent.[37]

This need not, however, be the end of the matter. The losing party could challenge the assize's verdict. He could proceed by 'attaint', that is by obtaining – often at notable expense – a jury of twenty-four men who might convict the recognitors of having made a false oath. Or he might proceed by 'certification', that is by re-assembling the assize justices, the opponent, and generally the recognitors before another court, normally the king's. Either procedure might

---

writ, at the same time that the defendant was summoned, and before any pleading took place; a jury was summoned to answer a question raised in pleadings. See Pollock and Maitland, i 149.

34. *Bracton*, f. 185, Thorne, iii 72; Sutherland, *Novel Disseisin*, p. 73, although note that his earliest evidence comes from the 1220s.
35. *Glanvill*, xiii 38, Hall, p. 170.
36. E.g. *Lincs.*, nos 103, 409; Sutherland, *Novel Disseisin*, pp. 52–4. Flower, *Introduction*, pp. 473–9, assembles clues as to the relationship between damage and damages.
37. Note amercements for withdrawing or not pursuing complaint, e.g. *CRR*, iii 129, 137; *Lincs.*, nos 52, 252.

lead to the reversal of the judgment.[38] Alternatively, the defeated party might accept the assize's verdict but obtain a writ of right. Pleading in a case of 1212 is particularly revealing concerning such 'dual process':

> Herbert replied that he was not bound to answer . . . because he had obtained this land against Nicholas by judgment in the court of the lord king. Nicholas replied that he had only recovered seisin by writ of novel disseisin, and so he was nonetheless bound to answer him concerning right.

Thus dual process represents a practical manifestation of the distinction between seisin and right.[39]

(ii) Mort d'ancestor

We first learn of *mort d'ancestor* from the Assize of Northampton:

> If the lord of the fee denies to the heirs of the dead man the seisin of the deceased which they demand, the justices of the lord king are to make to be held concerning this a recognition by twelve lawful men as to what sort of seisin the deceased had thereto on the day on which he was alive and dead, and as it is recognized, so they are to make restitution to his heirs.[40]

Here the concern clearly is with the lord refusing seisin to the heirs. He might be trying to hold on to the land for himself, or a third party might have entered the land, either seised by the lord or at least having gained his recognition. Family gifts caused various problems, as did the succession of heiresses. Other disputes turned on the nature of the tenure, sometimes on whether the ancestor really had held in fee, most notably on whether the tenement was held in villeinage.[41]

---

38. Sutherland, *Novel Disseisin*, pp. 74–5; *Lincs.*, no. 120; cf. *Lawsuits*, no. 650. Note, however, that *Glanvill* is silent on these points.
39. *CRR*, vi 291; note also e.g. PRS, ns 31 (1957), p. 106; see above, p. 150.
40. *EHD*, ii no. 25, c. 4.
41. See *Lincs.*, nos 155, 414, 416, Milsom, *Legal Framework*, p. 167, Biancalana, 'Legal reforms of Henry II', 509.

Quite possibly from its creation, the assize was of limited scope. The plaintiff and the current tenant must not be kin, a point on which a significant number of claims fell.[42] Moreover, the assize was available only to those relatives of the deceased tenant whose claims to succeed were generally accepted: sons, daughters, brothers, sisters, nephews, nieces.[43] If such close heirs had been excluded from their inheritances it was very hard to deny that there had been a default of justice which justified a remedy in the king's court. Also, in such cases, a group of neighbours was likely to know who was the closest heir. It is notable that the scope of the assize was not extended, only in Henry III's reign being supplemented by the actions of aiel, besaiel and cosinage. These were available against more distant relatives, and *Bracton* noted that some lords objected that their jurisdiction was being infringed.[44]

In *mort d'ancestor*, the plaintiff obtained a royal writ which he took to the sheriff:

> The king to the sheriff, greeting. If G. son of O. gives you security for prosecuting his claim, then summon by good summoners twelve free and lawful men from the neighbourhood of such-and-such a place to be before me or my justices on a certain day, ready to declare on oath whether O. the father of the aforesaid G. was seised in his demesne as of his fee of one virgate of land in that place on the day he died, whether he died after my first coronation, and whether the said G. is his closest heir. And meanwhile let them view the land; and you are to see that their names are endorsed on this writ. And summon by good summoners R., who holds that land, to be there then to hear the recognition. And have there the summoners and this writ.[45]

As in novel disseisin, the plaintiff had to give security that he would pursue his case, and the disputants were

---

42. Flower, *Introduction*, pp. 153–4; *Lincs.*, p. lxxiv, noting that this limitation was apparently poorly understood.

43. Biancalana, 'Legal reforms of Henry II', 486, 508; Hudson, *Land, Law, and Lordship*, p. 114 n. 26.

44. F. W. Maitland, *The Forms of Action at Common Law* (Cambridge, 1936), p. 25; F. W. Maitland, ed., *Bracton's Note Book* (3 vols, London, 1887), pl. 1215, *Bracton*, f. 281, Thorne, iii 318.

45. *Glanvill*, xiii 3, Hall, p. 150.

summoned to be present at the selection of recognitors. These then made the view of the tenement. However, unlike in novel disseisin, the tenant was allowed two essoins; if he failed to appear on the third day, the assize proceeded without him.[46] If both parties were present in court, the tenant might vouch a warrantor.[47] If not, he was then asked 'whether he wishes to show cause why the assize should not proceed'. He might put forward various exceptions, based on technical objections to the writ or on the facts of the particular case.[48] The latter might be that the plaintiff had been in seisin and then 'sold or given as a gift or quitclaimed or in some other lawful way alienated the tenement to him', or that the plaintiff was illegitimate or a villein. Unless the plaintiff simply admitted his exception, the defendant had to ask for a jury decision, or – in the case of alleged conveyances – offer proof by battle. If no exception was pleaded, 'the recognition shall proceed in the presence of both parties and by the oath of the twelve recognitors, according to whose verdict seisin shall be adjudged to one or other of the parties'. If the case ended in the demandant's favour, another writ ordered that the sheriff deliver him seisin, and he was also to recover seisin of everything found on that fee at the time when seisin was delivered.[49] Again the writ of right was available to defeated parties.

Glanvill classified *mort d'ancestor* and novel disseisin with various other recognitions both in procedural terms and as pleas which were concerned 'only with seisins', as opposed to right. The emphasis is upon speed, notably through the reduction of the number of essoins compared with procedure determining right. Whilst there came to be four main recognitions, novel disseisin, *mort d'ancestor, utrum* and darrein presentment, this number was far from

46. See *Lincs.*, no. 496 for an assize proceeding by default.
47. S. J. Bailey, 'Warranties of land in the reign of Richard I', *Cambridge Law Journal* 9 (1945–47), 202, *Lincs.*, pp. lxxiv–lxxv; cf. *Glanvill*'s doubts, xiii 30, Hall, p. 166. See also above, pp. 110–11, on warranty.
48. See e.g. *Lincs.*, no. 404, *Rotuli Curiae Regis*, i 56–7; someone held after person named in writ: *Rotuli Curiae Regis*, i 139–40, *CRR*, i 96; *Lincs.*, p. lxxiv.
49. *Glanvill*, xiii 7–11, Hall, pp. 151–6, quotation at pp. 155–6; *Lincs.*, no. 392 for a split decision – note compromise settlement.

preordained. There were others in *Glanvill,* for example concerning whether land was held in fee or only wardship, and this and other procedures also existed in Normandy.[50] The limitation in the number of such recognitions was accompanied by the appearance of writs of entry.[51] Again, the developing common law was taking a variety of directions, not conforming to some initial overall plan.

(iii) Writ of right and grand assize

The reversal of decisions of recognitions was only one of the uses of the writ of right. It could initiate hearings concerning disputes begun by two parties claiming to hold of the same or different lords, by an aspiring tenant, or by a lord seeking to take land from a tenant and restore it to his demesne. Such disputes occurred in various circumstances, for example when an inheritance was claimed outside the scope of *mort d'ancestor,* when a lord retained land because of doubt as to the correct heir, when problems arose from various kinds of family gifts, or when remarriage had led to a difficult inheritance dispute.[52] The demandant obtained a writ, generally addressed to the lord of whom he claimed to hold:

> The king to Earl William, greeting. I command you to do full right without delay to N. in respect of ten carucates of land in Middleton which he claims to hold of you by the free service of one hundred shillings a year for all service, which land Robert son of William is withholding from him. If you do not do it the sheriff of Devonshire will, that I may hear no further complaint for default of right in this matter.[53]

We know of some writs producing hearings in lords' courts,[54] and of duels being fought there, but unfortunately

---

50. *Glanvill,* xiii 1, 14, Hall, pp. 148, 157–8; see also e.g. xiii 26–30, pp. 164–6; *TAC,* xix, lxxxvi–vii, Tardif, pp. 20–1, 96–8.
51. See above, p. 136, on the way in which these writs brought cases directly before the royal justices and focused a recognition's attention on a specific flaw in the tenant's title.
52. Milsom, *Legal Framework,* p. 84, 86, 90, 132, 137; *CRR,* i 1; 75; *CRR,* v 241–2.
53. *Glanvill,* xii 3, Hall, p. 137.
54. E.g. PRS, ns 31 (1957), pp. 87–8, *Rotuli Curiae Regis,* i 64; note also e.g. *CRR,* iii 132.

cannot tell whether these are only the tip of the iceberg: if the lord's court came to an acceptable decision, no evidence may survive since our records concern primarily the royal courts. However, as we shall see, there are reasons for believing that lords' courts were growing less important. On occasion lords' courts defaulted and the cases were dealt with by the county. Alternatively, the king or his justices might determine cases over right to land, either summoned directly by writ *praecipe* or transferred from the lord's or county court.[55]

Bringing the relevant parties to court was often a very lengthy process because of the wide use of essoins. Once there, the plaintiff made his claim. At the time of the earliest plea rolls, he could seek to establish his right through an ancestor's seisin on the day of Henry I's death, although some looked back to the Conquest and beyond.[56] The tenant might ask for a view of the land in order to distinguish which of his lands in the place named by the writ were disputed, and he also might well vouch his lord to warranty. If such questions were not raised, the tenant put forward his counter-claim. The tenant might then choose to defend himself by battle. The demandant had to be represented by a champion, that is by one who would back up his plea supposedly as a witness; in practice in the late twelfth century champions were not real witnesses but men required as a matter of form to say that they or their fathers had witnessed the seisin on which the demandant based his claim. Failure of the champion to act as witness lost the case.[57] The tenant might defend himself in person or by a champion. Hired champions should not be allowed.[58] The vanquished champion was liable to a penalty and 'to lose all his law; that is to say, he shall never again be allowed as a witness in court and therefore can never make proof for anyone by battle'. If the tenant's champion was defeated, the tenant had to restore the land to the demandant, together with the produce found on the fee at

55. On the transfer of cases, see below, p. 231, on *praecipe*, below, p. 225. For the county dealing with another writ of right, *Lawsuits*, no. 659.
56. See e.g. *CRR*, i 93; also Brand, *Making*, pp. 221–2 on the possibly fairly recent origin of the 1135 date.
57. *CRR*, i 71.
58. *Lincs.*, no. 260.

the time when seisin was delivered. Cases settled by battle in the king's court were, according to *Glanvill*, settled for ever.[59]

However, the tenant had an alternative to battle – the grand assize. *Glanvill* presents this as a benefit, but sometimes the procedure may not have been very desirable for the tenant. In a dispute with the prior of Spalding, which had reached the king's court,

> the abbot of Crowland had not used due precaution, because he had not brought with him the royal charter nor any strong young man who could offer gage upon the ownership of the marsh on behalf of the abbot. . . . And because the abbot could not choose the duel, he was bound to consent to a recognition, although dangerous to him. For the knights of the shire are very far away from the marsh of Crowland and know nothing of its boundaries and there is hardly anyone in the county of Lincoln who is not in some way bound either to the house of Spalding, or to William de Roumare, or to one of those who had moved a claim upon the marsh.[60]

The grand assize automatically took the case into a royal court. The demandant had to decide whether or not he too would put himself upon the assize, and if he was unwilling so to do, must show his reason. *Glanvill* singled out the possibility of kinship between the parties. If the tenant then admitted the kinship, 'the assize shall not proceed'; verbal pleading and enquiry would determine the rightful heir, to whom the land went unless it could be shown that an ancestor had wholly alienated or lost that right. If the tenant denied the kinship, the question of their relationship was put to the parties' relatives who were summoned to the court. If kinship was established, the procedure was as already outlined. Otherwise, 'if the court and the lord king's justices take the contrary view, then the demandant, who by pleading that the parties were of the same stock maliciously attempted to frustrate the assize, shall lose his case'.[61]

59. *Glanvill*, ii 3, Hall, p. 25.
60. *Lawsuits*, no. 641.
61. *Glanvill*, ii 6, Hall, pp. 26–8; also e.g. Flower, *Introduction*, pp. 139–40. On the increasing use of exceptions, see Brand, *Legal Profession*, pp. 40–2.

If the assize went ahead, 'the tenant . . . should first purchase a writ of peace' in order to stop the case temporarily:

> The tenant who puts himself upon the assize secures peace by such writs until the demandant comes to court and purchases another writ, which provides that four lawful knights of the county and of the neighbourhood shall elect twelve lawful knights of the same neighbourhood, who are to declare on oath which of the parties has the greater right in the land sought.

Again, many essoins were available, and the procedure was slow despite *Glanvill*'s praise for its relative speed.[62] Eventually, twelve knights were elected and arrived in court. Their recognition went ahead whether or not the tenant was present, but the demandant was allowed essoins. According to *Glanvill*, if the twelve knights could not agree, further knights were added, until at least twelve agreed in favour of one party; however, lack of later evidence for such added knights suggests that this practice soon died out. If the knights declared

> that the tenant has the greater right therein, or make some other form of declaration from which it sufficiently appears to the lord king or his justices that this is the case, then the court shall award that the tenant be sent away, quit for ever from the demandant's claim; moreover the demandant shall never again effectively be heard in court on this matter. . . . On the other hand, if the judgment of the court based on the assize is in favour of the demandant, then the other party shall lose the land in question, and shall restore with it all produce and profits found on it at the time seisin is delivered.[63]

Yet it would again be wrong to assume that most cases came to such a decisive end. Of the assizes heard at Lincoln in 1202, in one the demandant would not let the assize swear and admitted the tenant's right, in another two the jurors answered the question put to them by the justices. In ten others it is specified that a final concord was made, and the remainder reached no conclusion at Lincoln.[64]

---

62. *Glanvill*, ii 7–10, 12, Hall, pp. 28–32.
63. *Glanvill*, ii 18, Hall, p. 35.
64. *Lincs.*, p. lxix; nos 149; 61, 188; 22, 76, 82, 117, 133–4, 139, 145, 148, 157; in addition nos 186, 196 were to end with final concords, but this is not mentioned on the roll.

. . .

THE IMPACT OF CHANGE

(i) Procedure

The reforms' most obvious impact was to bring a greater number of parties and cases into contact with royal justice. This is reflected in the development of royal courts, the changing role of local courts, and the decline of lords' courts. The chronology is necessarily unclear, since formal records of the royal courts only begin to survive from the 1190s.[65] These records do, however, confirm the importance of the eyre: in the Michaelmas term 1194 the court at Westminster heard twenty novel disseisin cases, whilst the eyre heard twenty such cases in Wiltshire alone.[66] Various criteria helped to determine whether a case went to the central court or the eyre. The plaintiff's choice was one influence, as was his willingness and capacity to pay for a hearing at his court of choice: the central court was probably always more expensive than the eyre. Another influence might be a defendant's privilege of only answering before the king.[67] In addition, there were some upper limits to the scale of cases the eyre should hear; the Assize of Northampton mentions half a knight's fee, whilst the articles of 1194 set a maximum of lands worth 100 shillings a year for grand assizes before the eyre.[68] However, this did not mean that the central courts only heard cases about large amounts of land. Indeed, the records of both the eyre and the court at Westminster were largely concerned with lawsuits between minor men about small amounts of land. Thus nearly one-third of the Norfolk final concords made before the 1209 eyre concerned less than five acres. Although such minor actions involving royal justice were not new in the late twelfth and early thirteenth centuries, they were surely

---

65. E.g. Hyams, 'Warranty', 478 sees the 1170s as a turning-point.
66. Sutherland, *Novel Disseisin*, p. 60 n. 1.
67. E.g. *Lincs.*, no. 437.
68. *EHD*, ii no. 25, c. 7 and iii no. 15, c. 18 respectively; these amounts are reflected in the earliest register of writs. All royal courts seem to have insisted that esplees, the products of the lands or the value of services, should be a minimum of 5s. p.a.

Kate is absent even if she lives. She's in the hospital, and people talk about her in the same self-centered and regretful ways. If she dies, people are sad, but nobody actually grieves. Nobody is ruined. Nobody finds themselves staring at a ceiling for hours, wishing it would collapse on them. Nobody forgets to eat for two whole days until they crumple to the asphalt in a pharmacy parking lot.

I played two games of *Life is Strange* concurrently. The one in which Kate died, and another one in which I went all the way back to the beginning, did everything perfectly, and stopped her from stepping off of that roof. The differences were only marginal shading on the edges of Max's life. A few odd sentences changed in the occasional conversation. There was no seismic difference, no sense of cataclysm.

This is less realistic than the time-travel, to be honest. Nothing in my life is unchanged by grief. I can't forget how thin the world is.

Somewhere, there are two versions of my life playing out concurrently. One in which Kat dies, and one in which she lives. I know that if I actually had the power to save and load lives, I'd keep testing and tinkering. I'd end up spending all of my time in the spaces where she lived. Over time, her lives would proliferate. The more I saved and re-loaded and branched out, the ugly reality where she died would take up a narrower sliver of space, and the realities where she lives would bloom and branch apart. The "Kat is alive" timelines would be so voluminous, they'd crowd out the opposition. Ninety-nine percent of realities would be ones in which she lives. They'd ensnare buildings, overturn cars, and grow to every possible height. My friend would be alive so much more than she'd be dead.

Over time and underneath it, the fabric of spacetime would curl around us like a blanket. She'd take off her glasses to nuzzle into my shoulder, and I'd re-load that moment, again and again, a .GIF playing endlessly in space, until I'd finally lived there long enough to be okay with living here, too.

becoming more common.[69] How far they were econom-
ically rational is very hard to tell. Rather, they show a
willingness to invest in litigation, to stand up for one's
rights and honour, and to look for the most decisive
possible source of justice.

Change affected not just the place but also the form of
litigation. The use and examination of written documents
became more extensive. An interesting instance records
that a party in a dispute kept its charters locked in a chest;
when needed, the chest was produced and opened in
court.[70] Certainly there was a continuing preference for
human witnesses, and an insistence that livery of seisin, not
the writing of a charter was crucial to a conveyance.[71]
However, the treatment of documents in court was
becoming more sophisticated, increasingly subjecting them
to technical close reading. Specific failings in writs, or
variation between the writ and the pleading might lead to
the dismissal of the case, at least until a better writ was
obtained.[72]

In general, pleading grew more specific and technical,
tending to focus upon a single point of law or fact. This
might be the case in any court, notably with the pleading of
exceptions, but was in particular associated with the use of
the jury in royal courts.[73] The parties might agree to be
bound by a jury verdict concerning an issue of fact, or one

---

69. B. Dodwell, ed., *Feet of Fines for the County of Norfolk, 1201–15* (PRS,
ns 32, 1958), pp. xxvi–vii; for central court records, see e.g. *CRR*, i
35, 37, 38 etc.. For earlier cases involving small amounts of land, see
above, p. 108 for Henry I's reign, p. 127 and Stenton, *English Justice*,
pp. 28, 43 for the early years of Henry II.

70. *CRR*, vii 272; for careful examination of documents early in Henry
II's reign, see Pollock and Maitland, i 157–8.

71. Note M. T. Clanchy, *From Memory to Written Record* (2nd edn,
Oxford, 1993), esp. pp. 260–6; P. R. Hyams, 'The charter as a
source for the early common law', *Journal of Legal History* 12 (1991),
184; but the situation might have changed, see Bailey, 'Richard I',
199.

72. See Flower, *Introduction*, pt. III ch. 1, esp. p. 344; *CRR*, iv 238; *Lincs.*,
nos 293, 320, 401; also below, p. 235.

73. Note e.g. *Lincs.*, no. 405; also *Lawsuits*, no. 641 (p. 684); see above,
p. 110 for Anglo-Norman precursors, and *Lawsuits*, no. 408, the
Anstey case from early in Henry II's reign; also Hyams, 'Ordeal',
119.

party might buy from the king an enquiry into the other party's claim.[74]

The enquiries whereby justices guided the handling of cases also led to greater precision. Furthermore, the justices might well be outsiders, less likely to be sympathetic to local custom or the politics of local affairs. With the desire for speedier justice, they might be more prepared than earlier court presidents to rule certain matters out of court. These tendencies are illustrated by *Glanvill*'s statement that 'the court of the lord king is not accustomed to protect private agreements'.[75] Moreover, from the later years of Henry II's reign the justices themselves, not the suitors, appear to have made judgments.[76] Even if these rested heavily on the verdicts of recognitions, the justices had considerable influence, and the reformers' willingness to look to the discretion of justices surfaces occasionally in *Glanvill*.[77] The justices' perceptions of correct procedure, lordship, and land-holding practice might conflict with and predominate over those of some others involved in the case. The spread of royal justice was thus likely to produce a more standardized, more rule-based legal procedure.

Change was not limited to procedure within court. The availability of the new royal actions led lords to modify their extra-judicial activities, for example in enforcing their rights.[78] The increasing influence of royal justices came to marginalize or delegitimize certain forms of self-help or of aid which lords provided for their followers. In the 1170s or 1180s, Roger de Mowbray received the hospital of St Leonard, York, into his own hand and defence, and ordered his men to guard and maintain it in his absence. His seneschal was to make anyone acting against the tenor of his charter observe it 'as he loves me and the salvation of my soul'.[79] Yet whilst

---

74. See e.g. *Lincs.*, nos 36, 119, 177, 511; also Pollock and Maitland, i 149, ii 611–18.

75. *Glanvill*, x 18, Hall, p. 132; also x 8, p. 124, *Bracton*, ff. 34, 100, Thorne, ii 109, 286, and see above, p. 189.

76. See above, p. 151.

77. E.g. *Glanvill*, ii 12, Hall, p. 32; on *privatae conventiones*, see above, p. 189.

78. See above, p. 192, below, pp. 213–14.

79. D. E. Greenway, ed., *Charters of the Honour of Mowbray, 1107–1191* (London, 1972), no. 313, cited with other examples at Hyams, 'Warranty', 449.

warranty was to remain part of common law, such active 'maintenance' would be, from the lord and his followers' point of view, at best a private affair, at worst the target of royal action.

Greater care was also needed in transfers of land and the recording of grants. Whilst grants continued to be made in lords' courts, the county or the king's court became increasingly attractive alternative or additional venues.[80] Charter usage of honorial addresses – to the donor's men and officials – declined, being replaced by more general forms, for example to all people present and future who might see the charter.[81] Moreover, the preferences of the royal justices may have had an effect on the very form of the transfer or 'livery' of seisin. In the earlier twelfth century a symbolic livery away from the land, for example by a knife, sufficed. However, in the late twelfth and early thirteenth centuries a successful conveyance required not only an initial making of a gift but also an actual livery on, or possibly in sight of, the land. The symbolic livery perhaps had sufficed to announce the conveyance to the suitors of the lord's court, but not to the potential jurors upon whom the royal justices would rely.[82]

The drafting of charters also became more careful. This was not a purely English phenomenon,[83] but it was surely affected by the treatment of charters in courts, as discussed above. Charter draftsmen had to guard against omissions which might be exploited. For example, it became increasingly common to include a clause explicitly promising warranty to the tenant and his heirs. Parties paid to have transactions or agreements registered on Pipe Rolls, presumably in order to make them more than mere 'private agreements'.[84] In addition, the expansion of royal justice promoted the use of final concords as a form of conveyance and record. These recount that a plea had

---

80. See e.g. *CRR*, iii 129 for a gift made in a lord's court but then announced in the county. See also below, p. 216, on the partition of lands amongst heiresses.
81. Hudson, *Land, Law, and Lordship*, p. 272 n. 69 and refs.
82. S. E. Thorne, 'Livery of seisin', *Law Quarterly Review* 52 (1936), 345–64.
83. Hyams, 'Charter', 179.
84. Ibid., 181.

been brought before the royal justices, and that one party recognized and quitclaimed the disputed land to the other. Such a final concord or 'fine' was conclusive proof in future cases, and – unlike a charter – required no one to warrant it. Huge numbers of final concords survive, particularly from certain areas such as East Anglia: the 1202 eyre produced 150 Norfolk final concords within a few weeks at Norwich, forty-one Suffolk final concords within a few days at Ipswich. Obviously, their form makes it very difficult to assess whether such fines record genuine cases or collusion aimed at securing conveyances. Opinions differ, but even some of the more modest estimates of collusion cannot rule out the growing use of fines as records of conveyances.[85]

Fines thus relate to the enabling and preventative functions of law, enabling well-protected grants, preventing future challenge. They helped in making aspects of land-holding more certain, more predictable. Methods such as collusion reflect practical legal learning, and are connected with another contemporary development, the increasing need for more specialized legal expertise. This might take the form of counsel in court or advice in obtaining an appropriate and correctly drafted writ or charter. Meanwhile, the royal justices' enforcement to the letter of reforms and actions, including technicalities which the parties in disputes did not fully understand, increased the need for such legal expertise.[86]

(ii) Limits of procedural change

Having focused upon the impact of the Angevin reforms, it remains necessary to emphasize elements of continuity. The concentration of business upon the king's court may well have been gradual rather than immediate. At least at first

85. Dodwell, *Norfolk Fines*, esp. pp. xii–xiii, xx–xxi, xxiii, and review by G. D. G. Hall, *EHR* 75 (1960), 514–15; Flower, *Introduction*, p. 266; Hyams, 'Charter', 185.
86. Brand, *Legal Profession*, chs 2–4; Hyams, 'Charter', 184; cf. above, chs 2, 5, below, ch. 8. J. R. Maddicott, 'Law and lordship: royal justices as retainers in thirteenth- and fourteenth-century England', *Past and Present Supplement no. 4* (1978) dates the start of the retaining of royal justices by lords to the second quarter of the thirteenth century.

the reforms' concentration upon cases of default of justice implied a continuing role for the lord's court.[87] Conveyances continued to be made there. Heirs continued to come to ask for their inheritances. Actions concerning lands continued to take place, and quite probably to be concluded, in lords' courts, even if they were begun by royal writ. Disseisins were made by judgment of the lord's court.[88] Lords could claim their courts if they felt cases had been wrongly removed or started in the wrong court, and in 1215 they still saw their courts as worth defending.[89]

Within the courtroom, royal, local, or seignorial, the transformation of the late twelfth century was far from complete. Pleading might sometimes be technical, but eloquence, cleverness, and shaming retained their place.[90] Royal justices might generally seek to limit, but did not always exclude, personal and political considerations from the decisions of their courts. Such considerations remained influential in lords' courts, and in the multitude of compromise settlements.[91] And even in cases proceeding by the new actions, parties occasionally still came up with their own *ad hoc* methods of settlement.[92]

Moreover, much room remained for self-help, particularly against weaker opponents. Lords probably continued to see their forceful, indeed their violent actions as legitimate – although they would have been less willing to accept such actions by their opponents. Their perceptions clashed with those of royal justices, but sometimes victims must simply have been too scared to bring incidents to the king's notice.[93] The early plea rolls,

---

87. See Biancalana, 'Legal reforms of Henry II', esp. 441, 486–7, and above, p. 145; note also, Brand, *Legal Profession*, p. 29 and esp. n. 94. Cf. for lords' courts in Normandy, *TAC*, xli, Tardif, pp. 34–5.

88. E.g. *Lawsuits*, nos 623, 652; see above, p. 188, for the Cockfield case; *Lincs.*, no. 326, *CRR*, vii 235. Note also *Lincs.*, no. 260.

89. *Glanvill*, xii 7, Hall, pp. 139–40, on which see Milsom, *Legal Framework*, pp. 69–70, and below, p. 225, on Magna Carta c. 34. On the county court, see *Lincs.*, p. lxii.

90. E.g. Jocelin, p. 57; see also above, p. 110.

91. See above, pp. 188, 204; see *CRR*, i 96 for a compromise reached because of doubts concerning the facts; Flower, *Introduction*, p. 462.

92. E.g. *Lawsuits*, no. 643.

93. See e.g. Jocelin, p. 57 for parties appearing in court in such a way as to cow their opponents. On fear in cases, see above, p. 12.

therefore, reveal only that limited proportion of incidents which led to royal action.[94] Even so, they do shed increased light upon the ways in which violence entered into land disputes. A trial by battle might degenerate into an uncontrolled fight,[95] whilst out of court far more terrible events might occur. Nicholas of Trubweek had quarrelled with Hugh Sturmy over certain lands. Nicholas appealed Hugh on the grounds that, although Hugh had given him the king's peace, he had:

> sent his two sons John and Hugh and his nephew Desideratus to Nicholas's house. Wickedly and with premeditated assault at night they opened a window of the house, and when Nicholas was sitting at his hearth, one of them shot an arrow, whence John struck him in the skin of his throat and shaved it a little. Hugh shooting another arrow wounded him in his right arm thus that he is maimed, and Desideratus struck him with another arrow through the middle of a testicle, whence he is maimed, thus that there was a view in the county and the wounds were recent. And he said that they came from Hugh the elder's house to do that evil and returned there after the deed. Hugh and those appealed deny everything.

Particularly in the more distant areas of the realm, land disputes could develop into minor local feuds, scaled-down versions of the major conflicts of Stephen's reign.[96]

However, some self-help was acceptable to royal justices as well as to the self-helpers. Royal justice continued to allow certain forms of force, notably against villeins.[97] Cases also reveal that a disseised tenant, although not allowed to eject a disseisor who had enjoyed lengthy unchallenged

---

94. See e.g. Flower, *Introduction*, p. 248 for accusation of forcible entry to land during the female tenant's last illness; P. R. Hyams, *King, Lords, and Peasants in Medieval England* (Oxford, 1980), p. 254. See below, p. 215, for *Glanvill* on heirs resisting the violence of their lords. Note also e.g. the continuing use of money to obtain one's ends: e.g. *Lincs.*, no. 87; Jocelin, p. 34; Flower, *Introduction*, pt. III ch. 13; also below, ch. 8.

95. *CRR*, i 100.

96. *CRR*, i 101; also e.g. *Lawsuits*, no. 629, Thomas, *Vassals*, p. 64; see above, pp. 120–1.

97. See generally Hyams, *King, Lords, Peasants*; also e.g. Thomas, *Vassals*, p. 64.

possession, was permitted self-help when it occurred without undue delay; recent and unjust possession was not the same as the seisin protected by the assize. Moreover, self-help might be used against those who had enjoyed land for a limited term and were refusing to give it up. Forceful entry to the disputed tenement seems generally to have been as permissible. However, reseisin should not involve violence to the opponent's person or action against his personal property and perhaps should be carried out unarmed. Thus forceful action was limited rather than prohibited. Self-help was not to be private war.[98]

(iii) Land-holding: security of tenure, heritability, alienability

Having concentrated largely upon procedure, let us turn to more substantive issues. Regularized enforcement of procedural norms by royal justices during litigation may have encouraged the perception that the tenant was the true owner, or at least the true lord, of the land. In various cases pleading turned upon whether the correct person was answering the claim. A mere farmer of land should not do so, but nor should one seised only of the services. It was the person seised of the land in demesne who should answer. The confusions which arose may indicate that such matters had not previously required so standardized and definitive answers.[99] The reforms thus reinforced the free tenant's position, strengthening its proprietal aspect.

Similar developments are also evident with regard to the interrelated issues of security of tenure, heritability, and alienability. Although a tenant's position may sometimes have been threatened by a greater possibility of rivals bringing claims relating to the distant past, reopening previous decisions,[100] in general the land-holder's ability to do as he wished with his land grew. This can be associated

---

98. Sutherland, *Novel Disseisin*, pp. 97–125.

99. E.g. *Lincs.*, nos 360, 494; *Rotuli Curiae Regis*, i 20; *CRR*, i 93–4, 97. Note also *Glanvill*, iii 5, Hall, p. 40 on the tenant who chooses to answer without vouching his warrantor; also the implications of the deforciant clause in the writ of right, on the emergence of which see Biancalana, 'Legal reforms of Henry II', 449–50 n. 59.

100. Note esp. Milsom, *Legal Framework*, pp. 181–2, who may exaggerate the contrast between pre- and post-reform situations.

not only with the Angevin reforms but also with other developments, many already at work in the Anglo-Norman period. The centrality of lordship and the honour to social relations tended to weaken. The power of some vassals relative to their lords increased,[101] and long tenure continued to help to reduce the personal element in homage and in tenure.

The tenant's security during his life-time continued to strengthen. Despite instances such as Abbot Samson's treatment of Aubrey de Ver, the lord's disciplinary jurisdiction was shrinking. As Samson himself admitted, the assize of novel disseisin made it impossible to eject established intruders without judgment.[102] Even seisin not established by seignorial acceptance now had a routine form of royal protection. Also, royal justices might automatically apply the rule requiring a writ to compel a tenant to answer concerning his free tenement. These developments had a particular effect on newly succeeding lords, who, like Abbot Samson, generally held an enquiry concerning their predecessor's tenants. It was becoming increasingly difficult for them to eject unwanted tenants. The latters' position was stronger in part because of long-term changes distancing seisin from the lord's personal acceptance. Also they might call upon the assize of novel disseisin for protection, and the recognition's view of what constituted unjust disseisin was influenced by those same long-term factors as were favouring the tenant. A lord wishing to take effective action through an enquiry increasingly would be wise to obtain royal backing, in the form of a royal writ concerning the free tenement or a hearing in the king's court.[103]

101. See e.g. Thomas, *Vassals,* pp. 15, 23, 32, 36, 44–7; P. Dalton, *Conquest, Anarchy and Lordship: Yorkshire, 1066–1154* (Cambridge, 1994), pp. 249–55; Milsom, *Legal Framework,* p. 28. See also above, pp. 91–2, on the emergence of the classifications 'in villeinage' and 'in socage', showing a continuing hardening of the definitions of, and distinctions between, types of land-holding.

102. Above, pp. 191–2; also Milsom, *Legal Framework,* p. 57. On Samson's treatment of Aubrey in the general context of distraint, see Hudson, *Land, Law, and Lordship,* pp. 280–1.

103. Milsom, *Legal Framework,* ch. 2, esp. pp. 47, 54; Hyams, 'Warranty', 460–1, 494–6.

At the same time, royal involvement was affecting distraint. As we have seen, a *statutum regni* early in Henry II's reign required judgment before distraint by fee, and early thirteenth-century practice is congruous with such a requirement.[104] The insistence of royal justices may have pressured lords to follow routine stages for distraint, earlier more characteristic of shire or hundred, rather than honorial courts: the distrainee was summoned three times to answer concerning the services, and thereafter might be distrained first by chattels, and then by the tenement. There was also a further tendency away from distraint by land, perhaps because of the danger of complaint of disseisin and of acting without a royal writ; the tenant might say that the question involved the amount of services, in which case, at least by the time of *Bracton*, the lord seems to have needed a royal writ. The same factors prevented the lord's enforcement of forfeiture of a tenement for disciplinary reasons by judgment of his court. For *Glanvill*, such power was still real, but from the evidence of the plea rolls it seems to have disappeared during John's reign. Lords might still proceed by royal writ, but a more convenient solution was often to act without court judgment and distrain only by chattels. The changes thus left the tenant more secure in his position, although far from free to ignore his obligations to his lord.

The heritability of land, already fairly secure for closer relatives by 1135, continued to strengthen. Long tenure, the increasing use of charters, and the strengthening of assumptions of inheritance all had an effect: for example, jurors on occasion assumed that a grant for homage and service must mean that it was to the grantee and his heirs.[105] According to *Glanvill*, 'heirs of full age may, immediately after the death of their ancestors, remain in their inheritance; for although lords may take into their hands both fee and heir, it ought to be done so gently that they do no disseisin to the heirs. Heirs may even resist the

---

104. For this paragraph, see Brand, *Making*, pp. 307, 314; Milsom, *Legal Framework*, esp. pp. 9 n. 2, 26–34; Hyams, 'Warranty', 478; Hudson, *Land, Law, and Lordship*, p. 28; *Bracton*, ff. 156–156b, Thorne, ii 440–1; e.g. *CRR*, iii 133–4; see above, p. 128.
105. *CRR*, iv 34.

violence of their lords if need be, provided that they are ready to pay them relief and to do the other lawful services.'[106] There is no sign here that lords were regaining any real control of the land when there was a clear heir. They continued to act if the heir failed to do homage, and to exact reliefs, but their discretion even in the latter field was restricted as customary levels of relief emerged. The *Dialogue of the Exchequer, Glanvill,* and Magna Carta all took 100s. as reasonable for a knight's fee.[107]

Matters were markedly different when there was no clear heir:

> When anyone dies without a certain heir – for example, without son or daughter or anyone who is undoubtedly the nearest and right heir – the lords of the fees may, as the custom is, take and keep those fees in their hands as their escheats, whether such lord is the king or someone else. If anyone later comes and says that he is the right heir, and is allowed by the grace of his lord or by a writ of the lord king to pursue his claim, he shall sue and may recover such right as he may have; but the land shall meantime stay in the hand of the lord of the fee, because whenever a lord is uncertain whether the heir of his tenant is the right heir or not, he may hold the land until this is lawfully proved to him. . . . However, if no-one appears and claims the inheritance as heir, then it remains permanently with the lord as an escheat, and so he may dispose of it, as of his own property, at his pleasure.[108]

Overall, though, the existence of royal remedies, and in particular *mort d'ancestor,* strengthened the position of heirs. The possibility of claims to succeed not based on the norms of succession was still further reduced.[109] One model of inheritance grew still more dominant.

---

106. *Glanvill,* vii 9, Hall, p. 82; see also above, p. 132, for the Assize of Northampton, c. 4, which I take to be a statement of good custom, not a legislative innovation. By the end of our period such resumption could be referred to as 'simple seisin'.
107. Milsom, *Legal Framework,* pp. 168–9; Hudson, *Land, Law and Lordship,* p. 129. See also *Dialogus,* p. 121, and Milsom, *Legal Framework,* p. 163 on other limits of discretion concerning relief.
108. *Glanvill,* vii 17, Hall, p. 90. See above, p. 199, on *mort d'ancestor* leaving aside hard cases.
109. See e.g. Milsom, *Legal Framework,* p. 163 n. 4; however, see below, p. 226 on tenants in chief.

her—and hug you like you were trapped in a wind-tunnel together. She was basically always a little bit drunk.

Every time I write these details, my memory gets a tiny scratch on it.

•◦•◦•

Once you've used modding tools to fly a camera throughout their 3D environments, video games are harder to trust. The finished product may look stable and solid, but you know how fragile the illusion is. You know that the characters aren't made up of blood and organs, but an internal nightscape of angles and glitches. You know that behind those painted-on doors isn't the rest of the expected world, but a fractal void of junked textures and geometric refuse. You know that what you're standing on is thinner than paper.

That's what it was like when I got the call. I sank against a pillar, and didn't stop sinking. The world disintegrated into meaningless geometry.

I have no idea if anyone on the team that made *Life is Strange* has ever had a friend who committed suicide. When you say all the right things and Kate doesn't kill herself, the chapter ends with a song and you texting your friend Chloe, *"Let's find out what's going on!"* The whole mystery is still going on, after all—the town, the eerie weather, the Prescotts, and your superpowers. But when you say the wrong things and Kate does kill herself, the same song plays. You look out over the same cinematic shots of the bay. On the day of Kate's death, you end the chapter by texting that same friend, *"Let's find out what's going on!"*

Nobody sends a text with an exclamation point on the day that their friend kills themselves. They just don't. It's an error of realism so jarring, it's more like an error of continuity, like they just lost track of Max's personhood between shots. The game paints it as if watching your friend throw herself to her death—as a direct result of you failing to love her better—wouldn't traumatize you, but would rather galvanize you to go out and solve mysteries. The game makes it seem like the world in which Kate lives, and the one in which she dies, aren't separated by much. That, to me, is the worst part of it—just how little changes.

Inheritance by women further illustrates these points. As noted in chapter 4, the position of heiresses was strengthening, not just in England but elsewhere in Christendom. From the 1130s the regular pattern in England for inheritance by heiresses was division between them. Yet there remained notable flexibility, for example relating to the the actual division of the lands. The possibility of re-arrangements, for example as heiresses died, exacer- bated the problems. Room remained for the exercise of lordly discretion. In the latter stages of the twelfth century the norms hardened somewhat, as royal courts sought simple criteria by which to settle cases.[110] Divisions, meanwhile, increasingly took place in the king's court, sometimes involving a final concord, and the precise equality of shares was emphasized.[111] Certainly, some flexibility continued to exist, for example with a father still able to give his daughter at the time of her marriage more than her share of the inheritance. Also, difficult cases remained, notably when political interests became involved. Nevertheless, a hardening of custom could be welcome not only to the royal courts but also to tenants and lords, in restricting the scope for dispute, aiding the arbitration of partitions, and helping to ensure that the king fulfilled his role as a good lord.[112]

Alienability also seems to have strengthened. Whilst it remains unlikely that substitution could be made without the lord's participation, subinfeudation was far less

---

110. S. L. Waugh, 'Women's inheritance and the growth of bureaucratic monarchy in twelfth- and thirteenth-century England', *Nottingham Medieval Studies* 34 (1990), 76–83; S. F. C. Milsom, 'Inheritance by women in the twelfth and early thirteenth centuries', in his *Studies in the History of the Common Law* (London, 1985), esp. pp. 243–5; J. C. Holt, 'Feudal society and the family in early medieval England: iv. The heiress and the alien', *TRHS* 5th Ser. 35 (1985), 1–28. Adjudication was sometimes by *mort d'ancestor*, but this was not available between sisters. The alternatives were a writ of right 'concerning reasonable portion', or a writ *praecipe* which took the case directly to the king's court.

111. See Waugh, 'Women's inheritance', 83–8, who seems to assume that the cases in fines are collusive; for some examples, Dodwell, *Norfolk Fines*, pp. xxiv–v.

112. Waugh, 'Women's inheritance', esp. 76, 89, 91–2.

restricted.[113] Distinctions between inheritance and acquisition largely disappeared.[114] A few cases still raised issues of lords' and heirs' participation in grants or the notion that a donor must not disinherit his heirs,[115] but these were not a frequent subject of litigation in surviving court records. Meanwhile, mentions of participation grew even scarcer in charters from the 1160s. Rather, homage and warranty were taken to bar the lord or heirs of a donor from claiming the land from the donee or his heirs, and although *Glanvill* stated only that 'the heirs of donors are bound to warrant to the donees and their heirs reasonable gifts and things given thereby', the qualification of reasonableness seems soon to have disappeared.[116] With the addition of a plausible but unprovable enlivening of the land-market in the later twelfth century, the pressures for alienability are familiar from earlier discussions. For example, the weakening of the bond between lord and vassal and of the influence of this bond upon land-holding made alienation without the lord's assent all the more conceivable, whilst custom and new royal remedies protected the beneficiaries of alienation.

The tenant's freedom to alienate is reflected in attempts at restriction both by individual lords and more generally in the Magna Carta of 1217. Grants prohibited alienation to religious houses. A few cases in John's reign show lords seeking to use the king's court to regain control of lands given by their tenants to the Church. However, both the grants with their note of special concern and the disputes with their reliance on royal remedies can be taken to indicate that whatever degree of control lords had once enjoyed over their tenants' grants was in decline.[117] Magna

---

113. Substitutions: Brand, *Making*, p. 233 n. 4. Note that charters from the late twelfth century increasingly mention grants as to a man and his heirs and his assigns; Hudson, *Land, Law, and Lordship*, pp. 124, 226.

114. However, see e.g. PRS, ns 31 (1957), p. 109.

115. E.g. Flower, *Introduction*, pp. 196, 277; *CRR*, i 87; v 47–8 ; vi 342–3; vii 190, 322–5.

116. *Glanvill*, vii 2, Hall, p. 74; Bailey, 'Richard I', 194, 198–201; Hudson, *Land, Law, and Lordship*, pp. 57–8.

117. See Brand, *Making*, pp. 234–5; Flower, *Introduction*, p. 368; also Hudson, *Land, Law, and Lordship*, p. 223.

Carta of 1217 expressed particular concerns about alienation in two clauses. Clause forty-three will be considered in
the next chapter. Of more concern to us here is clause
thirty-nine, which stated that 'no free man may henceforth
give or sell to another so much of his land that he cannot
from the remainder adequately perform the service that he
owes to the lord': There is little sign that the clause was
enforced; the move toward alienability was too complete.[118]

. . .

CONCLUSIONS

During the Angevin period, therefore, the focus of
litigation in land cases shifted towards the royal courts, in
particular to the eyre. New procedures ensured that royal
justices heard even very minor cases, which the reformers
may not at first have intended to bring routinely to royal
courts and which might have been better settled in
seignorial ones. If the results of reform with regard to
crime did not quite match the reformers' high aspirations,
their more limited aims with regard to land-holding were
notably surpassed. Indeed, the pressure on the royal courts
was becoming such that attempts were made to limit
business; this may be suggested by changes in the
procedure of distraint, by the unwillingness to deal with
'private agreements', and also by the firmer exclusion of
the unfree from royal actions.[119]

The relationship between the reforms and the weakening
of lordship, the decline of the honour, are uncertain and
must have been complicated. Demand for royal actions
from sub-tenants may reflect loosening bonds of lordship,
but in turn the availability of actions such as novel disseisin
reduced seignorial elements in land-holding. Of course
lordship continued to be of importance in relation to
land-holding, for example with regard to warranty, but
increasingly it was lordship exercised through, or

---

118. Sutherland, *Novel Disseisin*, p. 88 finds just one case; concern over
services no doubt increased as the lord's capacity to distraint was
restricted, see above, p. 214. On clause forty-three, see below, p.
229.
119. See above, pp. 189, 207–8, 214, and below, p. 236; note also the use
of *justicies* writs to depute business to the county court. See also
Stenton, *English Justice*, p. 92 on eyres becoming overburdened.

reinforced by, royal measures, as epitomized in the attempt of the 1217 version of Magna Carta to control alienations by tenants.[120] The activities of seignorial courts are obscure. They may well have continued to be important, and certainly some strands of Angevin reform emphasized co-operation, not conflict, between courts. However, that honorial courts declined in part because of the Angevin reforms seems undeniable.

The proprietal element of land-holding was made the more secure by the protection offered to tenants by routine royal remedies. Lordly discretion was reduced. Whilst different perceptions of land-holding no doubt persisted according to the position of the party in relation to the land, these were constricted by royal justices more rigorously enforcing one model, and their model coincided more closely with that of the tenant than of the lord aggressively asserting his seignorial rights. Royal actions and justices must also have reduced any remaining regional or honorial variation, rendering still more anomalous forms such as Kentish gavelkind.[121] The consistency of custom and the strength of the position of the tenant which we saw in the Anglo-Norman period were thus supplemented by the new routine activities of royal courts to form the basis of common law property.

Excluded from this process of routinization, however, were two groups. The first were the unfree. Their position, and also the status of land as unfree, was more rigidly categorized as a result of the implementation of the new royal measures. Villeinage holdings could be categorized, indeed, as those not protected by the land reforms.[122] The other group were the tenants in chief, for as we have seen the reforms were aimed at sub-tenants; the king's position as lord was little affected. The results of this anomaly were to leave their mark on Magna Carta.

120. See also above, pp. 213–14, on customs and services, *quo warranto*. For later reassertion of certain elements of lordship over land, see e.g. Sutherland, *Novel Disseisin*, pp. 86ff.
121. On gavelkind, see PRS, ns 31 (1957), p. 106, *CRR*, vi 285. For a possible honorial custom concerning allocation of dower, see *Bracton's Note Book*, pl. 623.
122. Hyams, *King, Lords, and Peasants*.

Chapter 8

MAGNA CARTA AND THE FORMATION OF THE ENGLISH COMMON LAW

The Angevin reforms thus greatly increased the business of the king's courts. This growth may represent not just a higher proportion of a constant number of cases. Some men believed that litigiousness had increased, and various developments, including the reforms themselves, may have contributed to rising litigation.[1] However, whilst the royal remedies were often popular, the focusing of business on the royal courts helped to concentrate resentment of injustice upon royal administration. Criticisms of royal justices for their corruption and their lowly social origins were not new, but they almost certainly increased during the Angevin period. Ralph of Coggeshall's 'Vision of Thurkill', written in 1206, admits of a royal justice that he was 'famous throughout England among high and low for his overflowing eloquence and experience in the law', but criticises his avarice in taking gifts from both parties in cases, and details with black enjoyment the pains he was suffering in Hell following his intestate and apparently unrepentant death.[2]

Some of the very ideals of reform also encouraged criticism. The reformers sought to provide swifter remedies, and no doubt claimed much credit for doing so. When cases dragged on, therefore, the likelihood of complaint of delay or denial of justice was increased. Similarly, the reforms often emphasized the standardization of government and opposed forceful lordship, yet irregular

1.   Note e.g. Milsom, *Legal Framework*, p. 87.
2.   R. V. Turner, *The English Judiciary in the Age of Glanvill and Bracton, c. 1176–1239* (Cambridge, 1985), p. 7, and generally chs 1 and 6.

and often forceful exercise of power remained an essential part of royal rule.[3] Moreover, the reforms helped to educate potential critics by further involving them in royal administration, adding to their own legal interests.[4] The widespread participation of knights and others in the locality helps to explain why 1215 saw not just a rebellion but a highly articulated critique of John's kingship. Whilst the consumers of royal justice accepted the exercise of a certain amount of royal discretion, especially if in their favour, their ideals are expressed in proffers, requests, or demands to be treated according to the custom of the realm. Whole communities paid to enjoy certain privileges, privileges which prefigured the liberties generally granted by Magna Carta.[5]

. . .

KING JOHN AND THE ADMINISTRATION OF JUSTICE

The personal focus 'on the king increased with John's accession. Certainly, the survival of more detailed records reveals what is only hinted at in earlier reigns. The Assize of Northampton had conceived of the eyre justices referring cases to the king, for instance 'by reason of their uncertainty in the case'.[6] However, the loss of the Continental possessions ensured that John was present in England much more than had been his brother or his father. Although some of his involvement must stem from a desire not for justice but for financial benefit, John may also have had a personal interest in judicial and legal business. From the start of the reign, plea rolls include notes that the justices should speak to the king concerning

3. See e.g. R. V. Turner, *The King and his Courts* (Ithaca, NY, 1968), pp. 57–70; Holt, *Magna Carta*, pp. 81–4; also the classic study by J. E. A. Jolliffe, *Angevin Kingship* (London, 1955). On the tardiness of justice, not necessarily through royal delay, see e.g. *Lincs.*, pp. lxiii–lxvii.

4. For one discussion of a law-related matter, drawing both on book learning and personal experience, see D. L. and D. H. Farmer, eds and trans, *Magna Vita S. Hugonis* (2 vols, Oxford, 1985), i 19–21.

5. See Holt, *Magna Carta*, chs 3–4, and esp. pp. 64–6, 69–70, 92–3, 97–8; also pp. 72–3 for the complaints which Gerald of Wales made a Lincolnshire knight called Roger of Asterby take to Henry II.

6. *EHD*, ii no. 25, c. 7; note also no. 60.

a matter.[7] People may have considered such an interest as good kingship. Conceivably, though, royal administrators sometimes saw it as unwelcome royal interference in their routine, and a manifestation of John's characteristic lack of trust.

Whatever its causes, the focusing upon John is reflected in the growing judicial importance, at least from 1204, of the court which travelled with the king, the court *coram rege*. In 1209 all business from the eyres and the bench at Westminster was transferred there. In the king's absence in Ireland in the summer of 1210 all cases were adjourned, rather than being transferred to the justiciar's court. Contrary to what was considered good practice, judicial visitations to the localities in 1210 often consisted of the sheriff acting as justice in his own shire, supported by other specially recruited local men. A second visitation followed, by men described in the Pipe Rolls as 'autumnal justices'. The purpose of these, and also of a visitation throughout the kingdom by Richard de Marisco, appears to have been primarily financial. The bench was partially restored in 1212, but only when Peter des Roches became justiciar in February 1214 was there some return to normality.[8]

What of the quality of justice John provided? It was far from entirely unsatisfactory. Even when he had increased reliance upon the court *coram rege*, he often showed a readiness to ease access to his court, or to adjourn a case until he reached the litigant's area.[9] He sometimes employed notions of the custom of the realm, encouraging his subjects to look for such regularity. His own attempts to regain support from 1213 may have further whetted baronial appetite for reform.[10] However, the focusing of justice upon the king reduced any blame that might attach to a chief justiciar. The increased role of the court *coram rege* led to postponements and lengthy travel which restricted the availability of justice. Grievances also arose both from John's exercise of his royal will and his crushing

---

7. See e.g. *PKJ*, i nos 3117, 3118, 3136.
8. Stenton, *English Justice*, ch. 4; *PR12J*, pp. xiv–xxiij; *Surrey*, p. 12.
9. Stenton, *English Justice*, ch. 4; note also Holt, *Magna Carta*, pp. 149–50.
10. Holt, *Magna Carta*, pp. 96, 203–6, Turner, *Courts*, pp. 103–10.

of opponents through methods which had a basis in law. The administration of 'justice' might seem merely the expression of royal favour and disfavour. Even if John often ensured that justice was done, he left sufficient aggrieved parties to encourage opposition.[11]

Underlying such grievances were some structural rather than personal problems. Angevin reforms had established considerable controls over lords' actions and their courts. Few such enforceable controls existed over the king and his courts. Besides permitting abuses in the field of crime, this situation left the tenants in chief in an anomalous position in their dealings with the king, especially concerning land. Their own tenants employed the new regular actions to establish their rights. Such actions were rarely available against the king, writs could not be addressed against him, and there was no superior lord to deal with royal default of justice. The result was considerable royal discretion coupled with uncertainty in the tenant in chief's position, discretion and uncertainty all the more noticeable since they were now exceptional.[12] Cases involving tenants in chief were often particularly sensitive since they might challenge kings' past actions. Especially in complicated cases, room existed for profit by predatory royal officials and favourites, such as William Briwerre, or for the king himself to take huge payments. Payment might have to be made even if the case was lost; thus in 1199 William de Briouze offered £100 if he lost his case concerning Totnes, 700 marks if he won. An anomaly in warranty practice also encouraged such large proffers, often in our eyes lacking proportion to the limited value of the lands claimed. If a sub-tenant lost his land, his lord might be obliged to give him an exchange, and the sub-tenant could call upon the king to enforce this. No such regular mechanism was available to the tenant in chief, no exchange would necessarily appear to sweeten his loss, and hence it was all the more necessary to bid sufficiently high to ensure victory.

---

11. Note esp. Holt, *Magna Carta*, pp. 185–7; Stenton, *English Justice*, pp. 103–14; M. T. Clanchy, 'Magna Carta and the Common Pleas', in H. Mayr-Harting and R. I. Moore, eds, *Studies in Medieval History presented to R. H. C. Davis* (London, 1985), pp. 228–32.
12. For the rest of this paragraph, see Holt, *Magna Carta*, ch. 5, esp. pp. 152, 161–4; on proffers, note also *Dialogus*, esp. p. 120.

Even in John's reign a partial solution was being created for the anomalous position of the tenant in chief, with the appearance of the writ *praecipe in capite*:

> The king to the sheriff, greeting. Command B. that, justly and without delay, he render to A. half a knight's fee in N. which he claims to hold of the king for so much service and whereof he complains that this B. has deforced him; and if he does not do this and the said demandant shall have given you security for prosecuting his claim, then summon by good summoners that he be before our justices on that day to show why he has not done this, and have there the summoners and this writ.

This text appears in the earliest register of writs, which may date from 1210. If such a writ were readily available, it would give the tenant in chief a regular remedy for land of which he was being deforced by another tenant, although not necessarily for land which the king himself held. However, by 1215 it had not sufficed to end the great men's grievance.[13] They looked instead to rebellion and a royal grant of liberties.

. . .

MAGNA CARTA

Magna Carta sought to provide a solution for many grievances concerning law and justice. We have already seen the background to some clauses, for example clause forty laying down that 'to no one will we sell, to no one will we deny or delay right or justice'. Clause seventeen stated that 'common pleas shall not follow our court, but shall be held in some specified place'. Common pleas were those which involved the king's general or common jurisdiction over all people, very much the type of jurisdiction exercised by the general eyre. The clause aimed to prevent litigants having to pursue the king's court around the country. Rather, the location for pleading should be specified in the writ originating the plea. The location might be the bench at Westminster, but could also be a specific place during the eyre's next visit.[14]

13. E. de Haas and G. D. G. Hall, eds, *Early Registers of Writs* (Selden Soc., 87, 1970), p. 2; dating to 1210, Brand, *Making*, pp. 451–6.
14. Clanchy, 'Common Pleas', pp. 220–4.

Also concerned with courts was clause thirty-four: 'The writ called *praecipe* shall not in future be issued to anyone in respect of any holding whereby a free man may lose his court.' The writ more fully known as *praecipe quod reddat* brought land cases directly before the king's court, rather than via seignorial and local courts.[15] Before Magna Carta, lords in such cases could reclaim their courts by appearing before the king or his justices to prove their right to hear the plea. If such a capacity to reclaim was routine, clause thirty-four was merely of administrative convenience to the barons, in ensuring that cases should go directly to their courts rather than having to be reclaimed. Was John employing the writ with increasing frequency in an obnoxious fashion? Instances could be hidden by our records, but the evidence suggests a peak in 1204, and no great increase up to 1215. However, if the capacity to reclaim was not routine, but might necessitate considerable effort, the clause takes on rather more significance: it insists that cases proceed by due process rather than by a power struggle between court-holder and royal administration.

Indeed, some barons in 1215 perhaps were concerned, rightly or wrongly, that the king was intent on a general reduction of the jurisdiction of their courts. The *Histoire des ducs de Normandie* states that one of the desires of the barons in 1215 was 'to have all powers of *haute justice* in their lands'.[16] The chronicler seems to have lacked precise understanding of events in England, where few lords had the serious criminal jurisdiction referred to on the Continent as *haute justice*. Yet he may have understood baronial feelings rather better than modern historians who count actions on plea rolls: the barons of 1215, like their

15. Holt, *Magna Carta*, pp. 174, 325–6; N. D. Hurnard, 'Magna Carta, clause 34', in R. W. Hunt, W. A. Pantin and R. W. Southern, eds, *Studies in Medieval History presented to F. M. Powicke* (Oxford, 1948), pp. 157–79; M. T. Clanchy, 'Magna Carta, clause thirty four', *EHR* 79 (1964), 542–8.
16. Holt, *Magna Carta*, p. 271; note also the first clause of the Magna Carta of Cheshire, which suggests that the earl's barons feared that he was seeking to reduce their courts; G. Barraclough, ed., *The Charters of the Anglo-Norman Earls of Chester, c. 1071–1237* (Record Soc. of Lancashire and Cheshire, 126, 1988), no. 394.

INTRODUCTION

I N LATE 2016, ONE OF OUR MEMBERS READ A SHORT STORY ABOUT a character struggling to survive in their own skin after a crippling breakup. The writing style was emotional, raw, and visceral. It was a story that we could relate to, but one that also allowed us to step outside of ourselves and wonder how we might feel under similar circumstances. The story is called *A Beginner's Guide to Goodbye Sex*, by author Joaquin Fernandez, a dear friend of ours. We expressed interest in publishing it as a standalone chapbook and asked him to describe the theme in one word. His answer was "aftermath." That moment became the genesis of this anthology, one that weaves together the stories that are born from the experiences when grief seems too all-encompassing, too suffocating to see a way out of it.

The book you hold in your hands represents a milestone; it is the realization of a dream that goes back more than a decade. When Radix Media began as a one-person offset print shop in 2010, publishing was always in the cards. One of our very first projects

I've read over these messages so many times. These were the options I picked out of the sky. Every following day that I didn't text was another option in the sky. Everything I didn't say to her was another button I didn't click. Every hour I continue to live is a reminder of how far away from her I'm getting, and how I don't get to go back and do better. This will always be what I did.

People have done their best to convince me that there was nothing else I could have done. *Life is Strange*, though, destroys that reassurance. It makes the player the causally determinative factor in someone else's suicide. It's an irresponsible narrative gambit. But if I'm being honest, I was hungry for it. It confirmed every piece of molten self-incrimination that burned at the back of my skull.

For a long time after Kat died, I only referred to her as my friend. We were lovers, as well, but I didn't know how to say that without feeling like I was misrepresenting something, because we *were* friends. We were supportive friends to one another both when we were sleeping together and when we weren't. Lots of people had that kind of relationship with her, because she was so good at precisely that kind of relationship. She always made it obvious what her love was based on.

———◆•◆◆◆———

When you read information from a hard drive, the drive stays intact. When you write information, though, the tiny transistors in the drive's cells degrade. Every time you write, it exacts a tiny incremental toll on the hardware.

I don't know how to tell these stories without rewriting the information in them. I don't know how to prevent my memory circuits from degrading from the process. Every detail I mention makes it more likely that I'll forget the ones I don't.

Kat was a Star Wars dork. She was queer, polyamorous, and feminist. She wore black-rimmed glasses and tulle skirts and heavy Doc Martens. She was a writer who put an incredible amount of effort into making other people feel like they could call themselves writers. She said, "*Right??*" like you were the first person in the whole world to get it, like the search was finally over. She'd shiver with delight when you'd tongue her lip-ring—she called it the cheat code for making out with

predecessors faced with Henry II's decree concerning default of justice, may have felt that the king was taking away their courts.

The other point the *Histoire des ducs* singled out concerning 1215 was that John 'had to fix reliefs for land, which had been excessive, at such a figure as they wished'. The king's discretion in dealing with inheritance by tenants in chief was thereby much reduced.[17] John had taken very high reliefs, such as the 7000 marks John de Lacy had to offer for succession to the honour of Pontefract and other lands held by his father. The very first clause of the Articles of the Barons demanded that heirs pay only the ancient relief, and clause two of Magna Carta stated that:

> If any of our earls or barons, or others holding of us in chief by knight service shall die, and at his death his heir be of full age and owe relief, he shall have his inheritance on payment of the ancient relief, namely the heir or heirs of an earl £100 for a whole earl's barony, the heir or heirs of a baron £100 for a whole barony, the heir or heirs of a knight 100s. at most for a whole knight's fee; and anyone who owes less shall give less according to the ancient usage of fiefs.

Typically, Magna Carta established law on the stated grounds of recording good custom: there were precursors for these figures, stretching back to the mid-twelfth century, but the case for the £100 relief for baron or earl really being standard ancient usage was weak.

Court-holding and land were not the sole concerns of Magna Carta. Clause twenty demanded that:

> A free man shall not be amerced for a trivial offence, except in accordance with the degree of the offence; and for a serious offence he shall be amerced according to its gravity; and a merchant likewise, saving his merchandise; in the same way a villein shall be amerced saving his tilled land [*wainaggio*]; if they fall into our mercy. And none of the aforesaid amercements shall be imposed except by the testimony of reputable men of the neighbourhood.

The notion that penalties should be proportionate was an old one. Again, the clause reveals the involvement of

17. Holt, *Magna Carta*, pp. 52, 190–1, 196, 271, 298–301, 304–6, 309.

leading members of the local community in the administration of justice. And whilst the limitation on royal
amercement of villeins may partly have been designed to
protect the interests of their lords, the clause's phraseology
– 'in the same way' – suggests that the Charter was here
giving its protection from royal oppression not just to free
men but to villeins.

Examination of these clauses reveals Magna Carta's
relationship to the pattern of legal development already
discussed. It most obviously made use of writing; as reissued
under Henry III it would provide a model for legislation by
statute and took its place at the beginning of Statute books.
The Charter drew on a variety of sources, for example
sometimes restating custom, sometimes greatly extending
existing practices, sometimes assembling supposed customs
which justified breaks from the past, and transformed them
into more fixed, more regular rules. Not all Magna Carta's
suggestions succeeded. Clause eighteen's desire that
specially commissioned justices hold recognitions of novel
disseisin, *mort d'ancestor* and darrein presentment four times
a year shows the popularity of these assizes, but proved
impractical. Yet the aspiration of this clause and the rest of
the Charter shows the development of a more regular,
routine, and royally provided system of justice.

. . .

LAW AND LEGAL EXPERTISE

I argued in chapter 1 for the existence, although not the
absolute distinctness, of the categories 'law' and 'legal'
during the Anglo-Norman period. Categorization hardened
during the period 1066–1216. We saw the mixture of rights
listed in *Leges Henrici Primi*, c. 10.1. The treatises of the later
twelfth century distinguish more clearly between law and
finance. Indeed, it is obvious that the *Dialogue* was intended
primarily as a treatise concerning finance, *Glanvill* as one
concerning law and justice. There was also a specialization
of personnel and of courts, for example with the separation
of the bench from the exchequer. Magna Carta, sometimes
implicitly, sometimes explicitly demanded a separation of
finance and justice.

The hardening of the category 'legal' manifested itself in
other ways. Routinization of certain court activities brought

various processes more clearly into the category 'legal', for example the demand that settlements should only be made with the licence of the king or his justice. Courts sometimes narrowed the limits of matter relevant in a case. Lords gradually found themselves unable to discipline vassals in ways which they and others considered quite suitable but which were not permitted by royal justice. Perhaps increasingly, although surely not unprecedentedly, individuals were amerced for technical reasons when a more general sense of justice seemed on their side.

Moreover, whilst law had certainly not previously been a simple reflection of normal social behaviour, the changes during the Angevin period encouraged legal activity and norms to become more distanced from customary perceptions of proper social practice. A very interesting instance comes in *Glanvill*. Having pointed out that a man with a son as his legitimate heir could not easily give land to his younger son without the heir's consent, he asked 'Can a man who has a son and heir give part of his inheritance to his bastard son? If he can, then the bastard son will be better off in this matter than the legitimate son; notwithstanding this, he can do so.'[18] The socially obvious answer, that the bastard should be worse off than the legitimate younger son, had to be rejected in favour of the legally correct answer. The problem may not have been new, but in the stark form given by *Glanvill*, it witnesses to the impact of the Angevin reformers' thinking on law.

At the same time, men started to play with legal norms and devices in order to achieve not the usual outcome of these practices, but ends they found socially desirable. Early instances appear in towns. In Northampton in *c.* 1190 it was laid down that 'no one can gage land to any one for a long term or a short one unless the gagor and he who took the gage will swear that they do not do this to defraud the lords or the kin of their rights'. This suggests that, for example, dying men were making limited term grants of lands, so that when the grant ended, the land would revert to the grantor's heir, thereby freeing him from paying relief.[19]

---

18. *Glanvill*, vii 1, Hall, pp. 70–1.
19. *Borough Customs*, i 288; such grants might also be used to avoid wardship if the heir were a minor. Cf. the later enfeoffment to use.

Outside towns, the most famous record of such developments is clause forty-three of the 1217 Magna Carta:

> it is not permitted to anyone to give his land to any religious house thus that he resume it to hold from the same house, nor is it permitted for any religious house to receive the land of anyone thus that they hand it over to him from whom they accepted it to hold. Moreover, if anyone ... gives his land to any religious house in this way and is found guilty of it, his gift will be utterly voided and that land fall to his lord of that fee.

The concern seems to have been primarily the avoidance of incidents; since a church never died, the lord lost his rights of relief and wardship, and of course the marriage of a church was an impossibility. Such learned and artificial devices were to become a feature of late medieval conveyancing. The still familiar relationship between legislator, court, parties, and lawyers was beginning to develop.[20]

Such developments, therefore, relate to the emergence of men specializing in law or the administration of justice.[21] In chapter 5, we analysed developments in the administrative mentality and the role of justices, particularly under Henry II. The judiciary under his sons displayed many similar characteristics. A large proportion of those named as justices appeared only on a few occasions, the bulk of the work being done by a core of less than twenty in any one reign. These tended to come from families with traditions of administrative involvement. There were no dramatic changes in their social origins, although under John the proportion of clerics declined. Increasingly, however, some concentrated on one field, be it finance or justice. Growing business, with courts sitting for ever lengthening terms rather than single days, coupled with the possible influence of increased legal learning, produced an ever more specialist and expert judiciary.[22] Simon of

---

20. For other devices, see e.g. S. J. Bailey, 'Warranties of land in the thirteenth century', *Cambridge Law Journal* 8 (1942–44), 293 and n. 145 on the avoidance of claims to provide exchange.
21. Cf. above, pp. 149–51.
22. See Turner, *Judiciary*; Brand, *Making*, pp. 93–4; also above, chs 5–7 on the standardizing impact of justices.

Pattishall seems to have been the first to specialize in a judicial career, serving continuously for twenty-six years from Richard I's reign. His witnessing of unusual writs and his pronouncements recorded in plea rolls testify to his pre-eminence in legal matters. Continuity and solidarity was also provided by justices who had served as clerks of their predecessors, for example Simon of Pattishall's clerk Martin. Others drew upon a family tradition of legal involvement at a local rather than royal level, as is the case with the eyre justice Henry of Northampton, whose father was named first amongst forty burgesses of Northampton responsible for recording the town's laws.[23]

More full-time and expert justices, enforcing more precise rules and more complicated procedure, required greater expertise from litigants. Greater skill was needed in pleading and especially in bringing exceptions. The use of expert counsellors and also of pleaders to make one's case in court was thereby encouraged. Meanwhile, particularly given the distance to the royal court, the use of representatives, of attorneys, grew more frequent.[24] Usually these were relatives or friends, but by John's reign some men acted on behalf of litigants who may otherwise have been strangers to them. Occasionally, royal justices or clerks were used as attorneys, as when in 1198 the bishop of Ely appointed his archdeacon Richard Barre as his attorney for all pleas at Westminster: Richard was not just an archdeacon, but also a royal justice.[25] Such developments in the judiciary, in representation, and in pleading laid the foundation for the emergence of a legal profession by the end of the thirteenth century.

. . .

THE COMMON LAW

At the end of chapter 1, it was suggested that general applicability throughout the realm should be a key characteristic of common law, and in the intervening

23. Brand, *Legal Profession*, pp. 27–8; Stenton, *English Justice*, pp. 82–3, 85–6; Turner, *Judiciary*, p. 163. See above, p. 36, on Glanville's father.
24. For this paragraph, see Brand, *Legal Profession*, chs 2–4.
25. Turner, *Judiciary*, p. 282; note also pp. 152–4.

chapters we have related such general applicability to royal administration of justice. Clearly there remained important non-royal elements in law and justice in 1215. A mass of minor offences was dealt with in local courts, be it hundred, shire, or some form of seignorial court. A very significant proportion of those serious offenders actually put to death may have suffered at the hands of privileged lords, holders of the right of infangentheof.[26] Some areas on the periphery of the realm were not and would not be covered directly by royal administration, whilst others enjoyed more limited privileges.[27]

Yet there had been a considerable shift not just in important business but in mental orientation towards the king and his courts. More people were travelling to the king's court or to the chancery to obtain writs. More were expectantly or fearfully awaiting the arrival of the royal justices in their locality. Some great men were appointing attorneys at the royal court in order to reclaim any cases which they believed belonged to their own courts.[28] Moreover, the local elements were being integrated more closely into the royal, the jurisdictional framework was becoming clearer, more of a system. The ideology of royal-dominated justice is very clear in *Bracton*, for whom all jurisdiction relating to the realm, as opposed to the Church, was either exercised by the king himself or delegated by him. *Glanvill* is not so explicit, but the pressures for integration are clear at the time he was writing. For example, cases could be transferred from lords' courts to the county by the process known as tolt and, in turn, from the county to the king's court by that called *pone*. Cases could also be transferred between royal courts, most commonly from the eyre to the bench at Westminster, on grounds such as the difficulty or seriousness of the case. It was also possible to miss out the intermediate stages and go straight to the king. We have seen some resistance to this

---

26. See above, pp. 165–6, 182.
27. See e.g. R. R. Davies, 'Kings, lords and liberties in the March of Wales, 1066–1277', *TRHS* 5th Ser. 29 (1979), 41–61; also above, pp. 45–7; and note e.g. *Lincs.*, nos 378, 380.
28. E.g. *CRR*, vii 5. Note also Turner, *Judiciary*, pp. 110–11 on churches making grants to royal justices.

in the case of the writ *praecipe* for land, but in practice the fact that the king's court gave decisions which it was extremely hard to overturn must have encouraged its use as a court of first resort. Royal control continued to grow after 1215, for example with a greater royal willingness to prosecute criminal cases in which the appellor had withdrawn.[29]

When successful, integration would lead to the reduction of any variation of custom between courts; lords' courts, like the eyre, would have to follow the custom of the king's court. Certainly, inconsistencies in law remained, even outside privileged or peripheral areas. With reference to county and honorial courts, *Glanvill* still wrote of the diversity of custom, perhaps primarily procedural diversity. However, *Glanvill* may have chosen to exaggerate such diversity in order to highlight the consistency and hence the advantages of his royal courts. There was both much consistency in Anglo-Norman law and further pressure for consistent and routine administration under the Angevins. Even in highly privileged areas such as the bishopric of Durham, pleading in the bishop's court was, according to a charter of John in 1208, to proceed according to 'the common and right assize of the realm of England'.[30]

Yet a theoretically consistent body of law would be of limited use if court-holders could override it. Angevin kings emphasized and exercised their will. *Glanvill* left royal justices and the king's court a certain degree of discretion. Political considerations sometimes led to judgments which at least the defeated party saw as inconsistent with law.[31] The ambiguous position of the justices exacerbated the problem. They were not a judiciary separated from the executive; rather they were the king's servants.[32] They recognized their duties such as raising revenue for the king, and in return enjoyed various special privileges and

---

29. Note e.g. C. A. F. Meekings, ed., *Crown Pleas of the Wiltshire Eyre, 1249* (Wilts. Archaeological and Natural History Soc., Rec. Branch, 16, 1961), p. 70.
30. Holt, *Magna Carta*, p. 102.
31. See e.g. *Glanvill,* ii 12, Hall, p. 32; *Lawsuits*, no. 641; and above, p. 223.
32. Note e.g. *Bracton,* f. 109, Thorne, ii 309; Turner, *Judiciary*, pp. 268–77.

protections, as well as rewards. Further pressures, for example from relatives and other connections, as well as money, could play on the justices.[33]

Another element of developing common law, therefore, was the exclusion or at least restriction of discretion. Law was contrasted with will, kingship with tyranny. According to an early thirteenth-century London text, 'Right and justice ought to rule in the realm rather than perverse will; law is always what makes right, but will and violence and force are not right.'[34] Law should proceed reasonably, with judgment. The Angevin reforms had further restricted the exercise of discretion by lords. Meanwhile, developing notions of proper practice which would be encapsulated in Magna Carta also helped to impose limits on the continuing personal elements in kingship. Royal administrators themselves displayed awareness of the distinction between royal arbitrariness and common law. Richard fitz-Nigel contrasted standard procedure with Forest Law: 'The forest has its own laws, based, it is said, not on the common law of the realm, but on the arbitrary decree of the king; so that what is done in accordance with the forest law is not called "just" absolutely, but "just" according to the forest law.' In the early plea rolls the great bulk of cases went ahead without special interference from king or justices; the growth of business made routine inevitable and desirable. Interestingly, the core justices of his reign did not all side with John in 1215. William Briwerre continued to condemn Magna Carta into Henry III's reign, on the grounds that it was extorted by force. On the other hand, five justices incurred the king's suspicion sufficiently to lose their lands temporarily in the period 1215–16. Recipients and providers of justice recognized the value of due process.[35]

A further characteristic of a common law, we suggested, was that it should affect the whole population. Certainly

---

33. See e.g. Turner, *Judiciary*, pp. 122–3, 164, 167, 282–5; also above, p. 203.
34. Liebermann, i 635; see generally Jolliffe, *Angevin Kingship*, Holt, *Magna Carta*.
35. *Dialogus*, pp. 59–60; Turner, *Judiciary*, pp. 168–71. At least until John's reign, arbitrary executive action may have been less common than under the Norman kings; see *Royal Writs*, on executive action and judicialization.

Angevin justice intruded into many individuals' lives. Indeed, the very frequent eyres of Henry II's later years may have created greater contact between his subjects and central government than would occur again for some generations. But how large a proportion of the population enjoyed access to the benefits of law? To some in Henry II's reign it was certainly too large a proportion, as men complained that near rustics were bringing royal writs. A more positive attitude was taken on occasion by the providers of royal justice, allowing different procedures for poor litigants.[36] The royal courts were used for disputes and agreements concerning very small parcels of land.[37] Lesser men did bring actions against greater ones.[38] And whilst a man's status might determine the categorization of his activities, men of influence, members of the knightly classes, were sometimes prosecuted under the same criminal law as much poorer men.[39] There was no specially legally privileged nobility. And famously, Magna Carta granted liberties to freemen and very occasionally to villeins, a more extensive body of beneficiaries than in equivalent Continental grants.

However, if the availability of royal justice to all was one ideal, clearly access was not in practice truly equal. Fear might deter the weak from seeking justice, especially since the agents of justice in the localities were themselves sometimes the perpetrators of lawlessness.[40] Wealth eased access to justice, for example through payments for hastening hearings.[41] More generally, certain groups enjoyed only limited access to, protection by, or freedom within the law of the realm.

The position of women was complicated. Law and social practice gave husbands very extensive control of their wives, and the developed common law provided no civil remedy

36. E.g. D. W. Sutherland, *The Assize of Novel Disseisin* (Oxford, 1973), p. 65. Note also *PKJ*, iii no. 743 on the offender's hunger being used to explain a crime.
37. See above, p. 205.
38. Note *Surrey*, pp. 116–17, 120 on officials being sued.
39. See e.g. H. M. Thomas, *Vassals, Heiresses, Crusaders, and Thugs* (Philadelphia, PA, 1993), pp. 61, 77–8, 83–4.
40. See e.g. Thomas, *Vassals*, ch. 2.
41. E.g. Turner, *Courts*, pp. 90ff.

for abused wives. The husband enjoyed control over his wife's moveable goods, and it was almost certainly difficult for her to ensure that her husband provided for her maintenance. Women could inherit lands; for example a dead man's daughters succeeded if he had no sons.[42] However, the heiress did not control her own lands as an heir would; if unmarried her lord controlled them, if married, her husband.[43] Her husband's alienations of her land might require her assent, but according to *Glanvill,* the wife was bound to consent to all his acts 'which do not offend God'. In practice, though, women seem to have had rather greater control of the alienation of lands they brought to their marriage than *Glanvill* would suggest. Women made grants in their own name with their husbands' consent, and following her husband's death a wife might revoke grants he had made without or even perhaps with her consent.[44] In litigation, too, women played a more significant part than might at first be apparent. Women appointed their husbands as attorneys, but husbands sometimes appointed their wives. In cases concerning lands she had brought to the marriage, a married woman had to be sued jointly with her husband. In such a case, if a writ failed to mention her where appropriate, it could be quashed, or a husband might vouch his wife as warrantor.[45] As widows, women were particularly prominent litigants, with numerous actions concerning dower.

As for criminal law, according to the opinion of a royal justice recorded in a plea roll, women could not bring appeals except concerning the death of their husband or concerning rape, whilst Magna Carta clause fifty-four mentions only the death of her husband. In rape cases, any settlement was almost invariably out of court, suggesting

---

42. In technical terms, although males of the same proximity to the decedent were preferred to females, females were preferred to males of the next closest degree; sons were preferred to daughters, daughters to brothers, and so on.
43. For a dispute involving a woman purchasing land, see PRS, ns 31 (1957), p. 83.
44. See *Glanvill,* vi 3, Hall, p. 60; Pollock and Maitland, ii 409–13.
45. E.g. *Lincs.,* no. 131. Note also the case in Pollock and Maitland, ii 409.

from the outside, going back on your meds seems wise. That stuff you were saying about wanting to 'touch base with yourself' and see what life is like without them is fair enough, and maybe something to explore when the rest of your life is stable enough to support that kind of experiment ... but that time is probably not now, hey.

Just something to think about. Go easy, take things slow, and watch lots of Buffy. You'll get through <3

Delivered

iMessage

that the law's protection was somewhat indirect. In homicide cases, the courts sometimes required that the woman actually witness the death of her husband. However, although these instances suggest a very narrow restriction in women's access to criminal law, there are other signs that women could bring accusations concerning not just rape but any physical harm done to them and on occasion other offences as well.[46]

Despite the protection given to them by Magna Carta and developments in Henry III's minority, tenants in chief were still disadvantaged by having a lord with no superior, a situation Edward I exploited.[47] Also excluded particularly in the field of land law were villeins; indeed, the Angevin reforms contributed to a hardening of the legal definition of villeinage. In criminal law, villeins had in theory some capacity to sue their lords for very serious physical harm suffered, and somewhat greater rights against people other than their lords, but in practice they probably found it very hard to pursue criminal cases in the royal courts. However, as we saw, they were defended as to amercements by clause twenty of the Charter.[48] Finally, churchmen and church matters were only covered by the common law to a limited degree. Property matters, such as advowsons and some land cases did come under royal courts, but Henry II had failed to bring clerical wrongdoing under royal control.

Thus, at the time of Magna Carta, limitations remained in the scope and regularity of the developing common law. Even royal manuals such as *Glanvill* and the *Dialogue* show inconsistencies and uncertainties.[49] Yet such limitations would survive into *Bracton*'s time and well beyond. The

46. *Lincs.*, pp. lv–lvi, and e.g. nos 690, 834, 841, 855; *PKJ*, ii no. 730; *Glanvill*, xiv 1, 3, 6, Hall, pp. 173–6; *Surrey*, pp. 123–5; *Wiltshire*, pp. 88–90. More generally, note Pollock and Maitland, i 482–5. For a short and lucid treatment of these and other aspects of women's position in common law, see P. A. Brand, 'Family and inheritance: women and children', in C. Given-Wilson, ed., *Illustrated History of Late Medieval England* (Manchester, 1996), ch. 3.
47. Holt, *Magna Carta*, ch. 5; K. B. McFarlane, 'Had Edward I a "policy" towards the earls?', *History* 50 (1965), 149–59.
48. See above, p. 226; P. R. Hyams, *King, Lords, and Peasants in Medieval England* (Oxford, 1980), esp. ch. 9, cf. Pollock and Maitland, i 415–19; *Glanvill*, xiv 1, Hall, p. 173.
49. See above, p. 155.

achievement of the Norman and Angevin periods was immense. Key elements of thirteenth-century and later common law were established: a court system with a definite focus on royal courts, local or central; much substantive law with regard to land-holding; consistent forms of litigation in land cases; classification of offences against the person and moveable goods; the availability of the jury to decide criminal cases.[50] A common law had been formed, both in the sense of a law common throughout the realm and a law with definite continuity into the common law of later centuries.

. . .

CONCLUDING COMPARISONS

To complete our assessment, let us look more widely for standards of comparison. The king of France's realm was much more extensive than England, and by 1215 the entire lands of John could not rival those of Philip Augustus. Geography, therefore, helps to explain why the French king's exercise of justice within his realm was rather more limited than his English counterpart's. His own court was primarily for his tenants in chief, and tended to produce compromise settlements. Otherwise royal justice concentrated upon the lands directly controlled by the king, lands which were growing at this time, particularly with the fall of Normandy. Whilst reforms were introduced when Philip was setting off on Crusade in 1190, these too concentrated on the areas of direct royal control. Even royal hearings of cases of default of justice were limited to these areas, only very exceptionally extending beyond to cases arising in the mass of lords' courts.[51] When treatises on custom (*coutumiers*) appeared in France in the thirteenth century, some contained law in many ways similar to England's, but they covered regions, not the whole realm.

50. See also above, p. 179, on justices familiar with the custom of the king's court giving guidance towards judgment in criminal cases.
51. For this paragraph, see J. W. Baldwin, *The Government of Philip Augustus* (Berkeley, CA, 1986), esp. pp. 37–44, 137–44, 264–6. For further comparisons, see e.g. R. C. van Caenegem, 'Criminal law in England and Flanders under King Henry II and Count Philip of Alsace', in his *Legal History: a European Perspective* (London, 1991), pp. 37–60.

The impression of comparatively restricted central control is confirmed in two smaller areas more closely related to England. Norman sources give no sign of the requirement that land cases in lords' courts should begin only by writ, and the same rule is absent from Scotland until the later thirteenth century. Scotland, indeed, provides an interesting comparison, with a greater decentralization of law and justice, and the survival of significant seignorial courts. In such circumstances, features of land law such as distraint by fee, which disappeared in England with the Angevin reforms, continued to exist in Scotland.[52]

Why was England different? Certainly, the realm was small compared with Germany or France, but not with Normandy or Scotland. Size therefore was not the sole reason. There was the survival of the Anglo-Saxon legacy of strong royal and local administrative power, manifest for example in the shire court which would be so important in Angevin reform. In addition, there was the coherence of Norman custom, linked to the power of its duke. Conquest and settlement further strengthened the regime, without creating very numerous and strong independent lordships. The Anglo-Saxon legacy and the settlement pattern combined to ensure the importance of local self-government at the king's command, and the vital role of local free men and knightly society. Anglo-Norman England had a powerful royal regime and an already fairly coherent and consistent body of custom, to which could be applied the developments of Henry II's reign, notably of routinization and bureaucratization. The Becket dispute may have given a peculiar spur to royal thinking about law and government.[53] Before the other major kingdoms of northern Europe, England had available the variety of materials from which the common law was constructed.

People in the twelfth and thirteenth centuries also compared their laws with others, and this self-consciousness

---

52. See J. Yver, 'Le bref Anglo-Normand', *Tijdschrift voor Rechsgeschiedenis* 29 (1961), 319; H. L. MacQueen, *Common Law and Feudal Society in Medieval Scotland* (Edinburgh, 1993), esp. chs 2, 4.
53. Note also MacQueen, *Common Law, passim* on conflict with the Church stimulating legal development in Scotland.

gives us one final element in the appearance of the common law. Ranulf de Glanville lauded the speed of the royal courts in comparison with ecclesiastical ones.[54] Meanwhile English practices were being exported, for example to Ireland. In 1210, King John sought to regularize these practices by issuing a charter ordering that English law and customs be observed in the lordship of Ireland. The charter may have recorded the main rules of English law, making it the first official statement of that law. As part of the process, the earliest surviving register of writs was probably written, and sent with a covering letter:

> Since we desire justice according to the custom of our realm of England to be shown to all in our realm of Ireland who complain of wrongdoing, we have caused the form of writs of course, by which this is accustomed to be done, to be inserted in the present writing and transmitted to you.[55]

The transfer of English practice, although not wholly successful, is highly significant. It shows again the emphasis upon uniformity. It reveals that not just individual reforms but the whole law was sufficiently coherent to be considered reproducible. English law could be compared with and preferred to other laws. Such self-confidence was not limited to comparison with the laws of those regarded as barbarians. Let us end with a famous story from two decades after our period. Churchmen were seeking to bring English law in line with canonical practice by allowing the marriage of a bastard's parents to legitimize the child. The case was discussed and the barons produced a ringing endorsement of practice: 'we do not wish to change the laws of England.'[56] For the nobles in 1236 the common law of England was a subject of pride.

54. Walter Map, *De Nugis Curialium*, ed. and trans M. R. James, rev. C. N. L. Brooke and R. A. B. Mynors (Oxford, 1983), p. 508.
55. Brand, *Making*, pp. 445–56; *Early Registers*, p. 1.
56. *EHD*, iii no. 30, c. 9.

GLOSSARY

The aim of this glossary is to provide brief working definitions for the reader. The definitions are therefore short, general, and dogmatic; they conceal both many nuances of sense and development of meaning during the period. Cross references within the glossary are indicated by 'qv.'. Fuller discussion is given in the main text, and is accessible through the index. See also 'Note on sources', below.

Abjure	To leave a specified area, for example the realm, under oath never to return.
Acquisition	Lands or other rights acquired by the current holder, as opposed to those which he inherited.
Advowson	The right of nominating a cleric to an ecclesiastical benefice, e.g. a parish.
Aid	Payment from a vassal to his lord, particularly payments owed on certain occasions such as the knighting of the lord's son.
Alienate	To grant away land or other rights.
Alms	(i) Lands granted to a church for spiritual services; the tenure of such lands; (ii) any charitable gift.
Amercement	A monetary penalty, exacted from one who had fallen into the king's mercy because of an offence.
Appeal	A charge brought by one individual against another, normally relating to theft or violence.
Appellor	One who brings an appeal (qv.).

Approver	A criminal who turns king's evidence; he must accuse and fight his former criminal colleagues.
Assize	(i) Legislation; (ii) procedures arising from such legislation; (iii) the body carrying out such procedures; (iv) the trial itself.
Attach	To compel a defendant to provide gages and sureties (qv.) that he would appear in court on a specified day.
Attaint	A process for reviewing court decisions, through a jury generally of twenty-four men who might convict recognitors (qv.) of having made a false oath.
Attorney	A person who acts as a legal representative for another, particularly in litigation.
Bench	A tribunal of justices, most notably in our period the court of the royal justices – the Common Bench – which sat at Westminster.
Bocland, bookland	An Anglo-Saxon form of land-holding, at least initially meaning privileged land granted by charter (*boc*). By the late Anglo-Saxon period, land characterized by various privileges, and – in the case of holding by laymen – by heritability and alienability.
Bót	Compensation payable to a victim or his/her relatives; also payment e.g. to the king or lord for an offence.
Carucate	(i) A measure of land; (ii) a fiscal assessment unit. The equivalent of a hide (qv.).
Certification	A process for reviewing a court decision, by re-assembling the assize justices, the parties, and generally the recognitors (qv.) before another court, normally the king's.
Chattels	Moveable possessions.
Cirograph	An agreement written out twice (or on occasion three times), with the word CIROGRAPHUM written between the texts. The parchment was then cut through this word, and each party received one copy.
Collusion	A case brought to court by one party against another with the latter's agreement, notably

	in order to secure a conveyance (qv.). Collusion may underlie many 'final concords' (qv.).
Common pleas	Pleas relating to the king's general or common jurisdiction over all his people.
Compurgation	An oath taken with the formal support of a specific number of others, in order to prove or disprove a point in court.
Conventio	An agreement.
Conveyance	The transfer of land or other rights.
Crown-wearing	A ceremony at a feast during which the enthroned king wears his crown. Such ceremonies show some regularity of location and timing.
Danegeld	A form of taxation.
Danelaw	(i) The northern and eastern areas of England once under Danish domination; (ii) the law of that area.
Darrein presentment (assize of)	A procedure using a recognition (qv.) to determine who is the lawful possessor of an advowson (qv.).
Default	Failure to perform an obligation, e.g. failure to appear in court.
Default of justice/right	Failure to do justice.
Deforce	To dispossess.
Demesne	Land a lord kept for himself in his own direct power (although with peasant tenants), as opposed to land granted away to others; often contrasted with fiefs (qv.).
Disseisin	Dispossession; the taking away of seisin (qv.).
Distraint	(i) Temporary seizure of moveable goods and/or land in order to enforce obedience to a decision or order; (ii) the thing distrained.
Dower	Land apportioned for a widow to hold after her husband's death.
Enfeoff	To grant land as a fief (qv.) to be held of the grantor.
Entry, writ of	A writ setting in motion a recognition (qv.), and focusing upon one alleged flaw in the tenant's title (see p. 136).

Escheat	(i) The reversion of land to its lord; (ii) land which has thus reverted.
Esplees	The products of land or the services deriving from it.
Essoin	An excuse for non-appearance at court.
Exception	A plea by a defendant that his opponent's complaint or claim is inapplicable to the case, for reasons of fact or law; the defendant should not, therefore, be required to make a formal defence to the complaint or claim.
Exchequer	(i) The meetings where sheriffs' annual accounts were audited – from the *exchequer board* on which these accounts were visually calculated; (ii) a court, generally presided over by the chief justiciar, dealing primarily with financial matters in the earlier twelfth century; later in the century, until the separation of the bench (qv.) in the 1190s, the central royal court at Westminster, normally although not always presided over by the justiciar.
Exculpation	Proof whereby the accused clears himself of blame.
Eyre	A visitation by the king or his justices. General eyre: a visitation by groups of royal justices throughout the realm to deal with all pleas; each group covered a circuit of several counties.
Farm	(i) A fixed rent; (ii) land held at such a rent.
Fealty	Loyalty; the oath of loyalty.
Fee	See 'fief'.
Fee farm	(i) A fixed rent, generally from land held heritably; (ii) land held at such a rent.
Felony, felon	(i) Infidelity, treason. One guilty of infidelity to his lord; (ii) the most serious type of offence; one guilty of such an offence (see pp. 161–3).
Fief	Land, generally heritable land, held in return for service, usually military service.
Final concord	(i) An agreement, generally one made in the king's court; (ii) the record of such an agreement.

Fine	(i) Payment for an agreement, or the ending of a lawsuit; (ii) a final concord (qv.); (iii) foot of fine: the third and bottom part of a three-part cirograph (qv.) recording an agreement in the king's court.
Franchise	(i) A privilege; (ii) a privileged area. Also 'liberty'.
Frankpledge	A body of men, generally ten or twelve, but sometimes an entire village, acting as mutual sureties (qv.) that they would not commit offences, and bound to produce the guilty party when an offence was committed.
Fyrd	The Anglo-Saxon word for military service, or for a military force.
Gage	(i) A thing given as security; (ii) gage of land: land given temporarily as security in return for a sum of money which is to be repaid.
Gavelkind	A form of tenure in Kent, characterized in particular by the division of inheritance between heirs.
Hallmoot	The lord's local court for lesser men.
Hide	(i) A measure of land, generally 120 acres; (ii) a fiscal assessment unit.
Homage	(Related to Latin *homo* – man.) The ceremony of becoming a lord's vassal/man.
Honour	A lordship, generally one held directly from the king by a tenant in chief (qv.).
Hue and cry	The raising of the alarm and pursuit following the committing of an offence.
Indictment	Presentment (qv.) of felonies (qv.).
Infangentheof	The right of executing, after summary trial, thieves caught red-handed.
Knight's fee	A tenement owing the service of one knight; thus also e.g. half a knight's fee, twenty knights' fees, etc.
Lawful man	A man possessed of all the rights of a freeman.
Leges	Unofficial legal tracts mostly of the twelfth century, composed of collections of supposed laws, often based in part upon translations of Anglo-Saxon texts.

Liberty	(i) A privilege; (ii) a privileged area. Also 'franchise'.
Livery of seisin	The ceremony of transferring land or other rights.
Mainpast	Those for whom a head of a household stands as surety (qv.).
Mark	Two-thirds of a pound; 13s. 4d. (=66p).
Mercy	See 'amercement'.
Mesne judgment	A court's intermediate (=*mesne*) judgment as to which party in a dispute should provide proof.
Mesne lord/tenant	One who holds from a lord other than the king.
Minor	One who is not yet of age; that is, according to *Glanvill,* vii 9, Hall, p. 82, males under twenty-one for tenure by knight service, under fifteen for socage (qv.).
Mort d'ancestor	An assize (qv.) whereby an heir may claim his inheritance through a recognition (qv.).
Murdrum	(i) Secret homicide; (ii) communal penalty paid for the killing of a Frenchman (or perhaps any foreigner) when the slayer cannot be found; later a similar penalty for the killing of any freeman (see pp. 62–3).
Novel disseisin	A swift assize (qv.), making use of a recognition (qv.), to reverse recent, unjust disseisins (qv.).
Papal judge delegate	A judge delegated by the pope to hear a particular case or cases.
Peers	One's equals.
Pleas of the crown	The most serious pleas, particularly connected with the king's interests.
Pone	A process for transferring cases from the county to the king's court.
Praecipe	A writ conveying a command, disobedience of which will lead to the matter being heard before the king or his justices.
Praecipe quod reddat	A writ ordering restoration of land to a claimant; disobedience leads to the matter being heard in the king's court.
Presentment	An accusation brought by a sworn body of men.

moment?

I saw my doctor yesterday cause I have a concussion and he wants me back on my meds. But I don't know. I can't face a hospital right now. Can barely walk. Thanks for caring tho, that helps.

Any time.

I obviously don't know shit about shit ... but from the outside, going back on your meds seems wise. That stuff you were saying about wanting to 'touch base with yourself' and see what life is like without

  iMessage

Quitclaim	(i) The surrender of lands or other rights and all claim to them; (ii) a document recording such a surrender.
Recognition	A process whereby a body of neighbours gave a true answer to a question put to them by the public official who had summoned them.
Recognitor	One of the neighbours responsible for making a recognition (qv.).
Relief	A payment made to a lord by an heir for his inheritance.
Returnable writ	A writ setting specified judicial proceedings in motion, and returned by the addressee to the royal justices hearing the case with added information written upon it.
Sake and soke	Jurisdiction exercised by lords over various offences (see pp. 43–5).
Scutage	Payment in lieu of knight service.
Seise	To transfer lands or some other rights.
Seisin	(i) Possession based on some justifiable claim; (ii) the act of seising.
Sergeanty	(i) Tenure based on rendering some personal service to the lord, normally distinguished from knight service; (ii) land held thus.
Socage	(i) Tenure based on rendering fixed services, usually rent; (ii) land held thus.
Sokeman	A classification of men, generally free men; literally those owing suit of court (qv.).
Subinfeudation	The grant of land by a lord other than the king to a man to hold from him as a fief (qv.).
Substantive law	The elements of law determining rights, claims, obligations; e.g., law as to whom an inheritance should pass on the death of a tenant. Generally distinguished from procedural law, concerned with the mechanics of court action.
Substitution	A grant of land whereby the current tenant surrenders it to his lord, who in turn grants it to a new tenant to hold from him.
Suit of court	The obligation to attend court.

Suitor	A person attending court.
Surety	A person pledged to ensure another's appearance in court or fulfilment of some other obligation.
Team	The right to supervise processes whereby a man proved himself the rightful possessor of chattels; note also 'warranty' (i), below.
Tenant in chief	One who holds directly from the king.
Tenement	A land-holding.
Tenure	(i) The holding of land from a lord; (ii) the land itself held from a lord; (iii) the terms on which such land is held; (iv) doctrine of tenure: the doctrine, not spelt out in writing during our period, that all land is held directly or indirectly from the king.
Tithing	A grouping of ten men for mutual security; see also 'frankpledge'.
Toll	The right of taking tolls.
Tolt	A process for transferring cases from a lord's court to the county.
Tourn, sheriff's	The sheriff's biennial tour of hundred courts, notably to inspect the workings of frankpledge (qv.).
Trespass	(i) A wrong; (ii) a wrong less serious than, for example, a felony (qv.) (see p. 164).
Utrum	An assize (qv.) using a recognition (qv.), originally established to determine whether land was lay fee (qv.) or alms (qv.).
Virgate	A quarter of a hide (qv.); generally about 30 acres.
Vouch	See 'warranty'.
Wardship	(i) Custody of an heir who is not yet of age and/or the heir's land; (ii) land held for this reason.
Warranty, voucher to	The process whereby (i) a man vouches that he obtained a chattel (qv.) legitimately from another; or (ii) a man vouches that his lord granted him a piece of land or other rights. Lords who failed to warrant lands successfully to their vassals were obliged to provide them with equivalent lands in exchange.

247

Wer	The monetary estimate of a man's worth, used for the calculation of payment following his unlawful death (see '*wergild*') or injury, the value of his oath, and penalties to the king.
Wergild	Payment to the kin in compensation for the slaying of a person.
Wite	Payment by way of punishment, in general to the king.
Wreck	Royal rights relating to shipwreck.

NOTE ON SOURCES

A wide range of sources has been used in this book, and the approach which I have adopted reflects both the prevalence of certain types of evidence, and the degree of trust which can be invested in them. There are some general problems, most obviously the fact that much legal activity was never recorded in writing. Records which were made need not survive. The preponderance of ecclesiastical material reflects the greater emphasis the Church placed on both record-making and record-keeping. Most lay records come from the higher level of society, especially the king, but also the greater tenants in chief. Changes in the amount or type of evidence may seem to indicate developments in law and the administration of justice whereas in fact they only reveal what had previously left no record. Most sources are in Latin, but one can also look for help and inspiration to the vernacular literature of the period, its epics and romances. Such literature can both help with analyses of disputes and also suggest the vernacular words which lay behind the Latin of the records.

Leges: If one were seeking to produce a complete set of legal rules which applied particularly in the first half of our period, it would be very tempting to go to the various post-Conquest texts commonly referred to as *Leges* (Laws), most notably the *Leges Henrici Primi* (1114–18). These purport to be authoritative statements of law. In fact, however, they are archaizing texts, intent perhaps on giving some idea of what law should be, but also on preserving and translating the legacy of the Anglo-Saxon past as its language and practices became less widely comprehensible. The *Leges* draw on Anglo-Saxon legal texts and also on other written sources, for example canon law or early Continental law codes. Any such statements based on earlier texts must of course be treated with extreme caution: given the choice between current reality and past written authority, the authors often favoured the latter. More problematic are the statements which have no written source, and which may be based on personal experience, for example much of the *Leges Henrici's* treatment of court procedure. Here the best method is to accept such statements only if they seem congruous with other, less untrustworthy evidence.

Dispute reports: Rather than the *Leges*, in my treatment of the Anglo-Norman period I have relied heavily on accounts of cases, preserved in chronicles, other narratives, or charters. These allow analysis of the tactics adopted by parties in and out of court, and also of the way in which norms both conditioned disputing and were used by disputants. However, it must be remembered that such accounts are not impartial, almost invariably being produced by one party in the dispute, generally by the winner.

Charters and writs: The records of land transactions underlie much of my analysis of land law. Such charters generally record gifts or confirmations of land by a lord to a tenant or a church. Some variations in drafting practices continued throughout our period, and these can be informative. However, the form of charters, at least in the twelfth century, is generally quite standardized. This allows analysis of the frequency with which certain formulae appear, for example with regard to the consent of family members to gifts of land. However, there are also problems with analysis of land law through charters, and not simply that written records of grants to laymen are rare in the Anglo-Norman period. An apparently simple grant of land in a charter may in fact record the settlement of a dispute, hence the need for the grant to be recorded in writing. It is therefore desirable to find out as much as possible about the circumstances which underlie any charter.

The great majority of charters are in letter or 'writ' form, starting with an address to those to whom the document should be of concern, and then spelling out the transaction. They are therefore sometimes referred to as 'writ-charters'. The word 'writ' is normally used more narrowly for a letter, generally fairly brief, conveying an order or instruction. Such instructions can be of wide application, even constituting legislation, or very specific. In the current book, analysis of writs has been particularly important with regard to royal intervention in disputes; the surviving writs are valuable of themselves, and also give an indication of interventions for which written evidence either does not survive or never existed.

Royal records: For the Anglo-Norman period, royal records are relatively scarce. Domesday Book tells us much about patterns of land-holding and something of the land law of the period. It also records many disputes, but these generally appear only as brief notes of claims. For some towns and shires sets of customs are recorded, including customs concerning wrongs. The 1130 Pipe Roll records shire accounts made at the exchequer of Henry I. These provide much information, for example on the judicial activities of royal servants and the payments made to the king in relation to law, justice, and land-holding.

Royal records are much more extensive for the Angevin period. From 1155 we have a complete run of Pipe Rolls, allowing financial and administrative trends to be analysed. From the 1190s, when the first royal court rolls start to survive, we have a reasonably complete account of the forms of business coming before certain types of court. There is no official record of royal legislation, but a variety of texts do survive, most notably in the chronicle of the one-time royal justice, Roger of Howden.

Law books: Also at the end of Henry II's reign comes the first legal manual intended for the practical use of royal justices and their officers. This goes under the name of *Glanvill*, since it was once held to have been written by the chief justiciar, Rannulf de Glanville. Its significance is considered at some length in chapter 5. Another manual, for financial administrators, *The Dialogue of the Exchequer*, includes much of interest on law and justice. For the last decades of our period, careful use must be made of a far larger law book than *Glanvill*. Also called *On the Laws and Customs of England*, this is best known under the title *Bracton*, since it was once believed that its author was another royal justice, Henry de Bracton. However, it is no longer accepted that he was the author of the work and wrote in the 1250s. He was at most a substantial reviser of a work primarily composed in the 1220s and 1230s; for recent controversy over the date of the work, see J. L. Barton, 'The mystery of Bracton', *Journal of Legal History* 14 (1993), 1–142 and P. A. Brand, 'The age of *Bracton*' in Hudson, *Centenary Essays*, pp. 65–89.

*

Translations: I have, in general, adopted translators' versions of texts; most of my alterations have involved giving more literal renderings in order to clarify legal points.

. . . . .

FURTHER READING

. . .

SOURCES

R. C. van Caenegem, ed., *English Lawsuits from William I to Richard I* (2 vols, Selden Soc., 106, 107, 1990–91) usefully presents court cases with English translations. Other Selden Society volumes also contain much relevant material. For the later period, C. T. Flower, *Introduction to the Curia Regis Rolls* (Selden Soc., 62, 1944), provides summaries of many plea roll cases; see also D. M. Stenton, ed., *Pleas before the King or his Justices, 1198–1202* (4 vols, Selden Soc., 67, 68, 83, 84, 1952–67). R. C. van Caenegem, ed., *Royal Writs in England from the Conquest to Glanvill* (Selden Soc., 77, 1959) contains a long and important introduction, as well as a selection of writs with translations.

Also available in parallel text are L. J. Downer, ed. and trans, *Leges Henrici Primi* (Oxford, 1972), Glanvill, *Tractatus de Legibus*, ed. and trans G. D. G. Hall (Edinburgh, 1965), and Richard fitzNigel, *Dialogus de Scaccario*, ed. and trans C. Johnson, rev. F. E. L. Carter and D. E. Greenway (Oxford, 1983). Many relevant texts are available in translation in *English Historical Documents*, i, ed. D. Whitelock (2nd edn, London, 1979); ii, ed. D. C. Douglas and G. W. Greenaway (2nd edn, London, 1981); iii, ed. H. Rothwell (London, 1975).

Note M. T. Clanchy, 'Remembering the past and the good old law', *History* 55 (1970), 165–76 for ideas on law and law-making; H. G. Richardson and G. O. Sayles, *Law and Legislation from Aethelbert to Magna Carta* (Edinburgh, 1966), for provocative ideas on legislation and legal texts;

T. F. T. Plucknett, *Early English Legal Literature* (Cambridge, 1958), ch. 2 for the *Leges* and *Glanvill.*

. . .

GENERAL

Historians' starting point – and often finishing point – is Sir Frederick Pollock and F. W. Maitland, *The History of English Law before the Time of Edward I* (2 vols, 2nd edn with new introduction by S. F. C. Milsom, Cambridge, 1968). The *History* is supplemented by F. W. Maitland, *Domesday Book and Beyond* (Cambridge, 1897). A companion piece is J. G. H. Hudson, ed., *The History of English Law: Centenary Essays on 'Pollock and Maitland'* (*Proceedings of the British Academy*, 89, 1996).

Essential new work on the Anglo-Saxon period is now being produced by P. Wormald. A summary view is provided by his 'Maitland and Anglo-Saxon law: beyond Domesday Book', in Hudson, ed., *Centenary Essays.* His fullest statement is due to appear in *The Making of English Law* (Oxford, forthcoming). Note also, for example, his 'Charters, law and the settlement of disputes in Anglo-Saxon England', in W. Davies and P. Fouracre, eds, *The Settlement of Disputes in Early Medieval Europe* (Cambridge, 1986), pp. 149–68.

The Norman background is discussed in C. H. Haskins, *Norman Institutions* (Cambridge, MA, 1918) and D. Bates, *Normandy before 1066* (London, 1982); the latter contains references to relevant material in French, notably the works of J. Yver. D. M. Stenton, *English Justice between the Norman Conquest and the Great Charter* (Philadelphia, PA, 1964) is the best survey of the administration of justice in our period. R. C. van Caenegem, *The Birth of the English Common Law* (2nd edn, Cambridge, 1988), has similar concerns to this volume but a markedly different approach. P. R. Hyams, 'The common law and the French connection', *ANS* 4 (1982), 77–92, 196–202 sets Anglo-Norman law in a wider French context; see also J. Le Patourel, *The Norman Empire* (Oxford, 1976), an extremely important, wide-ranging book. Other relevant essays are contained in G. S. Garnett and J. G. H. Hudson, eds, *Law and Government in Medieval England and Normandy* (Cambridge, 1994), and P. A. Brand, *The Making of the Common Law* (London, 1992).

General introductions for post-Conquest England are provided by W. L. Warren, *The Governance of Norman and Angevin England* (London, 1987), and M. Chibnall, *Anglo-Norman England* (Oxford, 1986). Useful for comparative purposes is O. F. Robinson, T. D. Fergus and W. M. Gordon, *An Introduction to European Legal History* (Abingdon, 1985). Three more general works of considerable relevance are M. T. Clanchy, *From Memory to Written Record* (2nd edn, Oxford, 1993); S. M. G. Reynolds, *Kingdoms and Communities in Western Europe, 900–1300* (Oxford, 1984) and her *Fiefs and Vassals* (Oxford, 1994).

. . .

CHAPTER 1

Anthropological work has had considerable influence on historians of law and disputing; a good starting point is S. Roberts, *Order and Dispute* (Harmondsworth, 1979). For very good anthropologically influenced work, see S. D. White, ' "*Pactum . . . legem vincit et amor iudicium*": the settlement of disputes by compromise in eleventh-century western France', *American Journal of Legal History* 22 (1978), 281–308, and his *Custom, Kinship, and Gifts to Saints* (Chapel Hill, NC, 1988). On compromise settlement, see also e.g. M. T. Clanchy, 'Law and love in the middle ages', in J. Bossy, ed., *Disputes and Settlements* (Cambridge, 1983), pp. 47–67. Historians of law are increasingly using literary sources; see, for example, P. R. Hyams, 'Henry II and Ganelon', *Syracuse Scholar* 4 (1983), 22–35; S. D. White, 'The discourse of inheritance in twelfth-century France: alternative models of the fief in *Raoul de Cambrai*', in Garnett and Hudson, eds, *Law and Government*, cited above.

Two perhaps complementary, if not always mutually complimentary, studies of ordeal are P. R. Hyams, 'Trial by ordeal: the key to proof in the early common law', in M. S. Arnold, T. A. Green, S. A. Scully and S. D. White, eds, *On the Laws and Customs of England: Essays in Honour of S. E. Thorne* (Chapel Hill, NC, 1981), pp. 90–126 and R. J. Bartlett, *Trial by Fire and Water. The Medieval Judicial Ordeal* (Oxford, 1986).

Like, "fuck hospitals", sure - I can COMPLETELY understand why you'd feel that, but ... you might need one? And it seems like what's happening right now has an awful lot to do with you going off your meds?

Just try not to face it more alone than you need to be

Are you seeing your doctor / psych at the moment?

I saw my doctor yesterday cause I have a

 iMessage

. . .

CHAPTER 2

In addition to the works of Maitland, D. M. Stenton, and van Caenegem already cited, a useful introduction is A. Harding, *The Law Courts of Medieval England* (London, 1973). W. A. Morris, *The Early English County Court* (Berkeley, CA, 1926) is now supplemented by R. C. Palmer, *The County Courts of Medieval England* (Princeton, NJ, 1982). For the hundred, see H. M. Cam, *The Hundred and the Hundred Rolls* (London, 1930). F. M. Stenton, *The First Century of English Feudalism, 1066–1166* (2nd edn, Oxford, 1961) provides vital background and material for seignorial courts.

Important more specific studies include J. A. Green, *The Government of England under Henry I* (Cambridge, 1986), H. A. Cronne, 'The office of local justiciar in England under the Norman kings', *Univ. of Birmingham Historical Journal* 6 (1958), 18–28, and W. T. Reedy, 'The origin of the general eyre in the reign of Henry I', *Speculum* 41 (1966), 688–724. On privileged areas, see N. D. Hurnard, 'The Anglo-Norman franchises', *EHR* 64 (1949), 289–323, 433–60. On church courts, see F. Barlow, *The English Church, 1066–1154* (London, 1979); C. Morris, 'William I and the church courts', *EHR* 82 (1967), 449–63; J. A. Brundage, *Medieval Canon Law* (London, 1995).

. . .

CHAPTER 3

There is no single introductory work on theft and violence in this period, although note that T. F. T. Plucknett, *Edward I and Criminal Law* (Cambridge 1959) is largely concerned with the centuries before 1272. Wormald, *Making of English Law*, cited above, contains very important arguments. J. Goebel, *Felony and Misdemeanor* (New York, 1937) is an important if difficult book. N. D. Hurnard, *The King's Pardon for Homicide* (Oxford, 1969) is of considerably wider relevance than its title might suggest. Conflicting views on *ex officio* prosecution of offences are taken in N. D. Hurnard, 'The jury of presentment and the assize of Clarendon', *EHR* 56 (1941), 374–410, and R. C. van

Caenegem, 'Public prosecution of crime in twelfth century England', in his *Legal History: a European Perspective* (London, 1991), pp. 1–36. W. A. Morris, *The Frankpledge System* (New York, 1910) remains the only monograph on this subject.

. . .

CHAPTER 4

For Norman background see E. Z. Tabuteau, *Transfers of Property in Eleventh-Century Norman Law* (Chapel Hill, NC, 1988). For a straightforward introduction to land law throughout the Norman and Angevin period, and beyond, see A. W. B. Simpson, *A History of the Land Law* (Oxford, 1986).

So fundamental to the thinking behind this chapter that they barely appear in the footnotes are S. F. C. Milsom, *The Legal Framework of English Feudalism* (Cambridge, 1976) and various works by J. C. Holt, most notably 'Politics and property in early medieval England', *Past and Present* 57 (1972), 3–52 and 'Feudal society and the family in early medieval England', *TRHS* 5th Ser. 32–5 (1982–85). All too prominent in the footnotes, but giving a more extended exposition of my own views is J. G. H. Hudson, *Land, Law, and Lordship in Anglo-Norman England* (Oxford, 1994). Very important articles are S. E. Thorne, 'English feudalism and estates in land', *Cambridge Law Journal* (1959), 193–209 and P. R. Hyams, 'Warranty and good lordship in twelfth century England', *Law and History Review* 5 (1987), 437–503. R. V. Lennard, *Rural England, 1086–1135: A Study of Social and Agrarian Conditions* (Oxford, 1959) contains much of relevance.

. . .

CHAPTER 5

Note especially the works of Maitland, Milsom, Stenton, and van Caenegem mentioned above. Of fundamental importance are J. Biancalana, 'For want of justice: legal reforms of Henry II', *Columbia Law Review* 88 (1988), 433–536 and P. A. Brand, ' "Multis vigiliis excogitatam et inventam": Henry II and the creation of the English Common Law', in his *The Making of the Common Law* (London, 1992), pp. 77–102. W. L. Warren, *Henry II*

(London, 1973), gives a context for, and a clear exposition of, Henry's reforms. For a general account of Stephen's reign, see H. A. Cronne, *The Reign of Stephen* (London, 1970). Also important in contextualization are the works of M. Cheney, for example 'A decree of King Henry II on defect of justice', in D. E. Greenway, C. Holdsworth and J. Sayers, eds, *Tradition and Change: Essays in Honour of Marjorie Chibnall* (Cambridge, 1985), and 'The litigation between John Marshal and Thomas Becket in 1164: a pointer to the origin of novel disseisin?', in J. A. Guy and H. G. Beale, eds, *Law and Social Change in British History* (London, 1984). Note also J. Gillingham, 'Conquering kings: some twelfth-century reflections on Henry II and Richard I', in T. Reuter, ed., *Warriors and Churchmen in the High Middle Ages: Essays presented to Karl Leyser* (London, 1992), which plays down Henry's interests in matters of law.

. . .

CHAPTER 6

The works cited for chapter 3 remain relevant. R. F. Hunnisett, *The Medieval Coroner* (Cambridge, 1961) analyses a long-lasting innovation of this period. D. M. Stenton, ed., *The Earliest Lincolnshire Assize Rolls, A.D. 1202–1209* (Lincoln Record Soc., 22, 1926) provides a wide range of cases and a very useful introduction, as does C. A. F. Meekings, ed., *The 1235 Surrey Eyre*, i (Surrey Record Soc., 31, 1979). On trespass, see A. Harding, ed., *Roll of the Shropshire Eyre of 1256* (Selden Soc., 96, 1981). As records become plentiful, further analysis can be made of the social context of crime; see, for example, J. B. Given, *Society and Homicide in Thirteenth-Century England* (Stanford, CA, 1977).

. . .

CHAPTER 7

The works cited above for chapter 4 remain relevant. A very important study is D. W. Sutherland, *The Assize of Novel Disseisin* (Oxford, 1973). On villeinage tenure, see P. R. Hyams, *King, Lords, and Peasants in Medieval England* (Oxford, 1980). On women and land law, see S. F. C. Milsom, 'Inheritance by women in the twelfth and early thirteenth centuries', in his *Studies in the History of the Common Law* (London, 1985), pp. 231–60; J. C. Holt,

'Feudal society and the family: iv. The heiress and the alien', *TRHS* 5th Ser. 35 (1985), 1–28; and S. Waugh, 'Women's inheritance and the growth of bureaucratic government in twelfth- and thirteenth-century England', *Nottingham Medieval Studies* 34 (1990), 71–92. Very interesting for comparative purposes is H. L. MacQueen, *Common Law and Feudal Society in Medieval Scotland* (Edinburgh, 1993).

. . .

CHAPTER 8

Essential reading here is J. C. Holt, *Magna Carta* (2nd edn, Cambridge, 1992), which also contains much of relevance to earlier chapters. For detailed legal commentary on the Great Charter, see W. S. McKechnie, *Magna Carta* (2nd edn, Glasgow, 1914). On John, note also Stenton, *English Justice*, cited above. On the judiciary and the emergence of lawyers, see P. A. Brand, *The Origins of the English Legal Profession* (Oxford, 1992); also R. V. Turner, *The English Judiciary in the Age of Glanvill and Bracton, c. 1176–1239* (Cambridge, 1985).

INDEX

Sorry to hear you're a
mess. Is there anything I
can do?

Taking care of yourself,
honestly, is the #1 thing
you could do for me. The
other night scared me so
much

Don't get me wrong: I'm
really glad you talked
about it with me. I'm just
not a professional, and
can't give you the help
you need. I want so
badly for you to be okay

Like, "fuck hospitals",
sure - I can
COMPLETELY
understand why you'd